Bloom's Major Literary Characters

King Arthur

George Babbitt

Elizabeth Bennet

Leopold Bloom

Sir John Falstaff

Jay Gatsby

Hamlet

Raskolnikov and Svidrigailov

Bloom's Major Literary Characters

Jay Gatsby

Edited and with an introduction by
Harold Bloom
Sterling Professor of the Humanities
Yale University

CHELSEA HOUSE
PUBLISHERS
An imprint of Infobase Publishing

Bloom's Major Literary Characters: Jay Gatsby
Copyright ©2004 by Infobase Publishing

Introduction ©2004 by Harold Bloom
Consulting Editor: Brian L. Johnson

Chelsea House
An imprint of Infobase Publishing
132 West 31st Street
New York NY 10001

Library of Congress Cataloging-in-Publication Data applied for.

ISBN 0-7910-7673-3 (alk. paper)

Chelsea House books are available at special discounts when purchased
in bulk quantities for businesses, associations, institutions, or sales
promotions. Please call our Special Sales Department in New York at
(212) 967-8800 or (800) 322-8755.

You can find Chelsea House on the World Wide Web at
http://www.chelseahouse.com.

Contributing editor: Amy Sickels
Cover design by Keith Trego

Printed in the United States of America

10 9 8 7 6 5 4 3 2 1

This book is printed on acid-free paper.

All links and web addresses were checked and verified to be correct
at the time of publication. Because of the dynamic nature of the web,
some addresses and links may have changed since publication and
may no longer be valid.

Contents

The Analysis of Character   vii
    Harold Bloom

Editor's Note   xiii

Introduction   1
    Harold Bloom

Fitzgerald's Brave New World   7
    Edwin S. Fussell

The Great Gatsby: Finding a Hero   13
    Henry Dan Piper

The Great Gatsby: Apogee of Fitzgerald's Mythopoeia   27
    Neila Seshachari

The Great Gatsby   39
    Brian Way

"I Could Still Hear The Music":
Jay Gatsby and the Musical Metaphor   63
    Bruce Bawer

Money, Love, and Aspiration in *The Great Gatsby*   69
    Roger Lathbury

Inventing Gatsby   83
    Richard Lehan

The Great Narcissist: A Study of Fitzgerald's Jay Gatsby   91
    Giles Mitchell

The Sexual Drama of Nick and Gatsby   101
     Edward Wasiolek

Gatsby as Gangster   113
     Thomas H. Pauly

The Great Gatsby and the Good American Life   125
     Ronald Berman

Character Profile   137

Contributors   139

Bibliography   141

Acknowledgements   145

Index   147

HAROLD BLOOM

The Analysis of Character

"Character," according to our dictionaries, still has as a primary meaning a graphic symbol, such as a letter of the alphabet. This meaning reflects the word's apparent origin in the ancient Greek character, a sharp stylus. *Charactēr* also meant the mark of the stylus' incisions. Recent fashions in literary criticism have reduced "character" in literature to a matter of marks upon a page. But our word "character" also has a very different meaning, matching that of the ancient Greek *ēthos*, "habitual way of life." Shall we say then that literary character is an imitation of human character, or is it just a grouping of marks? The issue is between a critic like Dr. Samuel Johnson, for whom words were as much like people as like things, and a critic like the late Roland Barthes, who told us that "the fact can only exist linguistically, as a term of discourse." Who is closer to our experience of reading literature, Johnson or Barthes? What difference does it make, if we side with one critic rather than the other?

Barthes is famous, like Foucault and other recent French theorists, for having added to Nietzsche's proclamation of the death of God a subsidiary demise, that of the literary author. If there are no authors, then there are no fictional personages, presumably because literature does not refer to a world outside language. Words indeed necessarily refer to other words in the first place, but the impact of words ultimately is drawn from a universe of fact. Stories, poems, and plays are recognizable as such because they are human utterances within traditions of utterances, and traditions, by achieving authority, become a kind of fact, or at least the sense of a fact. Our sense that literary characters, within the context of a fictive cosmos, indeed are fictional personages is also a kind of fact. The meaning and value of every character in a successful work of literary representation depend upon our ideas of persons in the factual reality of our lives.

Literary character is always an invention, and inventions generally are indebted to prior inventions. Shakespeare is the inventor of literary character as we know it; he reformed the universal human expectations for the verbal imitation of personality, and the reformation appears now to be permanent and uncannily inevitable. Remarkable as the Bible and Homer are at representing personages, their characters are relatively unchanging. They age within their stories, but their habitual modes of being do not develop. Jacob and Achilles unfold before us, but without metamorphoses. Lear and Macbeth, Hamlet and Othello severely modify themselves not only by their actions, but by their utterances, and most of all through *overhearing themselves*, whether they speak to themselves or to others. Pondering what they themselves have said, they will to change, and actually do change, sometimes extravagantly yet always persuasively. Or else they suffer change, without willing it, but in reaction not so much to their language as to their relation to that language.

I do not think it useful to say that Shakespeare successfully imitated elements in our characters. Rather, it could be argued that he compelled aspects of character to appear that previously were concealed, or not available to representation. This is not to say that Shakespeare is God, but to remind us that language is not God either. The mimesis of character in Shakespeare's dramas now seems to us normative, and indeed became the accepted mode almost immediately, as Ben Jonson shrewdly and somewhat grudgingly implied. And yet, Shakespearean representation has surprisingly little in common with the imitation of reality in Jonson or in Christopher Marlowe. The origins of Shakespeare's originality in the portrayal of men and women are to be found in the *Canterbury Tales* of Geoffrey Chaucer, insofar as they can be located anywhere before Shakespeare himself, Chaucer's savage and superb Pardoner overhears his own tale-telling, as well as his mocking rehearsal of his own spiel, and through this overhearing he is emboldened to forget himself, and enthusiastically urges all his fellow-pilgrims to come forward to be fleeced by him. His self-awareness, and apocalyptically rancid sense of spiritual fall, are preludes to the even grander abysses of the perverted will in Iago and in Edmund. What might be called the character trait of a negative charisma may be Chaucer's invention, but came to its perfection in Shakespearean mimesis.

The analysis of character is as much Shakespeare's invention as the representation of character is, since Iago and Edmund are adepts at analyzing both themselves and their victims. Hamlet, whose overwhelming charisma has many negative components, is certainly the most comprehensive of all literary characters, and so necessarily prophesies the labyrinthine complexities of the will in Iago and Edmund. Charisma, according to Max Weber, its first codifier, is primarily a natural endowment, and implies a primordial and idiosyncratic power over nature, and so finally over death. Hamlet's uncanniness is at its most suggestive in the scene of his long dying, where the audience, through the mediation of Horatio, itself is compelled to meditate upon suicide, if only because outliving the prince of Denmark scarcely seems an option.

Shakespearean representation has usurped not only our sense of literary character, but our sense of ourselves as characters, with Hamlet playing the part of the largest of these usurpations. Insofar as we have an idea of human disinterestedness, we tend to derive it from the Hamlet of Act V, whose quietism has about it a ghostly authority. Oscar Wilde, in his profound and profoundly witty dialogue, "The Decay of Lying," expressed a permanent insight when he insisted that art shaped every era, far more than any age formed art. Life imitates art, we imitate Shakespeare, because without Shakespeare we would perish for lack of images. Wilde's grandest audacity demystifies Shakespearean mimesis with a Shakespearean vivaciousness: "This unfortunate aphorism about art holding the mirror up to Nature is deliberately said by Hamlet in order to convince the bystanders of his absolute insanity in all art-matters." Of *Hamlet*'s influence upon the ages Wilde remarked that: "The world has grown sad because a puppet was once melancholy." "Puppet" is Wilde's own deconstruction, a brilliant reminder that Shakespeare's artistry of illusion has so mastered reality as to have changed reality, evidently forever.

The analysis of character, as a critical pursuit, seems to me as much a Shakespearean invention as literary character was, since much of what we know about how to analyze character necessarily follows Shakespearean procedures. His hero-villains, from Richard III through Iago, Edmund, and Macbeth, are shrewd and endless questers into their own self-motivations. If we could bear to see Hamlet, in his unwearied negations, as another hero-villain, then we would judge him the supreme analyst of the darker recalcitrances in the selfhood. Freud followed the pre-Socratic Empedocles, in arguing that character is fate, a frightening doctrine that maintains the fear that there are no accidents, that overdetermination rules us all of our lives.

Hamlet assumes the same, yet adds to this argument the terrible passivity he manifests in Act V. Throughout Shakespeare's tragedies, the most interesting personages seem doom-eager, reminding us again that a Shakespearean reading of Freud would be more illuminating than a Freudian exegesis of Shakespeare. We learn more when we discover Hamlet in the Freudian Death Drive, than when we read *Beyond the Pleasure Principle* into *Hamlet*.

In Shakespearean comedy, character achieves its true literary apotheosis, which is the representation of the inner freedom that can be created by great wit alone. Rosalind and Falstaff, perhaps alone among Shakespeare's personages, match Hamlet in wit, though hardly in the metaphysics of consciousness. Whether in the comic or the modern mode, Shakespeare has set the standard of measurement in the balance between character and passion.

In Shakespeare the self is more dramatized than theatricalized, which is why a Shakespearean reading of Freud works out so well. Character-formation after the passing of the Oedipal stage takes the place of fetishistic fragmentings of the self. Critics who now call literary character into question, and who proclaim also the death of the author, invariably also regard all notions, literary and human, of a stable character as being mere reductions of deeper pre-Oedipal desires. It becomes clear that the fortunes of literary character rise and fall with the prestige of normative conceptions of the ego. Shakespeare's Iago, who wars against being, may be the first deconstructionist of the self, with his proclamation of "I am not what I am." This constitutes the necessary prologue to any view that would regard a fixed ego as a virtual abnormality. But deconstructions of the self are no more modern than Modernism is. Like literary modernism, the decentered ego came out of the Hellenistic culture of ancient Alexandria. The Gnostic heretics believed that the psyche, like the body, was a fallen entity, mechanically fashioned by the Demiurge or false creator. They held however that each of us possessed also a spark or pneuma, which was a fragment of the original Abyss or true, alien God. The soul or psyche within every one of us was thus at war with the self or pneuma, and only that sparklike self could be saved.

Shakespeare, following after Chaucer in this respect, was the first and remains still the greatest master of representing character both as a stable soul and a wavering self. There is a substance that endures in Shakespeare's figures, and there is also a quicksilver rendition of the unsettling sparks. Racine and Tolstoy, Balzac and Dickens, follow in Shakespeare's wake by giving us some sense of pre-Oedipal sparks or drives, and considerably more sense of post-Oedipal character and personality, stabilizations or sublimations of the fetish-seeking drives. Critics like Leo Bersani and René Girard argue eloquently against our taking this mimesis as the only proper work of literature. I would suggest that strong fictions of the self, from the Bible through Samuel Beckett, necessarily participate in both modes, the sublimation of desire, and the persistence of a primordial desire. The mystery of Hamlet or of Lear is intimately invested in the tangled mixture of the two modes of representation.

Psychic mobility is proposed by Bersani as the ideal to which deconstructions of the literary self may yet guide us. The ideal has its pathos, but the realities of literary representation seem to me very different, perhaps destructively so. When a novelist like D. H. Lawrence sought to reduce his characters to Eros and the Death Drive, he still had to persuade us of his authority at mimesis by lavishing upon the figures of *The Rainbow* and *Women in Love* all of the vivid stigmata of normative personality. Birkin and Ursula may represent antithetical and uncanny drives, but they develop and change as characters pondering their own pronouncements and reactions to self and others. The cost of a non-Shakespearean representation is enormous. Pynchon, in *The Crying of Lot 49* and *Gravity's Rainbow*, evades the burden of the normative by resorting to something like Christopher Marlowe's art of caricature in *The Jew of Malta*. Marlowe's Barabas is a marvelous rhetorician, yet he is a cartoon alongside the troublingly equivocal Shylock. Pynchon's personages are deliberate cartoons also, as flat as comic strips. Marlowe's achievement, and Pynchon's, are beyond dispute, yet they are like the prelude and the postlude to Shakespearean reality. They do not wish to engage with our hunger for the empirical world and so they enter the problematic cosmos of literary fantasy.

No writer, not even Shakespeare or Proust, alters the available stock that we agree to call reality, but Shakespeare, more than any other, does show us how much of reality we could encounter if only we retained adequate desire. The strong literary representation of character is already an analysis of character, and is part of the healing work of a literary culture, which implicitly seeks to cure violence through a normative mimesis of ego, *as if it were stable*, whether in actuality it is or is not. I do not believe that this is a social quest taken on by literary culture, but rather that we confront here the aesthetic essence of what makes a culture *literary*, rather than metaphysical or ethical or religious. A culture becomes literary when its conceptual modes have failed it, which means when religion, philosophy, and science have begun to lose their authority. If they cannot heal violence, then literature attempts to do so, which may be only a turning inside out of the critical arguments of Girard and Bersani.

I conclude by offering a particular instance or special case as a paradigm for the healing enterprise that is at once the representation and the analysis of literary character. Let us call it the aesthetics of being outraged, or rather of successfully representing the state of being outraged. W. C. Fields was one modern master of such representation, and Nathanael West was another, as was Faulkner before him. Here also the greatest master remains Shakespeare, whose Macbeth, himself a bloody outrage, yet retains our imaginative sympathy precisely because he grows increasingly outraged as he experiences the equivocation of the fiend that lies like truth. The double-natured promises and the prophecies of the weird sisters finally induce in Macbeth an apocalyptic version of the stage actor's anxiety at missing cues, the horror of a phantasmagoric stage fright of missing one's time, of always reacting too late. Macbeth, a veritable monster of solipsistic inwardness but no intellectual, counters his dilemma by fresh murders, that prolong him in time yet provoke him only to a perpetually freshened sense of being outraged, as all his expectations become still worse confounded. We are moved by Macbeth, however estrangedly, because his terrible inwardness is a paradigm for our own solipsism, but also because none of us can resist a strong and successful representation of the human in a state of being outraged.

The ultimate outrage is the necessity of dying, an outrage concealed in a multitude of masks, including the tyrannical ambitions of Macbeth. I suspect that our outrage at being outraged is the most difficult of all our affects for us to represent to ourselves, which is why we are so inclined to imaginative sympathy for a character who strongly conveys that affect to us. The Shrike of West's *Miss Lonelyhearts* or Faulkner's Joe Christmas of *Light in August* are crucial modern instances, but such figures can be located in many other works, since the ability to represent this extreme emotion is one of the tests that strong writers are driven to set for themselves.

However a reader seeks to reduce literary character to a question of marks on a page, she will come at last to the impasse constituted by the thought of death, her death, and before that to all the stations of being outraged that memorialize her own drive towards death. In reading, she quests for evidences that are strong representations, whether of her desire or her despair. Such questings constitute the necessary basis for the analysis of literary character, an enterprise that always will survive every vagary of critical fashion.

Editor's Note

My Introduction centers upon Gatsby's American version of High Romantic idealism, his quest to reverse time and find a perpetual earliness.

Edwin S. Fussell believes the central pattern of *The Great Gatsby* is the protagonist's capacity for Romantic wonder, while Henry Dan Piper meditates upon the self-destructiveness of such Romantic individualism.

Mythmaking renders Gatsby exempt from tragedy, in Neila Seshachari's reading, after which Brian Way exalts both the poetic language and the comic vision that blend in Gatsby's self-creation.

Musical imagery enhances the tragedy of Gatsby's end, in the analysis by Bruce Bawer, while Roger Lathbury commends Fitzgerald for the newness with which he endows Gatsby's aspiration.

For Richard Lehan, what matters most about Gatsby is his self-invention, an achievement allied with narcissism by Giles Mitchell.

Edward Wasiolek persuasively explores the repressed homoeroticism of Nick Carraway's love for Gatsby, after which Thomas H. Pauly clarifies the protagonist's criminality.

In a concluding essay, Ronald Berman sets forth the deliberate dissonance of Gatsby's book, and finds in it a metaphor of American social disorder.

HAROLD BLOOM

Introduction

It is reasonable to assert that Jay Gatsby was *the* major literary character of
the United States in the twentieth century. No single figure created by
Faulkner or Hemingway, or by our principal dramatists, was as central a
presence in our national mythology as Gatsby. There are few living
Americans, of whatever gender, race, ethnic origin, or social class, who do
not have at least a little touch of Gatsby in them. Whatever the American
Dream has become, its truest contemporary representative remains Jay
Gatsby, at once a gangster and a Romantic idealist, and above all a victim of
his own High Romantic, Keatsian dream of love. Like his creator, Scott
Fitzgerald, Gatsby is the American hero of romance, a vulnerable quester
whose fate has the aesthetic dignity of the romance mode at its strongest.
Gatsby is neither pathetic nor tragic, because as a quester he meets his
appropriate fate, which is to die still lacking in the knowledge that would
destroy the spell of his enchantment. His death preserves his greatness, and
justifies the title of his story, a title that is anything but ironic.

Gatsby, doom-eager yet desiring a perfect love, or perhaps doom-eager
out of that desire, is a wholly American personality, as tender as he is tough.
Indeed, Gatsby's Americanism is so central to him that any other national
origin would be impossible for him. Fitzgerald memorably remarked of his
protagonist that "Jay Gatsby ... sprang from his Platonic conception of
himself," and for "Platonic" we could substitute "Emersonian," the proper

1

name for any American Platonism. As a son of God, Gatsby pragmatically seems to have fathered himself. And that may be why Fitzgerald had to portray his hero in the Conradian mode, with Carraway mediating Gatsby for us as Marlow mediates Jim in *Lord Jim*. Gatsby does not reveal himself to us, but to Carraway, who plays Horatio to Gatsby's Hamlet. Perhaps a character who lives in a consuming and destructive hope always has to be mediated for us, lest we be confronted directly by the madness of a Wordsworthian solitary or a Blakean emanation. It is Gatsby's glory that he is not a "realistic" character. How could he be, since his essence is his aspiration, which again is at once sordid and transcendental?

Since Gatsby is a character in a romance, and not a realistic fiction, we cannot apply the criteria of moral realism to his love for the absurdly vacuous Daisy. She is to Gatsby as his enchanted Dulcinea is to Don Quixote: a vision of the ideal. Just as Daisy's love for her brutal husband can be sublimely dismissed by Gatsby as "merely personal," so her defects of character and taste cannot affect Gatsby's attitude towards her, as Carraway teaches us:

> There must have been moments even that afternoon when Daisy tumbled short of his dreams—not through her own fault, but because of the colossal vitality of his illusion. It had gone beyond her, beyond everything. He had thrown himself into it with a creative passion, adding to it all the time, decking it out with every bright feather that drifted his way. No amount of fire or freshness can challenge what a man can store up in his ghostly heart.

It must seem odd to argue for Gatsby's religious significance, since his mindless idealism has no relevance to Christian terms. But it takes on a peculiarly intense meaning if the context is the American religion, which is oddly both Protestant and post-Christian. Gatsby's mythic projection is one of a more-than-Adamic innocence, in which his perpetual optimism, amoral goodness, and visionary hope all are centered in an escape from history, in a sense of being self-begotten. Daisy Buchanan, according to the late Malcolm Cowley, is named for Henry James's Daisy Miller, and *The Great Gatsby*, for all its debt to Conrad, partakes more in the Americanism of Henry James, though the Jamesian dream of innocence is marked by a more pervasive irony. But then Gatsby's Daisy is a snow-queen, ice-cold, while Daisy Miller has more of Gatsby's own warmth. A heroine of American romance, she shares Gatsby's deprecation of time and history, and his exaltation of the questing self.

Is Gatsby, as Marius Bewley once wrote, a criticism of America? I hardly think so, since his effect upon Nick Carraway, and so upon the reader, is so wonderful, and so affectionate. Nick, like Fitzgerald, declines to culminate in the irony of irony; Gatsby saves Nick from that abyss of nihilism, as well as from the pomposities of mere moralizing. More subtly, he seems to give Nick an image of the male side of heterosexual love that can be placed against the sadistic masculinity of Tom Buchanan. We do not know what life Carraway will return to when he goes West, but evidently it will be a life somewhat illuminated by Gatsby's dream of an ideal, heterosexual Romantic love, though the illumination may not prove to be pragmatic.

What would it mean if we interpreted Gatsby the dreamer as an ignorant and failed American lyric poet, whose value somehow survives both ignorance and failure? Gatsby cannot tell his dreams; every attempt he makes to describe his love for Daisy collapses into banality, and yet we no more doubt the reality of Gatsby's passion for Daisy than we doubt the terrible authenticity of the dying Keats's intense desire for Fanny Brawne. It seems absurd to compare the vulgar grandiosity of poor Gatsby's diction to the supreme eloquence of John Keats, but Gatsby is profoundly Keatsian, a direct descendant of the poet-quester in *The Fall of Hyperion*. I take it that a repressed echo of Keats is behind Carraway's sense of a lost, High Romantic music even as he listens to Gatsby's turgid discourses:

> Through all he said, even through his appalling sentimentality,
> I was reminded of something—an elusive rhythm, a fragment of
> lost words that I had heard somewhere a long time ago. For a
> moment a phrase tried to take shape in my mouth and my lips
> parted like a dumb man's, as though there was more struggling
> upon them than a wisp of startled air. But they made no sound,
> and what I had almost remembered was incommunicable forever.

What Carraway (and Fitzgerald) almost remembered may be a crucial passage in *The Fall of Hyperion*, where the poet-quester is nearly destroyed by his silence and his inability to move:

> I heard, I looked: two senses both at once,
> So fine, so subtle, felt the tyranny
> Of that fierce threat and the hard task proposed.
> Prodigious seemed the toil; the leaves were yet
> Burning—when suddenly a palsied chill
> Struck from the paved level up my limbs,
> And was ascending quick to put cold grasp
> Upon those streams that pulse beside the throat:
> I shrieked, and the sharp anguish of my shriek
> Stung my own ears—I strove hard to escape

The numbness; strove to gain the lowest step.
Slow, heavy, deadly was my pace: the cold
Grew stifling, suffocating, at the heart;
And when I clasped my hands I felt them not.
One minute before death, my iced foot touched
The lowest stair; and as it touched, life seemed
To pour in at the toes ...

Carraway remains mute; the anguish of Keats's shriek reawakens the poet to life, and to poetry. Part of Carraway's function surely is to contrast his own recalcitrances with Gatsby's continual vitality and sense of wonder, But Carraway anticipates his own narrative of Gatsby's destruction. Gatsby's foot never touches the lowest stair; there is for him no purgatorial redemption. But how could there have been "something commensurate to his capacity for wonder"? The greatness of Gatsby is that there was no authentic object for his desire, as Daisy's inadequacies render so clear. Like every true quester in Romantic tradition, Gatsby is both subject and object of his own quest, though he never could hope to have learned this bewildering contingency.

Many readers sense that there is a "drowned god" aspect to Gatsby's fate, doubtless suggested to Fitzgerald by Eliot's *The Waste Land*. Yet it is difficult to fit such a figure into American myth, as we can see by contrasting the powerful but enigmatic figure of Whitman's drowned swimmer in "The Sleepers" to the more evocative and contextualized image of President Lincoln in "When Lilacs Last in the Dooryard Bloom'd." The American visionary can die as a father, or as a son, but not as a ritual sacrifice to rekindle the dead land, because even now our land is far from dead. Gatsby, a son of God, dies with a curiously religious significance, but one that is beyond Carraway's understanding. What is best and oldest in Gatsby cannot die, but returns to the living Fullness of the American Dream, itself undying despite all of its cancellations and farewells, which prove never to have been final.

What Carraway does come to understand is that Gatsby's freedom was invested in solitude, and not even in the possibility of Daisy, since marriage to the actual Daisy could not have sufficed for very long. If your belief is in "the orgiastic future that year by year recedes," then your belief is in what Freud called repression, a process that implies that everything significant is already in your past. Gatsby's deepest need was to reverse time, to see his lateness as an ever-early origin. To fulfill that need, you have to be Emerson or Whitman, or if you are a fictive self, then Huck Finn will serve as example.

Loving a dream of freedom will work only if you can detach that dream from other individuals, and Gatsby was too open and generous to exercise such detachment.

It does seem, after all, that Fitzgerald placed much of the best of himself in Gatsby. His relation to Gatsby is quite parallel to Flaubert's rueful identification with Emma Bovary. Even Flaubert could not protect himself by his own formidable irony; he suffered with Emma, and so do we. Fitzgerald did not protect himself at all, and he contaminated us with his vulnerability. Perhaps Gatsby does not suffer, being so lost in his dream. We suffer for Gatsby, as Carraway does, but what mitigates that suffering is the extent to which we too, as Americans, are lost in the same dream of love and wealth.

EDWIN S. FUSSELL

Fitzgerald's Brave New World

With *The Great Gatsby* (1925), Fitzgerald first brought his vision of America to full and mature realization. Notwithstanding its apparent lack of scope, this is a complex and resonant novel, and one with a variety of significant implications. No single reading, perhaps, will exhaust its primary meanings, and that which follows makes no pretense of doing so. But there is, I think, a central pattern that has never been sufficiently explored—this pattern is the story of America, or of the New World, the story that Fitzgerald had been intuitively approaching since he began to write.

Gatsby is essentially the man of imagination in America, given specificity and solidity and precision by the materials which American society offered him. "If personality is a series of successful gestures, then there was something gorgeous about him, some heightened sensitivity to the promises of life, as if he were related to one of those intricate machines that register earthquakes ten thousand miles away." It is Gatsby's capacity for *romantic wonder* that Fitzgerald is insisting upon in this preliminary exposition, a capacity that he goes on to define as "an extraordinary gift for hope, a romantic readiness." And with the simile of the seismograph, an apt enough symbol for the human sensibility in a mechanized age, Fitzgerald has in effect already introduced the vast backdrop of American civilization against which Gatsby's gestures must be interpreted. The image is as integral as

---

From *ELH* 19, no. 4 (December, 1952): 291–306. © 1952 by The Johns Hopkins University Press.

intricate; for if Gatsby is to be taken as the product and the manifestation of those motivations caught up in the phrase "the American dream," he is also the instrument by means of which Fitzgerald is to register the tremors that point to its self-contained principles of destruction. "What preyed on Gatsby, what foul dust floated in the wake of his dreams" is ostensibly the stuff of the novel, the social content of Fitzgerald's universe of fiction. But it is essential to realize that Gatsby, too, has been distorted from the normative by values and attitudes that he holds in common with the society that destroys him. Certainly, in such a world, the novel assures us, a dream like Gatsby's cannot remain pristine, given the materials upon which the original impulse toward wonder must expend itself. Gatsby, in other words, is more than pathetic, a sad figure preyed upon by the American leisure class. The unreal values of the world of Tom and Daisy Buchanan are his values too, they are inherent in his dream. Gatsby had always lived in an imaginary world, where "a universe of ineffable gaudiness spun itself out in his brain"; negatively, this quality manifests itself in a dangerous tendency toward sentimental idealization: his reveries "were a satisfactory hint of the unreality of reality, a promise that the rock of the world was founded securely on a fairy's wing."

Daisy finally becomes for Gatsby the iconic manifestation of this vision of beauty. Little enough might have been possible for Gatsby anyway, but once he "wed his unutterable visions to her perishable breath, his mind would never romp again like the mind of God." One notes how steadily if surreptitiously, through his metaphors and similes mainly, Fitzgerald is introducing the notion of blasphemy in conjunction with Gatsby's Titanic imaginative lusts. But the novel makes only tentative gestures in the direction of religious evaluation; Fitzgerald's talent indicated that Gatsby's visions be focussed rather sexually and socially. After this concentration of Gatsby's wonder on Daisy has been established, Fitzgerald can go on to an explicit statement of her significance to the thematic direction of the novel: Gatsby, we are told, was "overwhelmingly aware of the *youth* and mystery that *wealth* imprisons and *preserves*, of the freshness of many clothes, and of Daisy, gleaming like silver, safe and proud above the hot struggle of the poor" (my italics). Her voice is frequently mentioned as mysteriously enchanting—it is the typifying feature of her role as *la belle dame sans merci*—and throughout the action it serves to suggest her loveliness and desirability. But only Gatsby, in a rare moment of vision, is able to make explicit the reasons for its subtle and elusive magic: "It was full of money—that was the inexhaustible charm that rose and fell in it, the jingle of it, the cymbals' song of it ... High in a white palace the king's daughter, the golden girl...."

Possession of an image like Daisy is all that Gatsby can finally conceive as "success"; and Gatsby is meant to be a very representative American in the intensity of his yearning for success, as well as in the symbols which he equates with it. Gatsby performs contemporary variations on an old American pattern, the rags-to-riches story exalted by American legend as early as Crevecoeur's *Letters from an American Farmer*. But the saga is primarily that of a legendary Benjamin Franklin, whose celebrated youthful resolutions are parodied in those that the adolescent Gatsby wrote on the back flyleaf of his copy of *Hopalong Cassidy*. As an indictment of American philistinism, Fitzgerald's burlesque is spare and sharp; what accounts for its impression of depth is Fitzgerald's fictionally realized perception that Gatsby's was not a unique, but a pervasive American social pattern. Grounding his parody in Franklin's *Autobiography* gave Fitzgerald's critique a historical density and a breadth of implication that one associates only with major fiction.

The connection between Gatsby's individual tragedy and the tragedy of his whole civilization is also made (and again, through symbol) with respect to historical attitudes. Gatsby's relation to history is summed up in his devotion to the green light that burns on Daisy's dock. When Nick first sees Gatsby, he is in an attitude of supplication, a gesture that pathetically travesties the gestures of worship; Nick finally observes that the object of his trembling piety is this green light which, until his disillusion, is one of Gatsby's "enchanted objects." In the novel's concluding passage, toward which all action and symbol is relentlessly tending, one is given finally the full implications of the green light as symbol ("Gatsby believed in the green light, the orgiastic future").

Gatsby, with no historical sense whatsoever, is the fictional counterpart of that American philistine maxim that "history is bunk"; and he may recall, too, for those interested in such comparisons, the more crowing moods of Emerson and Thoreau, and the "timelessness" of their visions and exhortations. But for Fitzgerald, this contemptuous repudiation of tradition, historical necessity, and moral determinism, however un-self-conscious, was deluded and hubristic. When he finally came to see, as he did in *Gatsby*, that in this irresponsibility lay the real meaning behind the American obsession with youth, he was able to know Gatsby as a miserable, twentieth century Ponce de Leon. And his fictional world was no longer simply the Jazz Age, the Lost Generation, but the whole of American civilization as it culminated in his own time.

In the final symbol of the book, Fitzgerald pushes the personal equation to national, even universal, scope, and in a way that recalls the method of "May Day." The passage has been prepared for in multiple ways; indeed, nearly all the material I have been citing leads directly into it. Even the "new world" theme has been anticipated. Fitzgerald is commenting on Gatsby's state of disillusion just before his death:

> he must have felt that he had lost the old warm world, paid a high price for living too long with a single dream. He must have looked up at an unfamiliar sky through frightening leaves and shivered as he found what a grotesque thing a rose is and how raw the sunlight was upon the scarcely created grass. A new world, material without being real, where poor ghosts, breathing dreams like air, drifted fortuitously about ...

Such, then, was the romantic perception of wonder, when finally stripped of its falsifying illusions. Gatsby finds himself in a "new world" (Fitzgerald's symbol for the American's dream of irresponsibility takes on ironically terrifying overtones here) in which his values and dreams are finally exposed. And so Fitzgerald moves on to his final critique:

> And as the moon rose higher the inessential houses began to melt away until gradually I became aware of the old island here that flowered once for Dutch sailors' eyes—a fresh green breast of the new world. Its vanished trees, the trees that had made way for Gatsby's house, had once pandered in whispers to the last and greatest of all human dreams; for a transitory enchanted moment man must have held his breath in the presence of this continent, compelled into an aesthetic contemplation he neither understood nor desired, face to face for the last time in history with something commensurate to his capacity for wonder.

The most important point to be made about this passage is its insistence that Gatsby's abnormal capacity for wonder could have, in the modern world, no proper objective. The emotion lingered on, generations of Americans had translated it into one or another set of inadequate terms, but Gatsby, like all his ancestors, was doomed by demanding the impossible. There is, too, the ironic contrast between the wonder of the New World, and what Americans have made of it (the same point that Fitzgerald made in similar fashion with the Columbus image in "May Day"). But there is a final, more universal meaning, implicit in the language of the passage—the hope that the new world could possibly satisfy man's lusts was, after all, "the last and greatest of all human dreams," unreal. The most impressive associations cluster around the word "pander"—a word that implies, above all, the illicit commercialization of love, youth, and beauty—which effectually subsumes most of the central meanings of the novel. Because of the verbal similarity, it is valuable to compare this phrase "panders in whispers" with Fitzgerald's remarks (in "My Lost City" [1932], an essay collected in 1945 in *The Crack-Up*) about New York City, a good instance of how the myths of Benjamin Franklin and Ponce de Leon could be blended in his mind—"it no longer whispers of fantastic success and eternal youth." The two parallel themes do, of course, come together in the novel; in fact, they are tangled at the heart of the plot, for the greatest irony in Gatsby's tragedy is his belief that he can buy his dream, which is, precisely, to recapture the past.

HENRY DAN PIPER

The Great Gatsby: *Finding a Hero*

Max Perkins was tremendously impressed by the manuscript of *The Great Gatsby* which Fitzgerald sent him from St. Raphael on October 27, 1924. "Extraordinary ... magnificent...," he wrote Fitzgerald on November twentieth; it was a novel that suggested "all sorts of thoughts and moods." "It's got his old vitality," Perkins wrote Ring Lardner enthusiastically a few days later, "—vitality enough to sweep away the faults you could, critically, find with it, which relate, in my view, chiefly to Gatsby himself."[1]

It was to Gatsby's shortcomings as a character that Perkins devoted the greater part of his long letter of November twentieth, in which he summarized for Fitzgerald his reactions to the manuscript. He had two major criticisms of the hero:

> One is that among a set of characters marvelously palpable and vital—I would know Tom Buchanan if I met him on the street and would avoid him—Gatsby is somewhat vague. The reader's eyes can never quite focus upon him, his outlines are dim. Now everything about Gatsby is more or less a mystery, i.e. more or less vague, and this may be somewhat of an artistic intention, but I think it is mistaken. Couldn't *he* be physically described as distinctly as the others, and couldn't you add one or two characteristics like the use of that phrase "old sport"—not verbal,

From *F. Scott Fitzgerald: A Critical Portrait.* © 1965 by Henry Dan Piper.

but physical ones, perhaps.... I do not think your scheme would be impaired if you made him so.

The other point is also about Gatsby: his career must remain mysterious, of course. But in the end you make it pretty clear that his wealth came through his connection with Wolfsheim. You also suggest this much earlier. Now almost all readers numerically are going to be puzzled by his having all this wealth and are going to feel entitled to an explanation. To give a distinct and definite one would be, of course, utterly absurd. It did occur to me, though, that you might here and there interpolate some phrases, and possibly incidents, little touches of various kinds, that might suggest that he was in some active way mysteriously engaged.... Whether he was an innocent tool in the hands of somebody else, or to what degree he was this, ought not to be explained. But if some sort of business activity of his were simply adumbrated, it would lend further probability to that part of the story.

In December, Fitzgerald wrote Perkins from Italy, where he and Zelda had gone for the winter, that he was confident he could remedy these defects during his revision of the galley proofs.[2]

Strange to say my notion of Gatsby's vagueness was o.k. What you and Louise [Mrs. Perkins] and Mr. Charles Scribner found wanting was that:
I myself didn't know what Gatsby looked like or was engaged in and you felt it. If I'd known it and kept it from you you'd have been *too impressed with my knowledge to protest.* This is a complicated idea but I'm sure you'll understand. But I know now—and as a penalty for not having known first, in other words to make sure, I'm going to tell more....
Anyhow after careful searching of the files (of a man's mind here) for the Fuller McGee [sic] case ... I know Gatsby better than I know my own child. My first instinct after your letter was to let him go and have Tom Buchanan dominate the book (I suppose he's the best character I've ever done—I think he and the brother in "Salt" and Hurstwood in "Sister Carrie" are the three best characters in American fiction in the last twenty years, perhaps and perhaps not) but Gatsby sticks in my heart. I had him for a while, then lost him and now I know I have him again.

The trouble, as we know from "Absolution," was that Gatsby was nothing more than the figment of a small boy's imagination. How was Fitzgerald to make something as vague as "Blatchford Sarnemington" the hero of his novel? Quite likely, when Fitzgerald began to plan the book, he expected to model the mature Gatsby after some typical Midwestern tycoon—perhaps his own grandfather, or Grandfather McQuillan's friend, James J. Hill. "If he'd of lived he'd of been a great man," Mr. Gatz proudly tells Nick. "A man like James J. Hill. He'd of helped build up the country."[3]

If this was the case, then Fitzgerald, after coming to Great Neck, no longer continued to think of his novel as a Midwestern story of the Gilded Age. By 1923, it was evident that the Twenties would surpass even that earlier era in glitter and irresponsibility. Moving his setting to New York did not, however, materially alter the story's meaning. For what was New York but an extension of Fitzgerald's Midwest, with all its bustle and excitement and easy money? "I see now that this has been a story of the West, after all," Nick says at the end of the novel. "Tom and Gatsby, Daisy and Jordan and I, were all Westerners and perhaps we possessed some deficiency in common which made us subtly unadaptable to Eastern life."[4]

Almost every Sunday the society columns and rotogravure sections of the New York newspapers carried accounts of wealthy young Midwesterners like the Buchanans who had moved to Long Island to enjoy the yachting, polo, and other expensive pastimes of the very rich. The financial sections of the same papers almost as regularly reported the mysterious appearance of Gatsby-like figures who had suddenly emerged from the West with millions of dollars at their command. A typical example was Charles Victor Bob, who turned up in Wall Street from Colorado, claiming to be the owner of tin mines in South America and copper mines in Canada. He spent money like water, throwing lavish parties for Broadway celebrities who had never heard of him before, and selling gilt-edged mining securities. He was finally indicted on a six-million-dollar mail fraud charge, but, in spite of the evidence, three successive juries refused to convict him. So far as the Twenties were concerned, anyone as rich, colorful, and successful as Charles Victor Bob deserved a better fate than jail.[5]

Knowing of Fitzgerald's interest in "success" stories like this, his friends collected them for him. The outskirts of Great Neck, where palatial estates fronted on Long Island Sound, made an especially good hunting ground. "He [Ring Lardner] told me of a newcomer who'd made money in the drug business—not dope but the regular line," Max Perkins wrote the Fitzgeralds shortly after they went to France:[6]

This gentleman had evidently taken to Ring. One morning he called early with another man and a girl and Ring was not dressed. But he hurried down, unshaven. He [Ring] was introduced to the girl only, and said he was sorry to appear that way but didn't want to keep them waiting while he shaved.

At this point the drug man signals to the other, who goes to the car for a black bag and from it produces razors, strops, etc., etc., and publicly shaves Ring. *This* was the drug man's private barber; the girl was his private manicurist. But as he was lonely he had made them also his companions. Ring declares this is true!

Lardner himself sent the Fitzgeralds an account of a Fourth of July celebration that might have come from the pages of *The Great Gatsby*:[7]

On the Fourth of July, Ed Wynn gave a fireworks display at his new estate in the Grenwolde division. After the children had been sent home, everybody got pie-eyed and I never enjoyed a night so much. All the Great Neck professionals did their stuff, the former chorus girls danced, Blanche Ring kissed me and sang, etc. The party lasted through the next day and wound up next evening at Tom Meighan's where the principal entertainment was provided by Lila Lee and another dame, who did some very funny imitations (really funny) in the moonlight on the tennis court. We would ask them to imitate Houdini, or Leon Errol, or Will Rogers or Elsie Janis; the imitations were all the same, consisting of an aesthetic dance which ended with an unaesthetic fall onto the tennis court.

Of all Fitzgerald's Long Island neighbors, the one whose outlines are most clearly discernible in *The Great Gatsby* was a certain Great Neck resident by the name of Edward M. Fuller. This was the Fuller of the "Fuller–McGee" case which Fitzgerald told Perkins he had studied until he felt he knew Gatsby better than he knew his own child. A thirty-nine-year-old bachelor and man about town, Fuller was president of the New York brokerage firm of E.M. Fuller and Co., with offices at 50 Broad Street. Of obscure origins, he had emerged suddenly on Wall Street in 1918 as a member of the Consolidated Stock Exchange and the head of his own company. Before long, he was being mentioned in the newspapers as one of a fashionable set that included Gertrude Vanderbilt, Charles A. Stoneham, the owner of the New York Giants baseball team, and Walter B. Silkworth, prominent clubman and president of the Consolidated Exchange. Fuller, an aviation enthusiast, was one of the first Long Island residents to commute weekly by airplane from his Great Neck estate to Atlantic City while the horse-racing season was on.[8]

On June 22, 1922, however, E.M. Fuller and Co. declared itself bankrupt, with some six million dollars in debts and assets of less than seventy thousand dollars. Fuller and his vice-president, William F. McGee, were promptly indicted on a twelve-count charge that included operating a "bucket shop"—i.e., illegally gambling with their customers' funds. It took four trials to put them behind prison bars, and it is significant that the first opened two months after the Fitzgeralds moved to Great Neck, and ended several days later with a hung jury. The second trial, in December, ended in a mistrial after the state admitted its inability to produce a key witness, who had unaccountably disappeared. The third, which began the following April, 1923, also resulted in a hung jury. During this trial it was revealed that Fuller's lawyer, a prominent New York attorney named William J. Fallon, had tried to bribe one of the jurors. For this Fallon was subsequently convicted and imprisoned, disgraced for life.

During this third trial, a leading state's witness was temporarily kidnapped by another of Fuller's attorneys, and vital records and other evidence also disappeared. By now the "Fuller-McGee" case was being featured on the front pages of the New York newspapers, and the fourth trial opened on June 11, 1923, amid a rash of rumors that Fuller and McGee were going to throw themselves on the mercy of the court and make a full confession. A deal had been arranged, it was reported, whereby they were to receive light sentences in exchange for confessions implicating a number of prominent New York officials, politicians, and businessmen with whom they had been associated in their financial ventures. Instead, however, both Fuller and McGee merely pleaded guilty to the more innocuous charges and were promptly sentenced to five years in Sing Sing—a sentence that was subsequently reduced to twelve months for "good behavior."

By coincidence, McGee's wife, a former New York showgirl named Louise Groody, arrived in Paris the same day that Fuller and her husband confessed their guilt. According to the Paris newspapers, Mrs. McGee disembarked from the liner at Cherbourg covered with diamonds and other jewels valued at several hundred thousand dollars. It was subsequently revealed that she had cashed a check of her husband's for $300,000 just a few hours before E.M. Fuller and Company went bankrupt.

Actually, the state of New York had difficulty establishing conclusive proof for most of the charges brought against Fuller and McGee. Nonetheless, it was obvious that they were part of a tangled web of corruption that included some of New York's wealthiest and most powerful business and political leaders. Fuller, according to his testimony, owed his business success mainly to his friendship with Charles A. Stoneham, another mysterious Gatsby-like figure who began life as a board boy in a broker's office and rose swiftly in the Wall Street financial hierarchy, emerging eventually as president of the brokerage house of C.A. Stoneham and Company. In 1921, he had sold out his firm's interest to E.M. Fuller and Co. and three other investment houses (E.D. Dier and Co., E.H. Clarke and Co., and Dillon and Co.) and plunged heavily into big-time gambling and sporting enterprises. Besides his controlling interest in the New York Giants baseball club, Stoneham owned a race track, a gambling casino, a newspaper, and other associated interests in Havana. By 1923, all four of the firms which had bought the assets of Stoneham and Co. had gone bankrupt, with debts totaling more than twenty million dollars.[9]

Fuller testified under oath that, after the dissolution of Stoneham and Co., Charles Stoneham had become a silent partner in the Fuller firm; he further claimed that his friend had advanced some two hundred thousand dollars in checks drawn against the Giants club, in a fruitless attempt to stave off Fuller and Co.'s impending bankruptcy. Stoneham insisted, however, that the money had merely been a private loan to Fuller, which he had advanced at the request of his friend Thomas F. Foley, former New York sheriff and Tammany Hall official. Foley, who had himself loaned Fuller $15,000, explained that he had come to Fuller's assistance purely out of friendship for one of McGee's former wives, a certain Nellie Sheean, who had remarried and was now living in Paris (the residence, also, of the current Mrs. McGee).

Fuller and Company, it turned out, had a rather dubious financial history. In 1920, the firm was indicted for having systematically defrauded its customers over the past three years by sale of worthless oil securities, but the case was thrown out of court on the grounds of insufficient evidence. On February 24, 1923, while awaiting his third bankruptcy trial, Fuller was arrested on another charge along with seven other men and women, most of whom had criminal records. They were seized in a suite of the Hotel Embassy, where they were accused of having attempted to sell fraudulent securities over the telephone. It was further claimed by the police that Fuller and his friends were planning to organize a new securities firm for the purpose of selling worthless stocks. This case, however, was also dismissed, by the court because of lack of evidence.

On June 13, 1922, Fuller had again been involved with the polices but under more romantic circumstances. On this occasion, his Broad Street offices had been invaded by "a fashionably dressed young lady" who, according to the New York *Times*, had threatened Fuller with severe bodily harm. Later, in the police court, the woman identified herself as Nellie

Burke, twenty-seven, of 245 West Seventy-fifth Street. Miss Burke, who at the time of her arrest was wearing $20,000 worth of what she told newspaper reporters was "borrowed" jewelry, testified that she had become acquainted with Fuller in 1915, in the bar of the Hotel Knickerbocker. Their subsequent friendship had terminated in a breach-of-promise suit which she had brought against him in 1921. On June sixth of that year, she said, she had been visited by Fuller's friend, and business associate, the notorious Arnold Rothstein, who had promised her $10,000 if she would sign a paper dropping the suit and agreeing not to pester Fuller any more. She had signed the paper and received $5,000 from Rothstein, but the rest of the money had been withheld. Her visit to Fuller's office the following June had, she claimed, been merely to collect the $5,000 in cash still due her. The magistrate found her guilty of assault but agreed to suspend sentence if she would promise not to give Fuller any more trouble. (Fuller's failure to pay her the additional $5,000 was explained several days later, on June twenty-second, when his firm went into bankruptcy!)

Many intimations of a mysterious tie between Fuller and the gambler, Arnold Rothstein, appeared during the Fuller trials, but the precise nature of this relationship was never fully clarified. Rothstein—"the walking bank, the pawnbroker of the underworld, the fugitive, unhealthy man who sidled along doorways," as Stanley Walker has described him in *The Night Club Era*—testified that Fuller owed him $336,768, most of which consisted of unpaid gambling debts. Fuller countered this statement with the charge that Rothstein personally owed him some $385,000. In subsequent testimony, Rothstein admitted having borrowed $187,000 at one time from Fuller and Co., for which he had put up $25,000 worth of collateral. But Fuller and Co.'s financial records (those that could be located) were so confused that this testimony was of little significance. More informative was Rothstein's statement that Fuller was a shrewd gambler who usually won his bets. Beyond this, Rothstein refused to testify. It was generally suspected that the firm's assets had been squandered by Fuller, McGee, Rothstein, and their friends on racing, baseball, boxing, and other sporting interests. Rothstein was believed to have "fixed" the World Series in 1919, although, again, nothing conclusive was ever proved against him. He was also reputed to be engaged in numerous other criminal activities, including the operation of gambling houses, shops selling stolen gems, brothels, and a lucrative bootlegging business—enterprises which did not affect his social standing. Like Fuller, he was frequently seen in the company of respected New York business and society figures, whom he entertained lavishly in his expensive Park Avenue apartment.[10]

Another interesting friendship disclosed during the trials was that between Edward Fuller and Walter S. Silkworth, the president of the Consolidated Stock Exchange. For months prior to the collapse of Fuller and Company, Silkworth had repeatedly ignored requests from Fuller's customers that Fuller and Co. be suspended from the exchange for fraudulent practices. Silkworth's brother was one of Fuller's employees, and during the trial Silkworth himself was unable to account for $133,000 in his private banking account—$55,175 of which had been deposited in cash. After Fuller's and McGee's convictions, Silkworth was obliged to resign from his presidency of the Consolidated Exchange.

Fitzgerald borrowed heavily from the newspaper accounts of Fuller's business affairs in creating Gatsby than he had from the details of Fuller's personality. For example, it seems unlikely that Fuller's friendship with Nellie Burke inspired Gatsby's idealistic attachment to Daisy Buchanan. However, Charles Stoneham's paternal interest in young Fuller, as it came out during the trial, is paralleled in the novel by Dan Cody's friendship for Gatsby, and Meyer Wolfshiem obviously was suggested by Fuller's friend, Arnold Rothstein. From the newspaper accounts of Fuller's career Fitzgerald also borrowed such details as Gatsby's airplane, the young stock-and-bond salesmen who haunted his parties, his mysterious connections with "the oil business" as well as his efforts to find a "small town" in which to start up some new and unmistakably shady enterprise, and his connections with New York society people like Tom Buchanan's friend Walter Chase. "That drug store business was just small change," Tom says after he has investigated Gatsby's business connections with Chase, "but you've got something on now that Walter's afraid to tell me about." What that "something" was Fitzgerald had spelled out in more detail in one of the earlier drafts of *The Great Gatsby*. "Until last summer when Wolfshiem was tried (but not convicted) on charges of grand larceny, forgery, bribery, and dealing in stolen bonds," Nick Carraway says, "I wasn't sure what it all included." Later, however, Fitzgerald omitted this passage, preferring to leave most of the facts about his hero's business affairs to the reader's imagination.[11]

For after all, in a world where people like Tom and Daisy and Jordan Baker survived and continued to be admired, what difference did it make what crimes Gatsby had committed? Besides, who in the real world of the Twenties, or in the novel that mirrored it, was free of the universal stain? The files of the Fuller–McGee case prove concretely what *The Great Gatsby* implies indirectly: that society leaders, financial tycoons, politicians, magistrates, pimps, jurors, lawyers, baseball players, sheriffs, bond salesmen, debutantes, and prostitutes—all shared in some degree the responsibility for Gatsby's fate.

Gatsby's murder was a grimmer fate than that meted out to Edward

Fuller, who successfully delayed going to Sing Sing for several years and who was then paroled at the end of a year. Even so, Fitzgerald's premonition that careers like Fuller's and Rothstein's were destined to end violently was borne out by later history. Rothstein was fated to die in almost exactly the same manner as Meyer Wolfshiem's friend Rosy Rosenthal, who was shot "three times in his full belly" at four A.M. in the morning outside the old Metropole, where he had spent the night plotting with five of his mobsters. Rothstein was finally killed by an anonymous gunman in 1928 just as he was leaving a conference of big-time bootleggers and gangsters in the Park Central Hotel. In Rothstein's case, however, there were no witnesses to eulogize the manner of his passing, as Wolfshiem did so lyrically for Rosy Rosenthal. Afterwards, the New York police were not only reluctant to investigate Rothstein's murder, but devoted their efforts instead to seizing and suppressing his papers, lest his connections with other prominent New Yorkers be brought to light. Ultimately it was the public hue and cry over the police's inability to solve the mystery of the Rothstein slaying that triggered the historic Seabury investigation into New York City politics a year later, in 1929. As Judge Seabury gradually compiled enough evidence to force the resignation of Mayor Jimmy Walker and his top officials, intimate ties were disclosed between money, politics, sports, crime, and business—ties which Fitzgerald had already described in *Gatsby* some years earlier. The further the 1920's recede, the more that novel emerges as one of the most penetrating criticisms of that incredible decade.

The newspaper clippings of Edward Fuller's career, however, by no means account for Gatsby himself or for the novel's vitality as a literary work. Few heroes of fiction have spent so much time off stage and yet dominated the action as he does. He does not speak his first line until the story is one-fourth of the way along, and he is dead by the time it is three-quarters finished. So far as the narrative is concerned, we are much better acquainted with Nick Carraway than we ever are with his mysterious neighbor. Yet *The Great Gatsby* for many of its admirers remains exclusively Gatsby's story. To the suggestion that Nick Carraway is the real hero of the novel and Gatsby only a figment of Nick's imagination, John O'Hara, for example, objects strenuously. "Gatsby not real. Why he's as real as you are sitting there in that chair!"[12]

Fitzgerald himself was not, however, so confident of his success in establishing the credibility of his hero. "... [Y]ou are right about Gatsby being blurred and patchy," he wrote John Peale Bishop several months after his novel was published. "I never at any one time saw him clear myself—for he started as one man I knew and then changed into myself—the amalgam was never complete in my mind." When Fitzgerald wrote this in the summer of 1925, *The Great Gatsby* was selling badly and he was groping for reasons to explain its disappointing reception. But now that his novel has become an established classic, it is not so apparent that Gatsby's vagueness is the flaw Fitzgerald thought it was. The puppet-carver, for example, knows that it is a mistake to carve his puppet's features too meticulously. At the distance from which the audience views his figures, reality is as much a factor of the onlooker's imagination as the carver's faithfulness to literal detail.[13]

Gatsby, too, is a puppet figure. It is useless to demand that he approximate the reality of the other characters in the novel, since the question of his reality is itself the subject matter of the story. He is an ideal figure, and the focal distance that separates him from the reader is greater than that of any of the other characters. What credibility he finally attains in the reader's imagination is not due to any specific action that he performs as much as to what he represents. Essentially, Gatsby is a mythic character, and the reality he achieves is that of the myth that creates and sustains him.

Lord Raglan, in his classic study of *The Hero*, points out that the career of the typical hero of Western folk literature generally follows a familiar pattern. Nothing illustrates Gatsby's mythopoeic nature better than his many resemblances to this archetype. According to Lord Raglan, the traditional hero of legend is the son of royal parents who has been wrongfully deprived of his birthright and sent away to the hinterland to be reared by humble foster parents. He is ignorant of his origins, yet his natural grace and talents soon mark him as a superior being. Suspecting that he is different from his companions, he leaves home and sets off for the king's court to seek his fortune. There he proves himself by some onerous test and eventually regains his rightful heritage?[14]

Most striking of all is Gatsby's resemblance to one particularly well-known variation of this pattern—the so-called Great or Noble Fool. This story was especially popular with Celtic bards, and served as the source for the histories of two famous Arthurian heroes, Sir Galahad and Sir Perceval. Here the rude country lad on his way to court meets a beautiful lady of high degree, wins her favor and spends a memorable night with her. Proceeding to court, he is mocked by the king's followers because of his rude ways and given a menial position, usually in the castle' kitchen. There he is ridiculed by the evil cook (or steward) until an opportunity arrives for him to prove himself. The lovely lady whom he met earlier appears on the scene, begging the king for a champion to defend her against some evil being who has her in thrall—an enchanter or cruel dragon or, in some versions, a cruel husband. Since everyone else is too frightened to volunteer, our hero steps forth, follows her to battle, destroys the wrong-doer, and wins her hand in marriage.[15]

The resemblances between this ancient pattern and *The Great Gatsby* are self-evident. That Fitzgerald had them consciously in mind when he was writing his novel is unlikely. But there is no doubt at all about his familiarity with the great fool motif. As a boy he had not only read Sir Walter Scott's famous version, *Ivanhoe*, but had written an imitation in verse, "Elavoe." During the years that he was growing up, a number of popular sentimental treatments of the great fool theme appeared in fiction—notably Sir James Barrie's *Sentimental Tommy* and *The Little Minister*, and John William Locke's *The Beloved Vagabond*. In *This Side of Paradise* Amory listed all three among the favorite books of his childhood. Also, in a 1923 review of Sherwood Anderson's *Many Marriages*, written while Fitzgerald was planning *The Great Gatsby*, he refers to the theme of "the noble fool which has dominated tragedy from Don Quixote to Lord Jim."[16]

In one of the best-known renditions of this myth, the legend of Sir Parzival, the hero ultimately renounces the various worldly trophies that he has won by his prowess, including sexual love, and dedicates himself to the quest for the Holy Grail, the symbol of the perfect life. It was an unattainable goal in this world, but, purified by long years of self-denial and a simple life, Parzival is finally rewarded with a vision of the Grail as he dies and ascends to Heaven.

Gatsby too, as Fitzgerald says, had "committed himself to a following of the Grail." But the Grail he pursues is the modern one of worldly success. Much of the force of his story lies in the fact that it combines two of the most pervasive myths in modern Western culture, with each serving as a critique of the other. One is the medieval and fundamentally Christian myth of the grail knight, and his lifelong pursuit of the good, the beautiful, and the true. The other is the modern secular myth of the self-made man—based on the belief that anyone, no matter how lowly his origins, could rise and become a success, provided he worked hard and made the most of his talents. The symbols of success were those that Fitzgerald himself had pursued with such diligence—wealth, prestige, and the possession of a beautiful, popular girl.[17]

Somewhere between the closing of the Middle Ages and the beginning of the modern era, the Parzival myth was supplanted by the present-day myth of the poor boy who makes good. The most convincing evidence for this is the dramatic emergence of a popular culture hero embodying the values of the new industrial society—Dick Whittington, best-known and best-loved of modern business tycoons.

Within the space of a few years, from 1600 to 1610 or so, Renaissance London experienced a sudden outpouring of broadsides, ballads, plays, and stories in prose and verse, all glorifying this hitherto unknown hero of the new rising middle class. The real Sir Richard Whittington had been dead and forgotten for almost two hundred years. The facts of his life, except that he owned a cat and had been Lord Mayor of London, bore little relation to the new Elizabethan legend. What was needed was a popular folk hero whose history would inculcate the virtues of the new philosophy of hard work and the opportunity to rise in the world. So sudden and so dramatic was Dick Whittington's appearance on the scene, full-blown, that one suspects the machinations of an Elizabethan public relations expert—just as the American "Paul Bunyan" would later spring in full panoply from the brain of a smart lumber industry advertising executive.[18]

Thus was the tale of the great fool changed to suit the needs of the new dispensation. During the years that followed Dick became the established ideal middle-class hero. Nowhere was he better-known or more admired than in the U.S.A., where his history went through edition after edition. Among some of his more famous offspring were Benjamin Franklin's "Poor Richard" and Horatio Alger's poor-boy heroes—Ragged Dick, Frank Fearless, and the sturdy lads of *Making His Way, Strive and Succeed*, and *From Canal Boy to President*.

It was hardly necessary for Fitzgerald to know the writings of Alger or Franklin to have been familiar with their philosophy of business success. Their maxims were promulgated weekly in the pages of popular magazines like *The Saturday Evening Post* (which claimed to have been founded by Franklin). In fact, one scholar has recently shown that Fitzgerald actually based Gatsby's pathetic list of rules for self-improvement on "Poor Richard's" popular precepts for getting ahead in the world. And in a deleted passage of an early draft of *The Great Gatsby*, Fitzgerald actually called one of Gatsby's sinister business acquaintances "Mr. Franklin Dick." Such was his ironic tribute to the Dick Whittingtons, Ragged Dicks, Poor Richards, and their forerunners to whom Gatsby owed his shabby glamorous dreams.[19]

Like the rest of his generation, Fitzgerald also knew his Horatio Alger. In "Absolution," Rudolph Miller's tiny library consists exclusively of that author's works. In "Forging Ahead," another autobiographical story written several years later for the *Post*, celebrating the virtues of hard work and determination, Fitzgerald said that after his hero decided to become a business success he "took down half a dozen dusty volumes of Horatio Alger ... then much as a postwar young man might consult The George Washington Condensed Business Course, he sat at his desk and slowly began to turn the pages of 'Bound to Rise.'"[20]

Thus like Fitzgerald's earlier play, *The Vegetable*, *The Great Gatsby* was a conscious indictment of the American dream of success. Like *The Vegetable*, it was another attempt to atone for stories like "The Popular Girl," "The Offshore Pirate," and "Forging Ahead," which accepted this precept, and which he would continue to write (as long as his conscience would let him) whenever he needed money. But unlike *The Vegetable, The Great Gatsby* succeeded because, by turning to his own past, Fitzgerald was able to make use of the wealth of mythology that had shaped his own experience.

Gatsby, like Fitzgerald, wants it both ways. He must be a Grail Knight as well as a Wall Street tycoon. He expects Daisy to be the innocent maiden in distress waiting stoically for her knight-errant. At the same time he insists that she be a typical "popular" girl—rich, pretty, and consequently self-centered and unadventurous. Confused by these conflicting aims and goals, the vulnerable Gatsby is easily betrayed and destroyed. But story affirms the unique value as the limitations of the philosophy of romantic individualism. More than any other American novel, *The Great Gatsby* demonstrates the tragic quality of this faith—still one of the most pervasive and vigorous beliefs of Western man.

NOTES

1. MP to FSF, November 18 and 20, 1924, SF; J.H. Wheelock editor *Editor to Author: The Letters of Maxwell E. Perkins* (New York, Charles Scribner's Sons, 1950) 38–40; MP to Ring Lardner, November 29, 1924, SF.

2. To MP, n.d. (*ca.* Dec. 20, 1924) SF.

3. *Gatsby*, 202.

4. *Gatsby*, 212.

5. *time*, December 11, 1944, 84.

6. MP to FSF, August 8, 1924, PF.

7. Ring Lardner to FSF, August 8, 1925, PF.

8. The histories of E.M. Fuller and Co., of Edward Fuller, and of his business associates, can be traced through the New York *Times Annual Index*, 1920–28 and the annual index, 1922–24, of the *Commercial and Financial Chronile*; for Fuller's flying exploits se New York *Times*, July 11, 1921, 11:3.

9. Feature article on Charles Stoneham, New York *Times*, September 9, 1923, VIII:2:1; see also Gene Fowler, *the Great Mouthpiece: A Life Story of William J. Fallon* (New York, Blue Ribbon Books, 1931), 326–340.

10. Stanley Walker, *The Night Club Era* (New York, Fred A. Stokes Co., 1933), 10; Lloyd Morris, *Postscript to Yesterday* (New York, Random House, 1947), 75.

11. *Gatsby*, 161; pencil draft of *Gatsby* manuscript, 206, PF.

12. To HDP in conversation, February 6, 1950.

13. To JPB, n.d. (*ca.* Summer, 1925) PF.

14. Lord Raglan, *The Hero: A Study in Tradition, Myth and Drama* (New York, Vintage, 1956), 174–75; see also Arnold Toynbee, *A Study of History* (Oxford University Press, 1934) III, 259.

15. B.B. Bruestle, *"The Fool of Nature" in the English Drama of Our Day* (Philadelphia, University of Pennsylvania, 1932), 14–19; Jessie L. Weston, *From Ritual to Romance* (Cambridge University Press, 1920), 28.

16. New York *Herald Tribune*, March 4, 1923.

17. *Gatsby*, 179.

18. "Sir Richard Whittington," *Dictionary of National Biography*; Rev. Samuel Lysons, *The Model Merchant* (London, Hamilton, Adams, & Co., 1860); *The history of Sir Richard Whittington* by "T.H.", edited with an introduction by H.B> Wheatley, F.A.A. (London, for the Villon Society, 1885); see also Louis B. Wright, *Middle Class Culture in Elizabethan England* (Chapel Hill, North Carolina, University of North Carolina Press, 1938), 1–3, 616–617; on Paul Bunyan, Daniel F. Hoffman, *Paul Bunyan: Last of the Frontier Demi-Gods* (Philadelphia, University of Pennsylvania Press, 1952).

19. F.C. Watkins, *New England Quarterly*, 27:2, 249–52 (June 1954); pencil manuscript of *Gatsby*, Chapter III, PF.

20. *AOA*, 35.

NEILA SESHACHARI

The Great Gatsby:
Apogee of Fitzgerald's Mythopoeia

The Great Gatsby marks the apogee of Fitzgerald's craft of fiction, especially in its richness of mythopoeic implications and use of mythic symbols. In this novel Fitzgerald successfully blends local, national, historical, and primitive myths, as a result of which the significance of the novel seems to "enlarge in ever-widening ripples," not only in terms of the personal, historical, and metaphysical as Richard Lehan suggests,[1] but even in terms of the mythistoric leading to myth. *The Great Gatsby* is remarkable for the multi-level mythic interpretation that it suggests. The mythic quality of *The Great Gatsby*, therefore, manifests itself at various levels to different critics. For instance, *The Great Gatsby* variously suggests itself as the perfect expression of the ephemeral Jazz Age; as the enactment of the history of the New World[2]; as the embodiment of the American Dream[3]; as a damaging criticism of that Dream[4]; and as a novel where the hero is so impersonalized as to be a mythic character.[5] *The Great Gatsby* is all these and more, for it is truly polysemous in mythic overtones. Critics, who are all agreed that in this novel Fitzgerald gives a scathing criticism of the myth of the American Dream, have spoken of the American Dream and Gatsby's personal dream as if they were synonymous—as if that were the prime reason why *The Great Gatsby* offers, in effect, a criticism of the American Dream. A closer inquiry into the fundamental difference between the American Dream and Gatsby's personal quest might point to the suggestion that *The Great Gatsby*, which is

From *Fitzgerald/Hemingway Annual* 1976, ed. Matthew J. Bruccoli. © 1978 by Indian Head Inc.

a damaging commentary on the former, may in fact be an affirmation of the latter. Also, Gatsby may appear to be a mythic character not only because he is impersonalized and appears to be the romantic impulse[6] crystallized in the term American Dream, but also because Gatsby's story offers a complete parallel to the embryonic path of the mythic hero, so that Gatsby, in his death and apotheosis, seems a minor avatar of the truly great mythic heroes of the stature of Theseus, Jason, Karna, and others.

A close study of *The Great Gatsby* will reveal that there are basic generic differences between the traditional American Dream and Gatsby's own personal quest. The American Dream has been an affirmation of the romantic possibilities of the human imagination and a belief in man's inherent greatness. Gatsby's personal philosophy synchronizes with this outlook. However, apart from this common faith, the actual direction that Gatsby's personal dream took does not follow the pattern of the American Dream. The American Dream, historically, has been the outcome of the Renaissance spirit and the later era of economic development and opportunism. The actual opportunity that the new continent offered the seekers of an essentially human dream shaped the forms of that quest. Thus, in 20th-century America, the goals of success are youth and wealth; as Edwin Fussell has pointed out, one aspect of the American Dream is the mythistoric quest of Ponce de Leon, whereas the other is plainly, wealth.[7] Thus at the core, the American Dream may be said to be self-centered. A votary of the American Dream is given to thinking in terms of the glorification of the self; he strives to establish his personal identity and amasses immense wealth before he allows either the gospel or the Internal Revenue Service to channel his thoughts to philanthropy. The hero's yearning after the most beautiful girl in the world is one of the symptoms of his ego-satisfaction. The girl is simply an adjunct or addition to the hero's manifest wealth. She is a visual symbol of his greatness, as Daisy is to Tom Buchanan. It matters not whether there is true love between the two—in fact, true love would imply a recapitulation of ego-seeking values. True love implies an acknowledgment of the worth of the beloved and sharing of glory. In admitting a dependence on the object of love, it diminishes, to that extent, the belief in the absolute power of the self. The American male has not been inclined to share the glory of his conquests with the woman. In the unfolding of the Promethean imagination on the new continent, woman has not shared the victory or the glory of the adventurer. The Women's Liberation Movement is the modern-day protest of this state. The American Dream, thus, is founded on the concept of the expansion of the male self based on a romantic belief in the glory of the self. Gatsby's personal quest appears to be an extension of the American Dream because in the pursuit of his personal dream he was compelled to resort to the material acquisition demanded by the American society in which he lived and of which he was a part. But in reality Gatsby's dream transcends the accepted modes of the American Dream to envelop man's primordial concepts. For Gatsby's quest is not youth and wealth which are the symptomatic goals of the American Dream; Gatsby's personal quest centers wholly on his acquisition of the object of his love—woman—which is really the quest of the mythic ideal.

Woman, in her mythic concept, is the ultimate quest of the hero. She is the symbol of all that is knowable and worthy of being conquered or won. As Joseph Campbell asserts:

> Woman, in the picture language of mythology, represents the totality of what can be known. The hero is the one who comes to know. As he progresses in the slow initiation which is life, the form of the goddess undergoes for him a series of transfigurations: she can never be greater than himself, though she can always promise more than he is yet capable of comprehending. She lures, she guides, she bids him burst his fetters. And if he can match her import, the two, the knower and the known, will be released from every limitation. Woman is the guide to the sublime acme of sensuous adventure. By deficient eyes she is reduced to inferior states; by the evil eye of ignorance she is spellbound to banality and ugliness. But she is redeemed by the eyes of understanding. The hero who can take her as she is, without undue commotion but with the kindness and assurance she requires, is potentially the king, the incarnate god, of her created world.[8]

This symbol of woman standing for world conquest and ultimate glory is operative in fairy tales and folk tales where the union of the hero with his beloved and the assertion of "... and they lived happily ever after" imply that the hero has reached his zenith. The hero's union with his beloved implies here, a fulfillment of the purpose of life. Gatsby's quest for Daisy is thus the quest of the mythic ideal and not of the values of the American Dream.

Gatsby's one consuming passion to which all others are either subordinate or nonexistent is his hope of winning Daisy. His acquisition of wealth, his nebulous parties, his mysterious activities are all secondary to his purpose which is to win back his woman. Getting into her "class" of society and accumulating enough wealth to be worthy of her are self-purificatory rites that he has to undergo before he can be worthy of her. His sense of worship—wonderment, anxiety, nervousness—are all obvious when he arranges to meet her at Nick Carraway's home for tea. The entire chapter in which he meets Daisy for the first time since their separation five years previously exudes Gatsby's sense of worship of Daisy. The preparation for the worship is itself very elaborate. Two whole days before their meeting—in fact, on the day it is arranged—Gatsby's home is lit from tower to cellar in an unreal blaze. It isn't the occasion of another party, and when Nick comments to Gatsby that his house looks like the World's Fair, Gatsby answers absently, "I have been glancing into some of the rooms."[9] The self-assured son of God is visibly nervous even in preparation for the visit of his goddess. In his anxiety to have everything right for his beloved, Gatsby has Nick's lawn mowed and flowers provided abundantly. Gatsby's offer of monetary reward to Nick strangely smacks of the offerings made by a devotee to the high priest in a formal worship ceremony. On the appointed day, minutes before Daisy's arrival, Gatsby "in a white flannel suit, silver shirt, and gold colored tie," makes his nervous appearance. From then on, until Daisy actually arrives and the evening wears on, Gatsby is in a state of nervous tension and panic combined into one. When he disappears from Nick's living room and makes his formal entry befitting the occasion, he looks "pale as death," his eyes are "distraught," and he is generally "trembling" (pp. 104–105). In his anxiety he thinks there has been some terrible mistake somewhere. It is only after Nick discreetly gives them half an hour alone with each other and comes back after making all sorts of noises, that he notices "They were sitting at either end of the couch, looking at each other as if some question had been asked, or was in the air, and every vestige of embarrassment was gone. Daisy's face was smeared with tears.... But there was a change in Gatsby that was simply confounding. He literally glowed; without a word or gesture of exultation a new well-being radiated from him and filled the little room" (pp. 107–108). This comment is Nick's observation and approval of Gatsby's successful worship. Later, as Gatsby takes Daisy and Nick round his home, Nick notices that "He hadn't once ceased looking at Daisy, and ... he revalued everything in his house according to the measure of response it drew from her well-loved eyes. Sometimes, too, *he stared around at his possessions in a dazed way, as though in her actual and astounding presence none of it was any longer real*" (pp. 110–111. Italics mine). Since Gatsby's wealth was acquired with the explicit aim of winning Daisy back and not for its own value, it is natural that his possessions suddenly seem to lose their glamor when he repossesses her. Gatsby's sense of worship of Daisy is seen even when he displays his shirts to her. The reason such a display does not seem vulgar is precisely that there is so much sanctity and ritual involved in the act—the reader intuitively comprehends the seriousness of the situation and holds his breath in awe. The ritual of display has its effect; suddenly, with strained sound Daisy bends her head into the shirts and begins to sob stormily. "They're such beautiful shirts," she sobs, her voice muffled in the thick folds. "It makes me sad because I've never seen such—such beautiful shirts before" (p. 112). At this moment, what Lionel Trilling said of Gatsby himself becomes surprisingly true of even a worship scene such as this: Its "credibility becomes trivial before the larger significance"[10] it implies. This significance, in one vital sense, is the mythic, which Fitzgerald's conceptual imagination seems to have grasped, albeit unconsciously.

Fitzgerald's success in imparting mythic significance to his writings comes from his spotlighting scenes, events, and furnishings that are strongly mythic in their overtones. Gatsby's yacht, for example, functions as a vital mythic symbol. Daisy goes into raptures when she first sees a picture of young Gatsby in yachting costume. Gatsby's career begins when he sees Dan Cody's yacht drop anchor and pulls up in a borrowed rowboat to tell Cody that the wind might catch him and break him up in half an hour. In the mythological formula that outlines the basic life of the hero, the skiff or boat forms, as Joseph Campbell has noted, a very major symbol. With the aid of this, the hero is able to cross the turbulent waters (which is yet another symbol) that endanger his life. The boat or yacht is the symbol of the special talent or virtue that the hero possesses, by which he is ferried across the waters of the world. "And by a like miracle, so will each whose work is the difficult, dangerous task of self-discovery and self-development be portered across the ocean of life."[11]

"To young Gatz, resting on his oars and looking up at the railed deck, that yacht [belonging to Dan Cody] represented all the beauty and glamor in the world.... And when the *Tuolomee* left for the West Indies and the Barbary Coast Gatsby left too" (p. 120). We are told that the arrangement lasted *five* years, during which time the boat went *three times* around the Continent. As Norma Goodrich points out, "Numbers in mythology have essence."[12] Mythologically, five denotes the four quarters, North, South, East, West, and the Center of the Earth. The number three is symbolic of both Christian and Hindu Trinity, "the three persons of Language," or the Egyptian Triad. At the end of his mystical journey Gatsby is "left with his singularly appropriate education"; "the vague contour" of Jay Gatsby fills out "to the substantiality of a man" (p. 121). Thus the picture of Gatsby in his yacht, going three times round the world in five annual revolutions of the earth around the sun, channeling his energies to win his woman may be construed as a symbolic one.

These two symbols—the yacht and the girl—meant a great deal to Fitzgerald himself. In "My Lost City," he writes:

> There was first the ferry boat moving softly from the Jersey shore at dawn—the moment crystallized into my first symbol of New York. Five years later when I was fifteen I went into the city from school to see Ira Claire in *The Quaker Girl* and Gertrude Bryan in *Little Boy Blue*. Confused by my hopeless and melancholy love for them both, I was unable to choose between them—so they blurred into one lovely entity, the girl. She was my second symbol of New York. The ferry boat stood for triumph, the girl for romance.[13]

It is significant that these two symbols recur again and again in his novels beginning with *This Side of Paradise*. In this first novel, Amory Blaine is aware that he was "made for glory," for triumph. When the story begins, Amory is Narcissus—but he is not Narcissus sitting on the banks of a brook brooding admiringly over his image. Rather, he is Narcissus in the ferry boat, paying too much attention to his own image in the water to heed where the ferry is drifting. But even Narcissus knows he is on a mission—some mission—even if it can be described only as a mission of glory, triumph, and romance. Although Amory wants to be a hero, in his scheme of values girls are still secondary. Amory's quest is the quest of the dreamer for the mythic grail. The questor is too naive and his initiation is tantamount to an initiation *manqué*. The protagonist of *The Great Gatsby* is a maturer one and is truly a hero. He is the one who overcomes the confines of his birth and his obstacles through his personal triumph (yacht), wins his goddess (or conquers the world), and is purified in the water of life. Through his valor and achievement, he attains apotheosis.

The water symbol is very extensively used in *The Great Gatsby*. Through a linking of the bay that connects West Egg and East Egg, Gatsby's swimming pool and the yacht that takes him thrice around the waters of the world, his aquaplane, and the final rain that gently purifies everything at the time of Gatsby's funeral, Fitzgerald treats the water symbol as a *leit motif*. Water or rain seems to play a baptismal part in all the crucial events in Gatsby's life. His meeting with Dan Cody takes place over the vast waters of Lake Superior from where he is launched in a "skiff" round the waters of the world. Nick Carraway's first glimpse of Gatsby is that of his standing on the shore of the bay stretching his arms in near mystic contemplation towards the dark waters separating him from Daisy. After five years Gatsby and Daisy are reunited in pouring rain. Also, significantly, Nick picks up Gatsby's body from the waters of his swimming pool. A steady, sombre rain beats down on the day of Gatsby's funeral. At the cemetery, someone murmurs "Blessed are the dead that the rain falls on," and the owl-eyed man says "Amen to that."

Water, as a purifier, is a mythic symbol. The Vedas, for instance, refer frequently to water as a life-giving symbol. The *Rig Veda*, in a creation legend, states how the Vedic god Indra had to strike down the cosmic serpent Vritra in order to release life-giving waters and bring the world into manifestation.[14] The Christian baptism is a rejuvenation through immersion in life-giving or life-purifying waters. Gatsby's death in his swimming pool thus symbolically becomes the scene of his rebirth and apotheosis. Gatsby's death, as Wilfred Louis Guerin has remarked, is a "death by water-rebirth myth."[15] It is meet that the rain should fall at the time of Gatsby's funeral. The rain is a fertility symbol—it rejuvenates the hero and completes his apotheosis. When he emerges from his final test, Gatsby truly rises to the stature of a mythic hero.

In what is probably the most exhaustive study on the subject, Joseph Campbell describes "the standard path of the mythological adventure of the hero" as a "magnification of the formula represented in the rites of passage: separation—initiation—return" which he calls "the nuclear unit of the monomyth."[16] Campbell describes the basic formula of the monomyth in the following terms:

> The mythological hero, setting forth from his commonday hut or castle, is lured, carried away, or else voluntarily proceeds, to the threshold of adventure. There he encounters a shadow presence that guards the passage. The hero may defeat or conciliate this power and go alive into the kingdom of the dark (brother-battle, dragon-battle; offering, charm), or be slain by the opponent and descend in death (dismemberment, crucifixion). Beyond the threshold, the hero journeys through a world of unfamiliar yet strangely intimate forces, some of which severely threaten him (tests), some of which give magical aid (helpers). When he arrives at the nadir of the mythological round, he undergoes a supreme ordeal and gains his reward. The triumph may be represented as the hero's sexual union with the goddess-mother of the world (sacred marriage), his recognition by the father-creator (father atonement), his own divinization (apotheosis), or again—if the powers have remained unfriendly to him—his theft of the boon he came to gain (bride-theft, fire-theft); intrinsically it is an expansion of consciousness and therewith of being (illumination, transfiguration, freedom). The final work is that of the return. If the powers have blessed the hero, he now sets forth under their protection (emissary); if not, he flees and is pursued (transformation flight, obstacle flight). At the return threshold

the transcendental powers must remain behind; the hero re-emerges from the kingdom of dead (return, resurrection). The boon that he brings restores the world (elixir).[17]

The embryonic pattern of the life of the hero is thus broad and adaptable, and individual myths usually elaborate on some of these features. As Campbell admits, "The changes rung on the simple scale of the monomyth defy description."[18]

The predominant events of Gatsby's life follow the basic concepts of this monomyth. Gatsby, like the mythic hero, is a man whose origins are steeped in mystery. He is, simultaneously, the son of nobody and of God. He is the nowhere hero. As Nick appropriately points out, "The truth was that Jay Gatsby of West Egg, Long Island, sprang from his Platonic conception of himself. He was the son of God—a phrase which, if it means anything, means just that—and he must be about His Father's business, the service of a vast, vulgar, and meretricious beauty. So he invented just the sort of Jay Gatsby that a seventeen year-old boy would be likely to invent, and to this conception he was faithful to the end" (p. 118).

James Gatz's transformation into Jay Gatsby marks the call to adventure that every hero must answer. Gatsby's apprenticeship with Dan Cody may be termed the symbolic equivalent of the "descent into the underworld," or "withdrawal from the world" for meditation that marks the spiritual myths. The purpose of these is to equip the hero for the tasks ahead. Gatsby's voyage with Cody is simultaneously his voyage into self and into the world. It marks the hero's setting forth on his adventures. As Campbell has pointed out, "The adventure is always and everywhere a passage beyond the veil of the known into the unknown."[19] The first adventure of the mythic journey is usually with some protective or guardian figure—the fairy-godmother of fairy tales, or some wizard, hermit, etc. who gives the hero some advice and possibly amulets or charmed possessions with which to protect himself in extreme danger. The higher or macrocosmic mythologies assign this role to some sort of father figure—a teacher, saint, or ferryman conducting the souls in the underworld. Dan Cody is suggestive of such a ferryman. The most important lesson that the hero learns in the first adventure is the notion of self-annihilation or "self-achieved submission." The reason for this would be that "No creature can attain a higher grade of nature without ceasing to exist."[20] Or, to put in other words, "We must lose ourselves to find ourselves in the overall pattern of the cosmos."[21] After his apprenticeship with his guardian figure Dan Cody is over, Jay Gatsby, now a young lieutenant in the army, meets Daisy, his goddess, when stationed in Louisville. Their wonder romance culminates one October evening into what could appropriately be termed a "mystical marriage" with her. That evening, as they were walking, "Out of the corner of his eye Gatsby saw that the blocks of the sidewalks really formed a ladder and mounted to a secret place above the trees—he could climb to it, if he climbed alone, and once there he could suck on the pap of life, gulp down the incomparable milk of wonder" (p. 134). At that moment "He knew that when he kissed this girl, and forever wed his unutterable visions to her perishable breath, his mind would never romp again like the mind of God. So he waited, listening for a moment longer to the tuning-fork that had been struck upon a star. Then he kissed her. At his lips' touch she blossomed for him like a flower and the incarnation was complete" (p. 134). This event marks the hero's initial conquest of the woman and symbolically of the world.

The mythic hero's conquest of the world remains a temporary one if the forces have not yet blessed the hero, and there is often a theft of the boon, "bride-theft" or "fire-theft" etc. In Gatsby's case, the ogre who snatches his bride away is Tom Buchanan. Nick describes Tom as a domineering, aggressive tyrant who has supercilious manners and a powerful, cruel body (p. 8). His voice, in sharp contrast to Daisy's gold-filled, melodious, hypnotic one, is "a gruff husky tenor" and adds to the impression of "fractiousness" that he exudes. He is totally egotistical. He is the ogre who abducts Gatsby's goddess and keeps her in imprisonment. Not until the hero has successfully fought this ogre can he win his bride back.

The entire summer interlude of *The Great Gatsby*, in a sense, depicts the war of the hero for his lost bride or lost love. Tristram P. Coffin, in an article called "Gatsby's Fairy Lover," sees *The Great Gatsby* as an odd mixture of the Celtic fairy tale of *La Belle Dame Sans Merci* and a märchen that is classified as Aarne-Thompson #561.[22] If *The Great Gatsby* is to be interpreted in terms of a märchen type, then perhaps Aarne-Thompson #400 would suit the story better. Gatsby is really in search of his lost wife (or lost love) because he has been eternally wedded to Daisy in mystical rites and comes to claim what he believes to be, not somebody else's, but his own. All the events of the summer culminate in the New York hotel scene where Gatsby "wins" his final battle with Tom and gets back his bride. The open encounter between Daisy and Tom vindicates Gatsby's victory, even though it turns out to be a short-lived one, and Gatsby is dead soon after.

In the embryonic pattern of the mythological hero, the final stage of the hero's journey is his apotheosis; this apotheosis, however, is often reached through the preliminary stage of "crucifixion." Even Jesus, the mythic hero *par excellence*, was crucified as a common criminal. To suggest that Gatsby is similarly killed is not necessarily to imply that he is a prototype of the Jesus-hero of spiritual myths, but to suggest that Gatsby's mortal end falls within the pattern of the mythic heroes. The "extinction" of the hero in death in such cases is only a prelude to the final resurrection or apotheosis. The final pages of *The Great Gatsby* impart to the reader a philosophical sense of tragedy of a mythic ideal—the American Dream—rather than a sense of Gatsby's personal tragedy. It is a tragedy of society, of its shallowness, of its false values, and of its blindness. Gatsby, even in death, is untainted. As a matter of fact, Gatsby's stature may be said to rise in his death. Nick Carraway, who is like the antenna of a moral order of universe, is awed by Gatsby's stature in death, and in Nick's mind and values, there is a reaffirmation of Gatsby's real worth. This is the apotheosis and resurrection of the mythic hero. Through his resurrection, the mythic hero enlarges, the vision of the common man, "For the hero figure is," as Emma Jung points out, "one of those eternal archetypal images which slumber in the depths of every soul and which determine human life and destiny in unsuspected measure."[23] In this sense, Gatsby, the mythic hero, operates not only at the macrocosmic level but through the linking of the imagination of the common man, at even the microcosmic level.

Jay Gatsby is a mythic figure because he operates simultaneously at the macrocosmic and the microcosmic levels, without being personally affected by his role. For instance, *The Great Gatsby* is a critique of the American Dream and a criticism of its material values, but this criticism somehow never touches Gatsby's own personality. He is untouched by the implications of the novel. In a corrupt, materialistic world, Gatsby's pursuit remains idealistic and untainted; amongst a class of shallow liars, he turns out to be the one with unswerving values; Gatsby's own wealth and display of it remains totally dedicated to the service of his romantic ideal. And therefore, when the summer interlude ends on the bizarre picture of Gatsby's dead body floating in his swimming pool, even the tragedy does not seem to touch Gatsby's person. It is a tragic commentary on every other character in the novel (except Nick's) and on the American Dream itself, but not on Gatsby. Gatsby curiously appears to vindicate his position. The clue to this final impression that the novel leaves may lie in the fact that "whenever the mythological mood pervades, tragedy is impossible."[24] The death of a mythic hero is a tragedy only for the people; it is always a triumph or ultimate victory for the hero himself. For the hero, who in his life presented a dual perspective (as Gatsby did), in his death is a synthesizing image. So in Gatsby's death are reconciled all the conflicts and tensions of national and human vision, as well as Gatsby's own tensions.

NOTES

1. Richard Lehan, *F. Scott Fitzgerald and the Craft of Fiction* (Carbondale: Southern Illinois University Press, 1966), p. 118.

2. Edwin Fussell, "Fitzgerald's Brave New World," *The Great Gatsby: A Study*, ed. Frederick J. Hoffman (New York: Scribner's, 1962), pp. 244–262.

3. Frederick J. Hoffman, ed., "Introduction," *The Great Gatsby: A Study*, p. 8.

4. Marius Bewley, "Scott Fitzgerald's Criticism of America," *The Great Gatsby: A Study*, p. 263.

5. Marius Bewley, *The Great Gatsby: A Study*, p. 272.

6. Frederick J. Hoffman, *The Great Gatsby: A Study*, p. 11.

7. "Fitzgerald's Brave New World," *The Great Gatsby: A Study*, pp. 245–246.

8. *The Hero with a Thousand Faces*, Bollingen Series XVII (New York: Pantheon Books, 1949), p. 116.

9. F. Scott Fitzgerald, *The Great Gatsby* (New York: Scribner's, 1925), p. 98. All further references to this novel will be indicated in parentheses in the body of the article.

10. F. Scott Fitzgerald," *F. Scott Fitzgerald: The Man and His Work*, ed. Alfred Kazin (Cleveland: The World Publishing Company, 1951), pp. 201–202.

11. *The Hero with a Thousand Faces*, pp. 22–23.

12. Norma Lorre Goodrich, *Myths of the Hero* (New York: The Orion Press, 1962), p. xx.

13. *The Crack-Up*, ed. Edmund Wilson (New York: New Directions, 1945), p. 23.

14. Dorothy Norman, *The Hero: Myth/Image/Symbol* (New York: World, 1969), p. 14.

15. "Christian Myth and Naturalistic Deity: *The Great Gatsby*," *Renascence*, V (1962), 85.

16. *The Hero with a Thousand Faces*, p. 30. Campbell uses the word monomyth from James Joyce, *Finnegans Wake* (New York: Viking Press, 1939), p. 581.

17. *The Hero with a Thousand Faces*, pp. 245–46.

18. *The Hero with a Thousand Faces*, p. 246.

19. *The Hero with a Thousand Faces*, p. 82.

20. Ananda K. Coomaraswamy, "Akimcanna: Self-Naughting," *New Indian Antiquary*, III (Bombay, 1940), 6, note 14. Quoted by Joseph Campbell, *The Hero with a Thousand Faces*, p. 92.

21. David Adams Leeming, *Mythology: The Voyage of the Hero* (New York: Lippincott, 1973), p. 6.

22. "Gatsby's Fairy Lover," *Midwest Folklore*, X (1960), 79–85.

23. Emma Jung and Marie-Louis Van Franz, *The Grail Legend*, trans. Andrea Dykes (New York: Putnam, 1970), p. 46.

24. *The Hero with a Thousand Faces*, p. 69.

BRIAN WAY

The Great Gatsby

T he power of a great novel often depends, more than anything else, upon the firmness and suitability of its underlying structure. 'On this hard fine floor', Henry James wrote in his Preface to *The Awkward Age*, 'the element of execution feels it may more or less confidently *dance*.' A novelist cannot hope to compensate by mere 'treatment' for 'the loose foundation or the vague scheme.' He can best avoid this kind of weakness by making his work express as far as possible the necessities of dramatic form: 'The dramatist has verily to *build*, is committed to architecture, to construction at any cost; to driving in deep his vertical supports and laying across and firmly fixing his horizontal, his resting pieces.'[1] If a novel is to have this secure basis, it should be written, like a play, in scenes; and each scene should have a definite shape and a precise location—those qualities we associate with theatrical performance.

The most striking formal characteristic of *The Great Gatsby* is its scenic construction, and Scott Fitzgerald himself, as we have seen, spoke of it as a 'dramatic' novel. In this respect, it shows extraordinarily close affinities with the theory and practice of James's later fiction. James's vivid account of the little diagram he drew in order to explain the structure of *The Awkward Age* to his publisher, corresponds exactly with what we find in *Gatsby*:

From *F. Scott Fitzgerald and the Art of Social Fiction.* © 1980 by Brian Way.

I drew on a sheet of paper ... the neat figure of a circle consisting
of a number of small rounds disposed at equal distance about a
central object. The central object was my situation, my subject in
itself, to which the thing would owe its title, and the small rounds
represented so many distinct lamps, as I liked to call them, the
function of each of which would be to light with all due intensity
one of its aspects ... Each of my 'lamps' would be the light of a
single 'social occasion' in the history and intercourse of the
characters concerned, and would bring out to the full the latent
colour of the scene in question and cause it to illuminate, to the
last drop, its bearing on my theme. I revelled in this notion of the
Occasion as a thing by itself, really and completely a scenic
thing ...[2]

The 'central object' of *The Great Gatsby* is clearly Gatsby himself, and the
chapters of the novel are in the main a series of dramatic scenes, each
illuminating some new aspect of his character and situation. The scenes are
invariably 'social occasions'; often they are parties, in that special sense which
is so fundamental to Fitzgerald's understanding of the 1920s. Chapter I is
built around the dinner party at the Buchanans' at which Nick Carraway
discovers the subtle charm and the inner corruption of Daisy and of the
American rich—the woman and the class which Gatsby has made the object
of his dreams. Chapter II presents the 'foul dust' that floats in the wake of his
dreams. It opens with a poetic and atmospheric evocation of the valley of
ashes, but its main source of energy is once again dramatic—the raucous
Prohibition-style party in Myrtle Wilson's apartment. In Chapter III, Nick
visits one of Gatsby's own parties for the first time, and begins to understand
the equivocal nature of the latter's creative powers—his capacity to mix the
beautiful with the vulgar, the magical with the absurd. Chapter IV functions
like an act in two scenes, each revealing a contrasted aspect of Gatsby's
identity: the lunch in New York, at which Nick meets Meyer Wolfsheim and
has a glimpse of Gatsby's underworld connections; and the tea during which
Jordan Baker tells him the story of Gatsby's wartime affair with Daisy. The
dramatic focus of Chapter V is the tea party at Nick's house, when Gatsby
and Daisy are reunited; and in Chapter VI Nick attends a second party at
Gatsby's, at which Daisy herself is present. Chapter VII, like Chapter IV, is
an act in two scenes: the lunch party at the Buchanans' where Tom realizes
for the first time that Daisy and Gatsby are lovers; and the abortive cocktail
party at the Plaza Hotel in New York, where Tom not only ends the affair,
but succeeds in destroying Gatsby's 'platonic conception' of himself. Only in
the last two chapters does Fitzgerald largely abandon the dramatic method,

and, even here, some of the most vivid moments depend on effects which are scenic in character—Mr Gatz's arrival at Gatsby's house, Nick's second meeting with Meyer Wolfsheim in New York, and Gatsby's funeral.

Nick Carraway is a key element in the success of this scheme, indeed he is no less vital to the structure of *The Great Gatsby* than to its tone and meaning. He is both stage manager and chorus, re-creating situations in all their actuality, and at the same time commenting upon them. Sometimes he even devises the action—contrives the circumstances by which the actors are brought together on the stage: it is he who arranges the reunion of Gatsby and Daisy. Nick has a further value from the structural point of view: through him, Fitzgerald is able to maintain a kind of flexibility which James considered impossible in the dramatic mode of fiction. James believed that, in order to benefit fully from the firmness of dramatic construction, the novelist was compelled to relinquish the privilege of 'going behind' the action so as to analyse and comment upon it.[3] But, thanks to Nick Carraway, Fitzgerald has the best of both worlds: he moves from the dramatic concentration of 'the scenic thing' to the rich texture of narrative without the smallest effect of incoherence or inconsistency.

This principle of construction affects every aspect of Fitzgerald's artistry: in particular, the language of *The Great Gatsby* often rises at moments of intensity to the level of dramatic poetry; and the element of social comedy, which gives the novel its predominant tone and colouring, always finds expression through specifically theatrical effects of action and spectacle. The structure of a dramatic novel, however, is not an end in itself: each scene, to use James's metaphor, is a lamp illuminating a central object, and it is this object which must remain the reader's primary concern. For this reason, a scene-by-scene analysis is by no means the best way to approach *The Great Gatsby*, and a thematic treatment is far more likely to bring out the true nature of Gatsby himself. I shall therefore discuss his situation and character from three points of view: the external social reality—the way of life of the American rich—by which he has been deluded and betrayed; the texture of his inner imaginative life, which becomes, in Fitzgerald's hands, an image of the romantic sensibility and its maladies; and his dramatic identity—his essentially comic nature.

The evolution of Gatsby's dream is the history of his involvement with a social class, the American rich. The turbulent imaginings of his adolescence first take shape in the scheme of self-advancement which he draws up in imitation of Benjamin Franklin and Horatio Alger. At this time, he has a plan to make himself rich, but no clear mental picture of what wealth and success would be like. This gap is partially filled when Dan Cody's yacht anchors off the Lake Superior shore, and Gatsby meets Cody himself. At once Cody, the Western tycoon, who is spending his money in the flamboyant style of the Gilded Age, becomes Gatsby's image of the wealthy and successful man. He changes his name from Jimmy Gatz to Jay Gatsby in an attempt to embrace this new conception in all its aspects. Cody's swagger is the basis of his own social style, and, like the former, he sees the acquisition of wealth as essentially an activity of the frontier—if not the actual geographical and historical frontier, then the no-man's-land between business and criminality.

As well as an image of himself, however, Gatsby needs an image of something beyond him to which he can aspire, and this final stage in his imaginative development is completed when he meets Daisy during the War and becomes her lover. When he kissed her for the first time, he 'wed forever his ineffable vision to her perishable flesh': from that moment, she was the substance of his dream, and 'the incarnation was complete'. In his eyes, she is intensely desirable both as a woman and as the symbol of a way of life:

> Gatsby was overwhelmingly aware of the youth and mystery which wealth imprisons and preserves, of the freshness of many clothes, and of Daisy, gleaming like silver, safe and proud above the hot struggles of the poor.[4]

Daisy's charm involves a subtle fusion of two powerful sources of attraction, sex and money: one might say that, in her, money becomes sexually desirable. This quality is concentrated in her voice, the one facet of her beauty which can never fall short of Gatsby's dream. As Nick Carraway reflects, when he leaves them alone together for the first time after their five year separation, 'I think that voice held him most, with its fluctuating, feverish warmth, because it couldn't be over-dreamed—that voice was a deathless song.'[5] Nick's tone surrounds the metaphor of song with an aura of high romance, but it is Gatsby himself who uncovers the secret of those elusive cadences, when he remarks with impressive simplicity that 'her voice is full of money.' Many American novelists, including Henry James, Edith Wharton and Theodore Dreiser, were well aware that a beautiful woman may contain within herself all the beguiling characteristics of a social class, but no one apart from Fitzgerald has ever found so felicitous an image for the interior music of wealth.

Gatsby is incapable of seeing the American rich in any other way, but Fitzgerald, through Nick Carraway, makes us equally aware of their shortcomings from the very beginning of the novel. His introductory portraits of Daisy and Tom Buchanan are sketched in with delicate irony. Nick is half dazzled by their wealth, and yet knows that their lives are pervaded by an atmosphere of rootlessness and futility. Since their marriage, they have 'drifted here and there unrestfully wherever people played polo and were rich together'—a year in France, a season or two on Chicago's North Shore, and now a summer on Long Island. Tom's discontent seems an expression, in part, of his permanent immaturity. He had been a great football star at Yale, 'a national figure in a way, one of those men who reach such an acute limited excellence at twenty-one that everything afterwards savours of anti-climax.' Nick suspects that he will 'drift on forever seeking, a little wistfully, for the dramatic turbulence of some irrecoverable football game.'[6]

These weaknesses are serious enough, but worse is to follow, and when Nick accepts Daisy's invitation to dinner he quickly learns the full extent of the Buchanans' corruption. Their failure is presented as the failure of a civilization, of a way of life. Nick Carraway imagines that he will find among the sophisticated Eastern rich, the high point of American civilization. The expanse of the Buchanans' lawns, the graciousness of their house, the formality of dinner, the poised, confident social tone give all the outward signs that a high civilization has been achieved. Nick contrasts the occasion with parties in the Middle West, where people hurry from one phase of the evening to the next in a state of 'continually disappointed anticipation' or in 'sheer nervous dread of the moment itself'. 'Your make me feel uncivilized,' he says to Daisy, 'can't you talk about crops or something.' At once he is ludicrously disillusioned by Tom, who is provoked by Nick's remark into an incoherent account of a book he has just read which 'proves' that 'civilization—oh, science and art, and all that' is threatened by the rise of the coloured races. To our sense of the restlessness and futility of their lives is now added an element of brutality and arrogance. A telephone-call from Tom's mistress, and a tense whispered quarrel with Daisy offstage on which Jordan Baker eavesdrops shamelessly, conclude the scene. The rottenness of these people is conveyed with a fine sense of comedy.

Nick's disappointment has already been prefigured poetically in his first glimpse of the Buchanan household:

> A breeze blew through the room, blew curtains in at one end and out the other like pale flags, twisting them up toward the frosted wedding-cake of the ceiling, and then rippled over the wine-coloured rug, making a shadow on it as wind does on the sea.
>
> The only completely stationary object in the room was an enormous couch on which two young women were buoyed up as though upon an anchored balloon. They were both in white, and their dresses were rippling and fluttering as if they had just been blown back in after a short flight around the house.[7]

The house, the draperies, the young women themselves, seem positively airborne upon Nick's romantic sense of expectation, until Tom enters: 'Then there was a boom as Tom Buchanan shut the rear windows and the caught wind died out about the room, and the curtains, and the rugs and the two young women ballooned slowly to the floor.'[8] Tom brings everything quite literally down to earth. There is no more impressive instance of how much Fitzgerald's fiction gains from his sense of the specifically poetic possibilities of the novel. And, as I have already suggested in chapter 2, we are dealing here with dramatic poetry, not the large abstractions of symbol and myth. In a way which is both subtler and more flexible, the local effects of language are finely adapted to the immediate demands of the scene, the moment.

The element of physical brutality in Tom Buchanan's character is insisted upon from the beginning. An arrogant stare; a manner which is both supercilious and aggressive; 'a great pack of muscle shifting when his shoulder moved under his thin coat'—these are the details of his appearance which catch our attention. His brutality is constantly breaking through the veneer of his surface gentility, just as the movements of his 'cruel body' show under the 'effeminate swank' of his riding clothes. At that first dinner Daisy displays a finger he has bruised in some domestic tussle; he breaks Myrtle Wilson's nose with a singularly efficient application of force; and he takes a vindictive pleasure at the end in setting Wilson on Gatsby.

Tom's style of physical dominance, his capacity for exerting leverage, are not expressions merely of his individual strength but of the power of a class. Fitzgerald does not make the mistake of imagining that because the rich are corrupt, they must necessarily be weak. That fallacy was to be a part of the sentimentality of the 1930s—as we see in *The Grapes of Wrath*, where the rich appear as impotent scared little men hiding behind barbed wire and hired guns: Tom Buchanan is a far truer representative: he draws on the sense of self-assurance his money and position give him as directly as he draws upon his bank account. The consciousness that, in contrast to himself, Gatsby is 'Mr Nobody from nowhere', gives him a decisive psychological advantage in their struggle over Daisy.

The rich have subtler styles of dominance than the brute power of Tom's money or of his pampered athletic body. One of these appears in the behaviour of Jordan Baker when Nick first sees her stretched out at full length on the sofa in the Buchanans' drawing room. She takes no apparent notice of his entrance, but maintains a pose of complete self-absorption as if she were balancing some object on her chin. Far from resenting her discourtesy, Nick feels almost obliged to apologize for having interrupted her. After he and Daisy have chatted for a few moments, Daisy introduces Jordan to him:

> ... Miss Baker's lips fluttered, she nodded at me almost imperceptibly, and then tipped her head back again—the object she was balancing had obviously tottered a little and given her something of a fright. Again a sort of apology arose to my lips. Almost any exhibition of complete self-sufficiency draws a stunned tribute from me.[9]

This was the quality Fitzgerald had been trying to isolate in the character of Dick Humbird in *This Side of Paradise*. By the time he wrote *The Great Gatsby*, he had learnt enough about the novel of manners to be able to make such subtle notations with complete success. In terms of dramatic conflict, these are the forces which defeat Gatsby, although clearly there are self-destructive potentialities in his own romanticism.

By the end of his first dinner party at the Buchanans', Nick Carraway is already disillusioned with the American rich. He is forced unwillingly to observe the violent contrast between their opportunities—what is implied by the gracious surface of their existence—and the seamy underside which is its reality. In the Buchanans—and in Nick's reactions to them—we see once more how completely the American upper class has failed to become an aristocracy. Nick's disappointment is so sudden and complete that the episode has an effect of comic anticlimax. The chapter ends, however, not with his small disappointment but with Gatsby's first appearance. Gatsby is still totally committed to his dream: he stretches out his arms in a great yearning gesture, across the dark waters of the bay towards the green light at the end of Daisy's dock. He never discovers how he has been betrayed by the class he has idealized, and, for him, the failure of the rich has disastrous consequences.

Gatsby's unique quality is his capacity to dream—

> ... some heightened sensitivity to the promises of life, as if he were related to one of those intricate machines that register earthquakes ten thousand miles away ... an extraordinary gift for hope, a romantic readiness such as I have not found in any other person and which it is not likely I shall ever find again.[10]

His tragedy lies in the impact of reality upon his dreams: neither the circumstances of his own life, nor the pseudo-aristocratic style of the American rich to which he aspires, offer him anything 'commensurate with his capacity for wonder'. Most of the ironies of his situation arise from the balancing of illusion against reality. The clearest, though by no means the most important of the ways by which Fitzgerald gives poetic substance to this duality is that of creating two settings with strongly contrasted atmospheres. The glittering palaces on Long Island Sound are set against the ash-heaps on the outskirts of New York. Gatsby's dreams are concentrated upon the former; the sordid realities which shatter his illusions and destroy his life lurk among the latter. Among the ashes, in or near Wilson's garage, Tom's rottenness and Daisy's cowardice are fully revealed; while Wilson himself, the ash-grey phantom gliding on Gatsby's track, is a singularly appropriate instrument for murder—there is after all nothing more dangerous than the hatred of the mean-spirited.

The ironic relation between illusion and reality in Gatsby's situation is conveyed most interestingly, however, by the actual language of the novel. Fitzgerald takes some of his own most vicious forms of writing—his journalistic chatter, his false rhetoric, and the cheap style of his poorest magazine fiction—and turns them into something which is artistically satisfying. It is a strange process of transmutation, by which styles that seem fitted only for crude and vulgar sentiments are, paradoxically, made to carry subtle shades of meaning and emotion. The bad writing produced with uncritical facility in the inferior pieces is here employed with conscious and elaborate artistry. An obvious and highly successful example is the list of the 'names of those who came to Gatsby's house that summer' at the beginning of Chapter IV. This is, among other things, a parody of the style of the gossip columns—of the cheap journalistic tone Fitzgerald could slip into all too easily himself. But it is more than a parody, or a mere compilation of those funny names which are a consequence of the diverse origins of Americans. It is a poetic composition (critics have often pointed to a similarity with T. S. Eliot's use of proper names in *Gerontion*) which gives expression to the social chaos of the Jazz Age. The names and scraps of rumour are interwoven to show how people are being hurried indiscriminately together in the frenetic pursuit of money and pleasure—the wealthy, the criminal, the disreputable, the pretentious, the showy and the frivolous, the rootless and the abandoned—even the respectable. The whiff of violence is in the air, and the presence of disaster is never far away. This is the foul dust that floated in the wake of Gatsby's dreams—the motley crowd that flock to the glittering and lavish entertainments he conceives at West Egg.

Fitzgerald takes this kind of writing farthest in his treatment of Gatsby's love for Daisy. Gatsby's taste in language is as flashy and overblown as his taste in cars or clothes: when he talks about his feelings to Nick Carraway, the words he uses retain echoes from many cheap and vulgar styles. Fitzgerald is able to catch these inflections in Gatsby's voice, and yet give to the paltry phrases vibrations they never had before. In order to see how this happens, it is necessary to quote an example of Fitzgerald's own worst writing, before turning to some passages from *The Great Gatsby*. For this purpose I have chosen the opening of 'Love in the Night', a story which was published only a few weeks before *Gatsby* itself:

> The words thrilled Val. They had come into his mind sometime during the fresh gold April afternoon and he kept repeating them to himself over and over: 'Love in the night: love in the night'. He tried them in three languages—Russian, French and English—and decided that they were best in English. In each language they meant a different sort of love and a different sort of night—the English night seemed the warmest and softest with the thinnest and most crystalline sprinkling of stars. The English love seemed the most fragile and romantic—a white dress and a dim face above it and eyes that were pools of light.[11]

In the conversations with Nick in which Gatsby talks about Daisy, the same kind of writing is used:

> ... he had never been in such a beautiful house before. But what gave it an air of breathless intensity was that Daisy lived there.... There was a ripe mystery about it, a hint of bedrooms upstairs more beautiful and cool than other bedrooms, of gay and radiant activities taking place through its corridors, and of romances that were not musty and laid away already in lavender, but fresh and breathing and redolent of this year's shining motor-cars and of dances whose flowers were scarcely withered....[12]

In the first passage, Fitzgerald is tastelessly and embarrassingly self-indulgent; in the second the validity of his rhetoric is incontestable. It is the same style but it is now being used consciously and with controlling irony. Gatsby's feelings for Daisy, the moment he tries to define them, become the banal stereotypes of romantic magazine fiction, and so it is fitting that the language he uses should be vitiated by worn-out images and sentimental clichés. Fitzgerald indeed states this quite explicitly in the scene in which Gatsby drives Nick Carraway to New York, and tells him the story of his life. Gatsby recounts the autobiography he would like to have had—the wealthy family in the Middle West; the Oxford education; the grand tour—

'After that I lived like a young rajah in all the capitals of Europe—
Paris, Venice, Rome—collecting jewels, chiefly rubies, hunting
big game, painting a little, things for myself only, and trying to
forget something very sad that had happened to me long ago.'

    With an effort I managed to restrain my incredulous laughter.
The very phrases were worn so threadbare that they evoked no
image except that of a turbaned 'character' leaking sawdust at
every pore as he pursued a tiger through the Bois de Boulogne.[13]

The tale concludes with the amazing heroism of Gatsby's war service: 'Every
Allied government gave me a decoration—even Montenegro, little
Montenegro down on the Adriatic Sea.' 'It was', Nick comments, 'like
skimming hastily through a dozen magazines.'

    Nick has just dismissed him as an extravagant impostor, a liar on the
grand scale, when there is an astonishing volte-face: Gatsby produces the
Montenegrin medal and a photograph of himself with a cricket bat (superb
authenticating touch!) at Oxford. Nick veers to the other extreme—'Then it
was all true': he pictures Gatsby, surrounded by tiger skins, in a palace on the
Grand Canal, gazing into a chest of rubies to find relief from the 'gnawings
of his broken heart.'

    It is not 'all true', of course, nor is it all imposture: it is a question of
language, a question of images. From one point of view, it is of the essence
of Gatsby's greatness that he can make these threadbare phrases and
magazine stereotypes the vehicle for his stupendous capacity for wonder and
imaginative response, in the same way as much of Fitzgerald's greatness in
this novel lies in his ability to transmute a bad style into great art. From
another angle, however, it is Gatsby's tragedy that the purest element of truth
in his life-story should be conveyed in the most false and sentimental of his
words: 'trying to forget something very sad that had happened to me long
ago.' The fusion of wonder and vulgarity is caught with superlative tact again
and again in the novel.

    We find an illuminating parallel to Gatsby's case in the greatest of all
novels about the romantic sensibility—*Madame Bovary*. It is interesting to
note that *Madame Bovary* had been much in Fitzgerald's mind during the
period when he was writing *The Great Gatsby*. In an article which was
syndicated to a number of newspapers, he listed what he considered to be the
ten greatest novels ever written, and among these *Nostromo*, *Vanity Fair*, and
Madame Bovary were singled out for special emphasis.[14] When he wrote to
Maxwell Perkins about last minute revisions he was making to the text of
Gatsby, he warned him that the proof 'will be one of the most expensive
affairs since *Madame Bovary*'.[15] Flaubert's heroine shows the same capacity
for wonder, the same restriction to banal images, and the same failure to find

speech that can match the intensity of her feelings, as Gatsby does. This is particularly apparent in Flaubert's account of her affair with Rodolphe, a jaded middle-aged *roué*:

> 'I love you so much,' she burst out. 'So much I can't live without you! I long for you sometimes till my heart almost breaks with jealousy! I say to myself, Where is he now? Talking to other women, perhaps. They smile at him, he comes—Ah, no! no! Tell me there's none you care for! There are women more beautiful than I, but none that can love as I can. I am your slave, your concubine. You are my king, my idol—you are good, handsome, intelligent, strong!'
>
> He had listened to so many speeches of this kind that they no longer made any impression on him. Emma was like any other mistress; and the charm of novelty, gradually slipping away like a garment, laid bare the eternal monotony of passion, whose forms and phrases are for ever the same. Any difference of feeling underlying a similarity in the words escaped the notice of that man of much experience. Because wanton or mercenary lips had murmured like phrases in his ear, he had but scant belief in the sincerity of these. High-flown language concealing tepid affection must be discounted, thought he: as though the full heart may not sometimes overflow in the emptiest metaphors, since no one can ever give the exact measure of his needs, his thoughts, or his sorrows, and human speech is like a cracked kettle on which we strum out tunes to make a bear dance, when we would move the stars to pity.[16]

Emma Bovary is condemned to express herself in the enfeebled phrases of early nineteenth-century sentimental fiction, just as Gatsby uses the debased coinage of the magazines. In their predicament, both Fitzgerald and Flaubert show an awareness not only of the problems of the romantic sensibility, but, more specifically, of the agonies of the romantic artist—a sense that the artist himself is foredoomed to defeat whenever he tries to put his inexpressible visions into words. It has always been recognized that *The Great Gatsby* gives a wonderfully intimate picture of American manners in the 1920s, and that it is a profound exploration of the nature of American civilization, but no one has fully grasped the extent to which it is the great modern novel of romantic experience. In the entire history of the novel, only Flaubert has gone as deeply into the dangers and despairs of romanticism, and only Stendhal has seen as much of the comedy.

Gatsby himself is not an artist, however—unless one regards his parties as in some sense works of art—and he is certainly not aware that the language he uses is vulgar and ridiculous. For him, the most destructive aspect of romantic experience lies in a somewhat different direction: he finds that attaining a desired object brings a sense of loss rather than fulfilment. Once his dream loses its general and ideal quality and becomes localized within the confines of actuality, his life seems emptier and poorer. On the afternoon when Daisy first visits his house, they pause at a window to look out across the waters of the Sound, and Gatsby tells her that, but for the rain and mist which obscure the view, they would be able to see the end of her dock where the green light burns every night. Daisy takes his words as a movement of tenderness, and puts her arm through his, but Gatsby is far away—lost in what he has just said. His sense that the green light is no longer the central image in a great dream but only a green light at the end of a dock, is momentarily stronger than his response to Daisy herself touching him with her hand: 'His count of enchanted objects had diminished by one.'

This feeling is made still more explicit in the conversation in which Gatsby tells Nick how he first kissed Daisy. Gatsby has made a decisive choice—from this point onwards all his capacity for wonder is concentrated upon her. Even if she were far more remarkable than she is, she could not possibly measure up to such fabulous expectations, and the affair must inevitably end in some personal disaster for Gatsby. It is only because of their five-year separation that the catastrophe is delayed for so long—in Daisy's absence, Gatsby is able to dream and idealize once more without having to subject his visions to the test of actuality. Once he is reunited with her, ruin comes almost immediately: Her personal weaknesses and the inadequacies of the way of life she represents only serve to aggravate the self-destructive tendencies of Gatsby's own romanticism. This passage also raises once again, in a most interesting way, the question of language and the romantic sensibility. Nick Carraway, in the paragraph which follows it, comments explicitly on the way Gatsby talks, and on the difficulties he himself experiences in finding words for what Gatsby is trying to say:

> Through all he said, even through his appalling sentimentality, I was reminded of something—an elusive rhythm, a fragment of lost words that I had heard somewhere a long time ago. For a moment a phrase tried to take shape in my mouth and my lips parted like a dumb man's, as though there was more struggling upon them than a wisp of startled air. But they made no sound, and what I had almost remembered was incommunicable forever.[17]

The sober precision of Nick's account of his own difficulties with language makes a marvellous contrast with the turgid unrestraint, the 'appalling sentimentality', of the images which evoke Gatsby's first kiss. This seems to me to be the clearest evidence in the novel that the ironic use of bad writing in *The Great Gatsby* is the result of conscious artistry on Fitzgerald's part.

Gatsby's ruin is accomplished in a single afternoon, in the stifling hotel room in New York where he and Tom struggle for possession of Daisy, with Nick and Jordan as unwilling bystanders. The ease of Tom's victory shows the extent to which Gatsby's identity is an insubstantial fabric of illusions. There is no occasion on which Tom appears to greater disadvantage: his homilies on the sanctity of family life are as absurd as they are hypocritical; his manner towards Gatsby is crassly snobbish, towards Daisy disgustingly maudlin. He does not have the least conception of what exists between Gatsby and Daisy, nor the smallest understanding of the former's complex inner life, and yet he blunders, as unerringly as if he knew exactly what he was doing, into the area where Gatsby is most vulnerable. Through his crude accusations, he presents Gatsby, as if in a distorting mirror, with a picture of himself which is unfamiliar and yet horribly real. Tom forces him to realize that he does not necessarily appear to others in the forms which he assumes in his own magnificent conception of himself: to settled respectable people, perhaps even to a 'nice girl' like Daisy, he is simply a vulgar *arriviste*, a bootlegger, a cheap swindler, the associate of crooks and gambling operators like Meyer Wolfsheim. Gatsby cannot survive this attack, clumsy as it is. The identity he has constructed for himself out of dreams and illusions, banal images and sentimental clichés, is so fragile that it disintegrates at a touch: '"Jay Gatsby" had broken up like glass against Tom's hard malice, and the long secret extravaganza was played out.'[18]

After this, his dream of Daisy too begins to recede: while he watches her bedroom window all night from the grounds of her house, she seems to be moving steadily away from him; and when she fails to telephone him the next day, he is at last compelled to relinquish 'the old warm world' which he has inhabited for so long. In these final moments of his life, he is forced to contemplate 'a new world, material without being real', a world in which the loss of his dream changes the very quality of his perceptions. The common objects which surround him—sky, leaves, grass and flowers—come to seem unfamiliar, frightening, grotesque.

The core of Gatsby's tragedy is not only that he lived by dreams, but that the woman and the class and the way of life of which he dreamed—that life of the rich which the novel so ruthlessly exposes—fell so far short of the scope of his imagination. Daisy is a trivial, callous, cowardly woman who may dream a little herself but who will not let her dreams, or such unpleasant realities as running over Myrtle Wilson, disturb her comfort. That Gatsby should have dreamt of her, given his marvellous parties for her, is the special edge to his fate. Fitzgerald shows Gatsby watching over Daisy from the grounds of her house, on the night of the accident, imagining that she might still come to him, and that he is protecting her from her brutal husband. Meanwhile, Tom and Daisy are sitting comfortably in their kitchen over fried chicken and bottled ale, coming to a working arrangement for their future lives. There is a banal and shabby intimacy about their marriage, it is a realistic, if worthless, practical arrangement that suits their shallow personalities. Outside, in the night, stands Gatsby, the man of tremendous and unconquerable illusions, 'watching over nothing'.

By the close of the novel, Fitzgerald has completed his immensely difficult task of convincing us that Gatsby's capacity for illusion is poignant and heroic, in spite of the banality of his aspirations and the worthlessness of the objects of his dreams. The poignancy is conveyed through one incident in particular—that of the car which drives up to Gatsby's house one night long after he is dead. 'Probably it was some final guest, who had been away at the ends of the earth and didn't know that the party was over.' The heroic quality is there in his vigil in the garden, in the scale of his entertainments, the determination behind his criminality.

In the closing paragraphs of the novel there is a sudden enlargement of the theme—a vision of America as the continent of lost innocence and lost illusions. The Dutch sailors who first came to Long Island had an unspoilt continent before them, something 'commensurate with their capacity for wonder'. Gatsby's greatness was to have retained a sense of wonder as deep as the sailors' on that first landfall. His tragedy was to have had, not a continent to wonder at, but only the green light at the end of Daisy's dock, and the triviality of Daisy herself. The evolution of such triviality was his particular tragedy, and the tragedy of America.

It is easier to discuss Gatsby's significance and the nature of his experience, as I have done so far, than to say what kind of fictional character he is. A number of early readers of the novel including Edith Wharton and H. L. Mencken, felt that as a character he virtually didn't exist. Most later critics have evaded the problem altogether by elevating him to the status of a mythic figure. Approached in this way he becomes a symbolic abstraction, the vehicle for a few school-book platitudes about American history, and the question of whether or not he is a tangible dramatic and human presence conveniently disappears. If one simply reads the novel, however, his dramatic and human presence obstinately and delightfully remains:

Gatsby, his hands still in his pockets, was reclining against the mantelpiece in a strained counterfeit of perfect ease, even of boredom. His head leaned back so far that it rested against the face of a defunct mantelpiece clock, and from this position his distraught eyes stared down at Daisy, who was sitting, frightened but graceful, on the edge of a stiff chair.

'We've met before', muttered Gatsby. His eyes glanced momentarily at me, and his lips parted with an abortive attempt at a laugh. Luckily the clock took this moment to tilt dangerously at the pressure of his head, whereupon he turned and caught it with trembling fingers and set it back in place. Then he sat down, rigidly, his elbow on the arm of the sofa and his chin in his hand.

'I'm sorry about the clock', he said.

My own face had now assumed a deep tropical burn. I couldn't muster up a single commonplace out of the thousand in my head.

'It's an old clock', I told them idiotically.

I think we all believed for a moment that it had smashed in pieces on the floor.[19]

The reality of Gatsby's character here is, overwhelmingly, comic, and it is this comic Gatsby—not a shadowy abstraction—who dominates the novel.

The only warrant for considering him as a mythic figure is given on the last page of the novel and, while it would be foolish to deny that the language of this passage is the language of myth, it should be remembered that what Nick Carraway says here is an afterthought, an aspect of Gatsby's case perceived only after he is dead. The living Gatsby who dominates one scene after another is a creature of comedy not myth—a literary relative not of Davy Crockett but Trimalchio.

The Great Gatsby itself is best regarded as a social comedy, but the phrase doesn't perhaps sufficiently convey the extent to which the comic is the vital creative element in Fitzgerald's achievement. The term social comedy, usually implies a mode of writing which is satirical and moral, and this is certainly trite of his treatment of a number of characters and episodes—in particular of Tom Buchanan. But frequently his writing rises to a level of rich absurdity where comedy is not subordinated to a satirical or moral point, but is itself the point—the truly creative thing. Such a moment occurs in the episode in which Myrtle Wilson buys a dog:

We backed up to grey old man who bore an absurd resemblance to John D. Rockefeller. In a basket swung from his neck cowered a dozen very recent puppies of an indeterminate breed.

'What kind are they?' asked Mrs Wilson eagerly, as he came to the taxi-window.

'All kinds. What kind do you want, lady?'

'I'd like to get one of those police dogs; I don't suppose you got that kind?'

The man peered doubtfully into the basket, plunged in his hand and drew one up, wriggling, by the back of the neck.

'That's no police dog', said Tom.

'No, it's not exactly a police dog', said the man with disappointment in his voice. 'It's more of an Airedale'. He passed his hand over the brown washrag of a back. 'Look at that coat. Some coat. That's a dog that'll never bother you with catching cold.'

'I think it's cute', said Mrs Wilson enthusiastically. 'How much is it?'

'That dog?' He looked at it admiringly. 'That dog will cost you ten dollars'.

The Airedale—undoubtedly there was an Airedale concerned in it somewhere, though its feet were startlingly white—changed hands and settled down into Mrs Wilson's lap, where she fondled the weatherproof coat with rapture.

'Is it a boy or a girl?' she asked delicately.

'That dog? That dog's a boy'.

'It's a bitch', said Tom decisively. 'Here's your money. Go and buy ten more dogs with it'.[20]

To say that this incident illustrates the false gentility of Myrtle Wilson or the crudeness of Tom Buchanan's desires would be true but inessential. What really matters is the irresistibly joyous and liberating sense of the ridiculous which Fitzgerald conveys—that quality in literature which we call, not loosely but precisely, Dickensian. As Grahame Smith admirably expresses it in his study of Dickens à propos of Mrs Gamp—'we recognize that we are enclosed in a magic circle of pure comedy from which it is impossible to break out with explanations of satirical intent or didactic purpose'.[21] The whole ensuing scene of the party at Myrtle Wilson's apartment is conceived on the same level of pure comedy. Nick Carraway's two encounters with Meyer Wolfsheim have the same quality. Wolfsheim isn't in the novel to give us tangible proof of Gatsby's underworld connections—the cryptic telephone calls the latter occasionally receives are enough to do that. Wolfsheim's monstrous absurdity—his nostrils, his cuff buttons, his sentimentality and his philosophy of life—is an end in itself. It is significant that Edith Wharton considered him ('your wonderful Jew') the best thing in the novel.[22]

Fitzgerald's greatest success by far in this mode of comedy, however, is the character of Gatsby himself. It is the comic element in Gatsby which makes him seem credibly alive—which gives him an independent existence as a fictional character. We depend on Nick Carraway's testimony for much of what we believe about him. Without the benefit of Nick's wide privilege of interpretation, and the assurance of his sober integrity, we should not be able to guess at the stupendous imaginative life that lies beneath Gatsby's trivial aspirations. But we don't need Nick to tell us how funny Gatsby is— we see it for ourselves. Here, Nick no longer interprets and guarantees, he merely records—he might almost as well not be there. We should probably be less ready to take his word even for Gatsby's imagination, if Gatsby were less comic. His sole creative talent—it is one of which he is entirely unconscious—is his power to arouse wild incredulous laughter. His life has the aspect of a non-stop theatrical performance—an 'unbroken series of successful gestures'; even his name, Jay Gatsby, is a farcical stunt. He does not provoke the superficial kind of laughter which is a mere brief contortion of the facial muscles; he appeals to a profound comic sense which makes life seem richer and fuller than it normally is. When one laughs at his car, his clothes, his parties, his manner, his autobiographical confidences, one is not merely amused, one is responding, through him, to the fertile, creative ludicrousness of life itself.

Gatsby's account of himself during the car ride to New York (from which I have already quoted) is one of the finest of such moments. The episode is too long to give in full, but a single detail—the way in which the car itself is described—will serve to bring out the nature of Fitzgerald's comic vision. Gatsby's car is a fantasy of colours, shapes and noises: its horn emits bursts of music; its 'labyrinth of wind-shields' mirrors a dozen suns; its monstrous length is swollen with 'triumphant hat-boxes and supper-boxes and tool-boxes'. It is clearly not so much a means of transport as a theatrical gesture, a fantastic expression of personality, as characteristic in its way as Falstaff's belly. (Falstaff, as Grahame Smith points out[23] is as essential as Dickens to any discussion of pure comedy.) There are certain striking similarities between the ways in which Gatsby and Falstaff function as comic characters. One of these becomes apparent in the scene from *Henry IV, Part 2*, in which Falstaff comments on the ludicrous contrast between his tiny page and his own monstrous bulk:

> The brain of this foolish-compounded clay, man, is not able to invent anything that intends to laughter more than I invent, or is invented on me; I am not only witty in myself, but the cause that wit is in other men. I do here walk before thee like a sow that hath overwhelmed all her litter but one.[24]

Gatsby is never consciously witty as Falstaff is—indeed he seems to be totally without a sense of humour—but he is certainly 'the cause that wit is in other men'. Both characters need only to exist in order to be comic.

The Falstaff parallel is illuminating in a further sense. It is usual to speak of the wreck of Gatsby's dreams as a tragedy—a statement of the case which appears to contradict the view that he is essentially a comic character. Gatsby, however, clearly isn't a tragic hero in any strict sense: if one calls his end a tragedy, one is simply giving the word the meaning it has in everyday speech—that of the sudden and shocking ruin of a human life. No inconsistency is involved if a comic character dies in this way. Falstaff is cruelly rejected by the king, and the manner of his death as narrated by Mistress Quickly is deeply moving, but these circumstances do not alter his essentially comic nature. The emotions aroused by Gatsby's death, similarly, do not negate the effect of earlier scenes.

The most successful of Gatsby's theatrical gestures are his parties. At the simple level they are fun, an aspect of the novel's meaning which is as true and as important as Nick Carraway's moral disapproval of Gatsby's guests. We are reminded once again of what Henry James and Henry Adams were forced to concede, however reluctantly—that the charm, the success, of American life is in democratic manners, even in social chaos. The corresponding failure of the aristocratic experiment—the stuffy, boorish, hypocritical life of the Buchanans—is clear enough, and throws Gatsby's achievement into sharp relief. Daisy finds—and this is perhaps the sole basis of her love for Gatsby—that there are romantic possibilities in the disorderly riot of his world totally absent from her own. Even the dissipations he offers, or condones, at his house are frank, lively and diverting—very different from Tom Buchanan's crude and furtive relaxations.

Gatsby's parties, too, are virtually his only genuine acts of creation. His dream of Daisy and the way of life she represents, whatever imaginative intensity he puts into it, is an absurd and vulgar illusion. His 'platonic conception' of himself does not differ very significantly from the pattern of Dan Cody's career—the robber baron turned playboy. But his parties are triumphant expressions of that 'vast, vulgar and meretricious beauty' which, as we have already seen, is one of the most characteristic manifestations of American life. When Nick tells Gatsby that his house looks like the World's Fair, and reflects that his guests 'conducted themselves according to the rules of behaviour associated with an amusement park'; or when Tom Buchanan calls Gatsby's car a 'circus-wagon', the implications are clearly unfavourable. And yet, taken in relation to the parties themselves, these gibes help to direct our attention to something very different: 'There was music from my neighbour's house through the summer nights. In his blue gardens men and girls came and went like moths among the whisperings and the champagne and the stars.'

> The lights grow brighter as the earth lurches away from the sun; and now the orchestra is playing yellow cocktail music, and the opera of voices pitches a key higher. Laughter is easier minute by minute, spilled with prodigality, tipped out at a cheerful word. The groups change more swiftly, swell with new arrivals, dissolve and form in the same breath; already there are wanderers, confident girls who move here and there among the stouter and more stable, become for a sharp, joyous moment the centre of a group, and then, excited with triumph, glide on through the sea-change of faces and voices and colours under the constantly changing light.[25]

That Gatsby should have brought to life all this miraculous shimmering ephemeral beauty and excitement places him among the great artist-showmen of America—the architects who designed the World's Fairs and Expositions; the circus ring-masters, and the gifted mountebanks of the state and county fairs; the directors of Hollywood epics and musicals; and the scientists, astronauts and media men who, between them, turned the Apollo moon-shots into the best television entertainment ever made.

To these creative gifts, Gatsby adds the gift of comedy. His parties always seem about to bubble over into a burst of irresistible laughter. Even the mechanical housekeeping arrangements have a comic effect: the servants who toil 'with mops and scrubbing-brushes and hammers and garden-shears, repairing the ravages of the night before'; the caterers who, with tempting foods, yards of canvas, and hundreds of coloured lights, turn Gatsby's gardens into an enormous Christmas tree; the crates of oranges and lemons which arrive like expected guests from New York, have their juice extracted, and leave his back door in a 'pyramid of pulpless halves.' When, a little later in the evening, Nick Carraway speaks of 'the premature moon, produced like the supper, no doubt, out of a caterer's basket', the whole scene seems to hover between the magical and the absurd. A similar effect is obtained at the beginning of Orson Welles's *Citizen Kane*, in the newsreel which describes Xanadu—not Kubla Khan's pleasure-dome but Kane's monstrous Florida estate. A particularly felicitous touch is the reference to Kane's collection of animals—'a specimen of every animal, bird and reptile in the world—the largest private zoo since Noah's Ark.'

As Nick's evocation of the atmosphere of Gatsby's parties gradually modulates into his account of the first one he actually attended, the comic element becomes more explicit. At the beginning, it is like a ripple of suppressed laughter half-heard in the general concert of sounds, but soon, like the mounting hilarity of the guests themselves, it becomes unmistakably the dominant note. It is at this phase of the evening that Nick and Jordan find the owl-eyed man admiring Gatsby's library. Then the rhythm of the party changes again—from hilarity to comic uproar: a drunken soprano performs with tears of black mascara streaming down her face, and, in the riotous finale, the owl-eyed man reappears—as the uncomprehending passenger of a car which has lost one of its wheels. The presiding genius at this scene of comic revelry is Gatsby: he surveys his departing guests from the steps of his house, his hand raised, amid the din of motor-horns in a formal gesture of farewell.

It is in this respect that he most resembles Trimalchio, a character who was very much in Fitzgerald's mind while he was writing *The Great Gatsby*. When Gatsby abruptly stops giving his parties, Nick remarks that 'his career as Trimalchio was over'; and at one stage Fitzgerald actually considered *Trimalchio* and *Trimalchio in West Egg* as possible titles for the novel.[26] Trimalchio's banquet, the longest episode in the *Satyricon* of Petronius, is one of the great comic scenes of classical literature, and has certain obvious resemblances with Gatsby's parties. Both are set in times of wealth and decadence (Petronius himself is usually—though not certainly—identified with that Petronius Arbiter described by Tacitus, who presided over the revels at the court of Nero). The guests in each case are a motley collection of adventurers and entertainers, while the two hosts are *nouveaux riches* with the uncertain taste common to that position. In both entertainments the life and virtue are comic, and both reach their dramatic climaxes in scenes of comic disorder. Gatsby's pose—aloof, dignified, ceremonial almost—is in ludicrous contrast with the turmoil of farcical misunderstandings and caterwauling motor-horns in his drive. The *débâcle* of Trimalchio's banquet has the same relation to the whole, and contains similar comic incongruities. In order to parade his wealth and liberality, he has his will brought in and read aloud. As his slaves and guests weep drunkenly, he is inspired by the thought that they can pretend the occasion is his funeral wake. He lies down on a couch as if he were the corpse, libations are poured out, and a brass band is summoned to play suitable music. But the leading performer gives such a piercing blast on his instrument that the whole neighbourhood is awakened. The fire brigade is aroused, and the guests flee in terror as the firemen rush in with their axes and buckets of water.

While it is almost certain that Fitzgerald learned something from Petronius about the dramatic organization of such scenes—about the mounting rhythms that run through huge entertainments—his comic sense is entirely his own. In Trimalchio's banquet there is no trace of that magical lightness and beauty which hover over Gatsby's parties—indeed, the tasteless display, the revolting food, the boring songs and recitations, and the fatuous practical jokes are only redeemed by the comic vitality of Trimalchio himself. Petronius's comedy is excellent, but it is straight-forwardly Rabelaisian, neither very subtle nor very varied. One cannot but feel that Fitzgerald's comic sense is, by contrast, finer and more inventive. Gatsby's nature contains both grossness and delicacy; his oblique relation to his guests allows of many ironies which are outside Petronius's range; and his parties display an incomparable variety of mood and atmosphere. *The Great Gatsby* is the only work in which Fitzgerald realized the full potentialities of his comic genius, but in this one novel he equalled the masters of world literature.

Fitzgerald's vision of life in *The Great Gatsby* is a complex one: he appreciates the comic vitality of Gatsby and the grandiose scope of his romantic imagination; at the same time, there is an equally important element of moral rigour in the novel, which is most apparent in Fitzgerald's attitude to the American rich. The relation these conflicting elements have to each other has some similarities with the complex meaning of Falstaff's position in the *Henry IV* plays: the mere fact of Falstaff's existence is a creative and liberating force, and yet one cannot deny the baseness of most of what he does. As both Shakespeare and Fitzgerald recognize, these two perceptions do not cancel each other out, nor is there any convenient formula that will resolve them. Each artist seems to say in effect, life is like that—that is a part of its complexity. That this sense of complexity is so successfully conveyed in *The Great Gatsby* is due almost entirely to the figure of Nick Carraway.

Nick combines the role of stern moral critic with that of fascinated and disinterested spectator of life. Fitzgerald is careful to define these attitudes at the beginning of the novel in such a way that this double vision can be seen as a plausible expression of a single unified character. The way in which Nick describes his ancestry—light and almost flippant as it is—suggests that the explanation may lie there. According to family tradition, the Carraways are descended from the Dukes of Buccleuch, but in reality their story begins with Nick's great-uncle, who came West in 1859, sent a substitute to the Civil War, and started the wholesale hardware business which is still the basis of their fortunes. The sense of divided loyalties is clear—to a romantic, pseudo-aristocratic ideal on the one hand, and to the standards of a sober, practical, commercial respectability on the other. It is wholly characteristic of Fitzgerald that this conflict of allegiances should be presented partly in terms of social class. Only through an aristocratic conception of man can the largest human possibilities be realized, but middle-class life is the only source of moral integrity and of stability in personal relationships.

Fitzgerald makes the same distinction in somewhat different teens in the first words of the novel. Nick Carraway recalls how his father, in a somewhat enigmatic manner, had once reminded him that 'a sense of the fundamental decencies is parcelled out unequally at birth'—a superior moral sense is one of the many advantages a man inherits from being born into a good family. The awareness of this privilege has made Nick tolerant when he encounters lower moral standards in others, and his tolerance has, in turn, made him the recipient of many strange confidences. But there are times when his impulse towards tolerance and receptivity is met by an equally strong principle of moral restraint: 'When I came back from the East last autumn I felt that I wanted the world to be in uniform and at a sort of moral attention for ever.' Only Gatsby is exempt from Nick's recoil into disapproval—'Gatsby, who represented everything for which I have an unaffected scorn.'[27] This passage is the key to Nick's position as narrator: it explains why he is able gradually to recognize Gatsby's extraordinary qualities. It also accounts for his prompt reaction to the Buchanans—why it is that his initial fascination with their way of life turns to disgust in a single evening: 'To a certain temperament the situation might have seemed intriguing—my own instinct was to telephone immediately for the police'. Most interestingly of all, perhaps, Nick's self-analysis tells us why, having recognized the Buchanans' rottenness so early, he puts up with them socially for so long.

Nick's moral stand, the point at which the limits of his tolerance are reached, involves, we notice, a return from the East to the Middle Western city where his family lives. Almost at the end of the novel he remarks; 'this has been a story of the West, after all' and at least part of the significance of these words is the bearing they have upon his complex moral position. The Middle West is home, the place to return to after dubious, if exciting, adventures in the East, a place where the sober, provincial, domestic virtues continue to maintain an unquestioned authority. Like the contrast in class values, this difference in regional cultures adds a further element of interest to Nick's responses.

It would be a mistake to see Nick simply as a narrator, however: he is a definite and important character. One of his functions is as Gatsby's shadow, a man who would have the same dreams as Gatsby if he could. Like Gatsby, he is a Middle Western boy who finds, after the upheaval of the War, that, 'Instead of being the warm centre of the world, the Middle West now seemed the ragged edge of the universe'. He comes East to make a quick fortune in the bond business and to become a part of a more sophisticated way of life. The fact that he can neither dream, nor live out the implications of his dreams, as Gatsby does, makes him a useful foil to Gatsby: by the measure of his ordinariness, we appreciate Gatsby's greatness all the more. Nick, too, pays his own modest tribute, at many points in the novel, to Daisy's charm, adding the necessary touch of credibility to Gatsby's dreams. His own half-hearted romance with Jordan Baker—a girl who, like Daisy, is careless, dishonest and 'a rotten driver'—again reminds one by contrast of the stupendous scale of Gatsby's love. The only decisive step Nick ever takes towards Jordan, in fact, is on the afternoon when she tells him what she knows of Gatsby's affair with Daisy five years before in Louisville. Moved momentarily by the story of another man's love, he kisses her.

It would be absurd to attempt to sum up Fitzgerald's achievement in *The Great Gatsby* in a single concluding phrase; all one can do is to try, as I have done, to show some of the sources of its greatness. However, there is one general comment that is in place: the novel is remarkable for the extent to which it succeeds in combining imaginative power and vitality with faultless artistry. The depth and range of its analysis of American civilization, the intensity with which it evokes the life of the romantic sensibility, and the wonderful comic vision that led to the creation of its hero, are balanced and controlled by a miraculously precise attention to detail—a poet's sense of the possibilities of language. *The Great Gatsby*, in achieving this particular kind of success, is not only unique among American novels of the twentieth century, but an undoubted masterpiece of world literature.

NOTES

1. Henry James, *The Art of the Novel*, edited by R. P. Blackmur, New York, 1934, p. 109.

2. *Ibid.*, p. 110.

3. *Ibid.*, pp. 110–11.

4. *The Great Gatsby*, BH1, p. 243.

5. *Ibid.*, p. 201.

6. *Ibid.*, p. 129.

7. *Ibid.*, p. 131.

8. *Ibid.*

9. *Ibid.*, pp. 131–2.

10. *Ibid.*, p. 126.

11. 'Love in the Night', *Bits of Paradise*, edited by Matthew J. Bruccoli, London, 1973, p. 66.

12. *Gatsby*, BH1, p. 242.

13. *Ibid.*, p. 176.

14. Arthur Mizener, *The Far Side of Paradise*, Boston, 1951, p. 336.

15. *Letters*, p. 172.

16. Gustave Flaubert, *Madame Bovary*, translated by Alan Russell, Harmondsworth, 1950), p. 203.

17. *Gatsby*, BH1, p. 213.

18. *Ibid.*, p. 242.

19. *Ibid.*, pp. 192–3.

20. *Ibid.*, pp. 145–6.

21. Grahame Smith, *Dickens, Money, Society*, Berkeley and Cambridge, 1968, see chapter 1 throughout, and especially p. 5.

22. In a letter to Fitzgerald reprinted by Edmund Wilson in *The Crack-up*, New York, 1945, p. 309.

23. Grahame Smith, *op. cit.*, pp. 1–3.

24. Shakespeare, *Henry IV, part 2*, I ii 5–11.

25. *Gatsby*, BH1, pp. 155–6.

26. Matthew J. Bruccoli, *Apparatus for F. Scott Fitzgerald's 'The Great Gatsby'*, Columbia. S.C., 1974, p. 6 and fn.

27. *Gatsby*, BH1, pp. 125–6.

BRUCE BAWER

"I Could Still Hear The Music": Jay Gatsby and the Musical Metaphor

Chapter Three of *The Great Gatsby* opens in this way:

> There was music from my neighbor's house through the summer nights. In his blue gardens men and girls came and went like moths among the whisperings and the champagne and the stars. At high tide in the afternoon I watched his guests diving from the tower of his raft, or taking the sun on the hot sand of his beach while his two motor-boats slit the waters of the Sound, drawing aquaplanes over cataracts of foam. On weekends his Rolls-Royce became an omnibus, bearing parties to and from the city between nine in the morning and long past midnight, while his station wagon scampered like a brisk yellow bug to meet all trains. And on Mondays eight servants, including an extra gardener, toiled all day with mops and scrubbing-brushes and hammers and garden-shears, repairing the ravages of the night before.

Music is thus associated with Gatsby; Nick's life is in fact (as far as we can see) without music until he moves in next door to Gatsby—for, indeed, in the first two chapters of the novel there is no mention of music whatsoever. Note

From *NMAL* 5, no. 4 (Fall, 1981): 25–26. © 1981 by Edward Guereschi and Lee. J. Richmond.

that the music coming from the great mansion is undifferentiated, uncharacterized; there is no talk of jazz or slow waltzes or string quartets, just the single word "music," which could stand for anything from Bach to Berlin. Indeed the paragraph quoted above, which begins with the novel's first reference to music, covers a gamut as well: there is the magic of the summer nights at Gatsby's house—the girls like "moths," the "whisperings," the "champagne," the "stars"—as well as the reality of the morning after— the "mops" and "scrubbing-brushes" and "hammers" and "garden-shears" of the morning that repair the "ravages" of the previous night. Thus the music from Gatsby's house is associated with a wide range of impressions—from champagne to scrubbrushes—that makes up the atmosphere of a Gatsby party.

Indeed, Fitzgerald takes care to establish music as a key imagistic device in the depiction of the Gatsby party atmosphere. The description of the party that occupies the first few pages of Chapter Three continually reverts to the music metaphor. The bar is not simply busy: it is in "full swing." There are "floating rounds of cocktails," and an "opera of voices" that "pitches a key higher." The Britishers out for easy American money are "convinced that it was theirs for a few words in the right key." Thus drinking, talking, conniving are all presented through a musical image.

All the time of course there is real music playing: "a whole pitful of oboes and trombones and saxophones and viols and cornets and piccolos, and in low and high drums." It is an interesting assortment of pieces, not a mere jazz band nor even a typical orchestra; to the instruments one might expect at a fashionable twenties party (trombones, saxes, cornets, even an oboe) are added the viol and the piccolo—significantly, the pieces which reach the lowest and highest notes respectively in the canon of instruments. This image of extremes is reinforced by the mention of "low and high drums." If music is a metaphor for the Gatsby party, then clearly Fitzgerald is characterizing the party—and life at the East Egg mansion in general—as one that will have its highs and lows.

Indeed the music is not all of an ilk. There is "a celebrated tenor" singing in Italian, and a "notorious contralto" singing "in jazz": Fitzgerald puts the serious alongside the flippant, the ponderous alongside the joyful. Vladimir Tostoff's *Jazz History of the World* is played, and again there is an odd affiliation: the mention of "Carnegie Hall" in the same breath as the word "jazz," which in 1925 would have been a much stranger fusion than it is today. The very phrase "Jazz History of the World" is peculiar, because of the juxtaposition of jazz—a thing of the moment, the key to which is improvisation—and history. The alignment of jazz and history results in an interesting irony. Fitzgerald is playing with time, in reminding us that there are things that are timeless and things (like improvisational music, jazz) that are not—things that must be enjoyed for the moment, and cannot be duplicated. Thematically, this juxtaposition has an obvious function: to foreshadow Gatsby's failure to revive his relationship with Daisy on a permanent basis after six years. (Recall that later in the book Nick will tell Gatsby: "You can't repeat the past," and Gatsby will reply: "Why, of course you can!")

As Chapter Three began with music from Gatsby's house at night, so Chapter Four begins with the sound of bells from the church on Sunday morning. The contrast between Gatsby's house and the church is intensified in the second paragraph of the chapter:

> "He's a bootlegger," said the young ladies, moving somewhere between his cocktails and his flowers. "One time he killed a man who had found out that he was nephew to Von Hindenberg and second cousin to the devil ..."

Second cousin to the devil: the intended antithesis between Gatsby and God could not be more straightforward. And note that Fitzgerald has used music to bring Jay and Jesus together—Gatsby with his wild night music, God with his morning church bells. Again, there is a sense of foreshadowing in having Gatsby's wild party night followed by a delicate reminder of the Enduring Things, in the form of church bells that have rung every Sunday for generations. God is eternal, Fitzgerald reminds us, and Gatsby is not. Even before he has renewed his affair with Daisy, the musical metaphors have presaged his failure to make it endure.

And why will the affair fail to last? Further musical references illuminate a flaw in Gatsby's personality in which may lie his ultimate doom. For example, when Jordan and Nick are riding through Central Park, little girls are heard singing:

> I'm the Sheik of Araby.
> Your love belongs to me.
> At night when you're asleep
> Into your tent I'll creep—

The lyric of course recalls Gatsby and Daisy. But the irony emerges from the contrast between the two situations thus brought together: Gatsby is not creeping into Daisy's tent; he wants her to creep into *his* tent. One is reminded of the unnaturalness of Gatsby's attitude, his perhaps excessive romanticism alongside the realistic attitude of the times (the universality of the song's practical view of man–woman relationships is suggested by Fitzgerald's placement of the song lyrics into the mouths of babes—even the innocents have a more realistic view of sex than Gatsby!).

Gatsby's overly romantic perspective is re-emphasized by Klipspringer's playing of "The Love Nest" on the piano while Gatsby shows Daisy through his house. The room in which Klipspringer is playing is referred to by Nick as the "Marie Antoinette Music Room," and the huge room serves as an analogue for the entire house. Again, Gatsby's romantic opacity is thrown up alongside reality: his East Egg residence is no nest (indeed, not even a tent), but a sprawling mansion. The disparity between the ideal and the actual reinforces the effect of the "Sheik of Araby" lyric. Further, when Klipspringer plays "Ain't We Got Fun," the background is a loud wind outside and

> a faint flow of thunder along the Sound. All the lights were going on in West Egg now; the electric trains, men-carrying, were plunging home through the rain from New York. It was the hour of a profound human change, and excitement was generating on the air
> 'One thing's sure and nothing's surer
> The rich get richer and the poor get—children.'

Alongside the profundity and gloom of the scene, the lyrics of the song ("in the morning, in the evening, ain't we got fun—") seem frighteningly ominous in their simple, idealized view of life. Indeed, we are reminded, there is "nothing sure" in life, and the stark truth rises out of the deceptively cheerful lyric to play the hopes of Gatsby off against the hopelessness of the real world.

Another such juxtaposition is effected when, at the Plaza Hotel, Gatsby and his party hear the Mendelssohn Wedding March playing downstairs. The "portentous" tones of the march remind the reader of Daisy's wedding ties and suggest the doom they will spell for Gatsby's romantic dream. Though the wedding march is followed by some hot jazz, Daisy doesn't want to dance; she would, she says, "If we were younger." The wedding march has perhaps reminded her of her bond to Tom; and the victory it thus wins over the dance music is a telling augury. There is an interesting if subtle differentiation in Daisy's voice quality before and after the Wedding March, in both cases referred to in musical terms: before hearing the March, her voice is "a cymbals' song"; afterwards it "drops an octave lower." Again, it is a subtle but significant pointer in the direction that Gatsby's romantic fortunes will go.

The last song mentioned in the book is "The Rosary," a religious song, which someone whistles "tunelessly" in New York on the morning of Gatsby's funeral. The song recalls the antithesis that was set up earlier between Gatsby and God, between Gatsby's house and the church, through the use of music. We are reminded, subtly, that the Eternal Powers have prevailed over Gatsby, the fleeting and temporal.

The last reference to music hearkens back to the opening of Chapter Three, to Nick's (and the reader's) introduction to Gatsby. "I could still hear the music," Nick reflects, sitting in his again silent house after Gatsby's death. As music came into his life with Gatsby, so it is gone now that the star-crossed lover is dead; thus the identification of Gatsby with music is carried through to the end. With Nick, the reader remembers Gatsby the more sharply, in his highs and lows, by recalling the spectrum of music that has filled the great man's house; moreover, with that one line, "I could still hear the music," Fitzgerald evokes the entire structure of musical metaphor that has worked throughout the book to contrast Gatsby's romanticism with the world's reality. As we read the line we recall Gatsby's sense of triumph at the same time as we realize the inevitability of his tragic end.

ROGER LATHBURY

Money, Love, and Aspiration in
The Great Gatsby

One characteristic of popular American fiction is the implicit separation of love and money. Possession of one does not lead to possession of the other. If the protagonists of Horatio Alger's books become rich and win the girl, such winning is an adjunct to their sudden solvency, not a consequence of it. Alger wants his audience to believe, perhaps, that common sense and moral determination secure the love of a worthy partner; but that these qualities of common sense and moral determination are the property of those who must struggle for money is an assumption—not an issue Alger wants to explore. As a result, it is impossible to imagine what happens to Ragged Dick, Frank Fowler, or any of the hundreds of Horatio Alger heroes after their first success.

The separation of love and money characterizes serious American fiction too. The guilt that seems to lurk behind the source of Lambert Strether's wealth (the firm in Woollen "made something") underscores both his and, I suspect, his creator's distaste for tainting the finer emotions with anything so crass as commercialism. If the independence and energy that constitute Strether's as well as his earlier prototype's, Christopher Newman's, most appealing facets come from contact with the struggles of business, the novel prefers to treat this matter as background. The inamoratas of Strether and Newman are fascinating more for their richness of background and their exquisiteness of taste than for the fortune that sustains these qualities.

From *New Essays on* The Great Gatsby, ed. Matthew J. Bruccoli. © 1985 by Cambridge University Press.

What I have said so far seems to me to hold especially true for American fiction before World War I. The laissez-faire democratic ideal that America has always believed it believed is the product of an age when individual effort counted, when a man could rise by his own efforts, and when—if his affairs were not succeeding—he could at least escape by signing up for a whaling voyage or lighting out for the territory ahead of the rest. When the system failed, it was the fault of rapscallions and crooks; the vision itself remained an ideal and the standard from which criticisms and judgments could be made.

World War I shattered this vision. It ended once and for all the faith in individual effort that had been eroding since the Industrial Revolution and had persisted—sometimes naively and sometimes defensively—in the fiction that I have been mentioning. As Mark Schorer has pointed out, disillusionment with the American system and the efficacy of individual effort is the distinguishing characteristic of postwar American writing.[1]

Of course, not many, if any, ideals die totally and suddenly even after mortal blows, and during periods of transition the most complex and seminal works are often written. In this respect the 1920s bridge the gap between the older, simpler, more naive and idealistic America and the bewildering, disparate, rootless, cynical America of the present. *The Great Gatsby*, neatly published in the mid-1920s, is a key work, looking Janus-like in both directions. The opening words of the novel express this double vision.

> In my younger and more vulnerable years my father gave me some advice that I've been turning over in my mind ever since.
>
> "Whenever you feel like criticising any one," he told me, "just remember that all the people in this world haven't had the advantages that you've had." (p. 1)

The narrator, Nick Carraway, senses that he is too quick to condemn; his father has a perspective from which to make judgments. Nick has to remind himself of his father's more balanced, human appraisal. The younger Carraway has one foot in the past and one in the present; his allegiance to his father's older, more careful manner is maintained at the cost of constant surveillance.

When, in a following paragraph, Nick declares that after returning from the East he "wanted the world to be in uniform and at a sort of moral attention forever" (p. 2), he connects the war with his cynical, guilty disapproval of the New York the book is about to portray, but he goes on to make an exception for Gatsby, allying Gatsby to an older, more humane America—an ironic identification, since Gatsby "represented everything for which I have unaffected scorn" (p. 2). Thus, not only the narrator but also Gatsby is double, making the novel doubly double.

Such doubleness is important, because by it Fitzgerald creates a character whose naiveté can be simultaneously touching and absurd, and who can possess the most romantic and crass attitudes at the same time. By the end of the novel, Gatsby and what he stands for reach proportions of mythic profundity.

Expressing such resonances was a talent Fitzgerald had to develop. Some indication of his abilities is present in *This Side of Paradise*, and some of the rhythms of *The Great Gatsby* appear in embryonic form in the earlier book, but it is not until "Winter Dreams" in 1923 that Fitzgerald explicitly connects the themes of love and money. In this story, Dexter Green, a figure straight from the work ethic of Horatio Alger, loses Judy Jones, a child of wealth.

Yet the relationship between love and money in "Winter Dreams" is not as simple as in Alger. For one thing, Judy Jones, the heroine of the story, is a romantically attractive woman. In Horatio Alger's fiction, rich females are cold and cruel and loveless, but Judy Jones is exciting and desirable, capable of exciting love in others, but, once society has corrupted her, not herself capable of loving. Exciting others and promising love, however, matter more than the realizable dreams of wealth necessary to obtain Judy Jones; they give the story all its powerful emotion. The intangibility of the emotion, its transience and fragility, its evanescent illusory quality, and the fact that it is unrealizable account for its enchantment. What sustains the charm is the atmosphere that surrounds Judy Jones, an atmosphere engendered by wealth. This wealth destroys even as it creates; thus, the doubleness of Gatsby is prefigured here.

When Dexter Green is aware of how empty and bereft his life is because the dream of the old Judy Jones has gone, he has the impulse to "get very drunk." There are shades here of Amory Blaine, who similarly responds when Rosalind is not to be his. But not, seemingly, shades of Gatsby; although a bootlegger, Gatsby is abstemious and careful—a man aware of his own doubleness. Both dreamer and vulgarian at the same time, he is, like Dexter Green, a money maker and a romantic; unlike Dexter Green, he seems to balance between the two. He appears able to keep the halves in control.

Almost predictably, the object of Gatsby's romantic quest, Daisy Buchanan, comes to us in a double way. She is, of course, presented not by Gatsby or Fitzgerald but by Nick Carraway, and she comes to us through his filter of contradictory impressions and emotions. After Nick's description of Tom, with the latter's conceit and meanness, the reader is prepared to respond instantly to the charm of Daisy. Daisy comes to us laughing "an absurd, charming little laugh" (p. 10) that makes Nick laugh also. The pleasing impression of Daisy is largely vocal:

> ... there was an excitement in her voice that men who had cared for her found difficult to forget: a singing compulsion, a whispered "Listen," a promise that she had done gay, exciting things just a while since and that there were gay, exciting things hovering in the next hour. (p. 11)

But then Nick's doubleness reasserts itself. Just as we are seduced by her simpering mockery of her husband, captivated by her posturing, her "thrilling scorn" (p. 21), and the romantic glow with which Fitzgerald has surrounded her, Nick pulls us back.

> The instant her voice broke off, ceasing to compel my attention, my belief, I felt the basic insincerity of what she had said. It made me uneasy, as though the whole evening had been a trick of some sort to exact a contributory emotion from me. I waited, and sure enough, in a moment she looked at me with an absolute smirk on her lovely face, as if she had asserted her membership in a rather distinguished secret society to which she and Tom belonged. (pp. 21–2)

This identification with Tom comes as a surprise. So does its limited extension to Nick himself. (A few pages earlier, Nick has referred to the fact that he and Tom "were in the same senior society" [p. 9] at Yale.) The three-way identification of Tom, Nick, and Daisy momentarily demystifies Daisy and consequently makes the reader trust more in Nick's judgments. Nick can both glamorize Daisy so that the reader shares Gatsby's attraction to her and undercut Daisy so that the reader can see her from without. Such a set of contradictions strengthens the spell Daisy can cast and gives us a view of Daisy that contrasts to the one Gatsby will later present.

The double view of Daisy persists throughout the novel, although it is later replaced by the more compelling topic of Gatsby's feeling for her; it certainly continues through Chapter 5, when Gatsby meets Daisy again after five years. At this point, our contradictory feelings are transferred to their relationship. Fitzgerald deliberately recalls our reactions by a reference to the first scene with Daisy when Nick refers to a joke about the butler's nose. His description of Daisy's voice when Gatsby enters Nick's house, also recalls that previous episode:

> For half a minute there wasn't a sound. Then from the living-room I heard a sort of choking murmur and part of a laugh, followed by Daisy's voice on a clear artificial note:
> "I certainly am awfully glad to see you again." (p. 104)

Just when it seems as though the hollow, mannered, deliberate falseness is going to continue, Fitzgerald effects another peripeteia. When Nick returns after having left Daisy and Gatsby alone for awhile, Daisy is crying, and "every vestige of embarrassment" (p. 107) has disappeared. Daisy's throat, at this point, "full of aching, grieving beauty, told only of her unexpected joy" (p. 108). Love seems possible, especially for Gatsby. He dominates the rest of the chapter, as "a new well-being radiated from him" (p. 108).

It is no accident that this scene falls squarely in the middle of the novel. It might also be the emotional center of it, and it is noteworthy that in a letter to his editor, Maxwell Perkins, Fitzgerald mentioned this scene as his favorite.[2]

Yet, moving as it may be, the initial encounter of Gatsby and Daisy cannot really be the emotional center of *The Great Gatsby*. For one thing, however much we may be charmed by Daisy, Nick's previous depiction of her undercuts our ability to give unquestioning credence to her feelings on this occasion. And, more comically, the means by which Gatsby expresses his feelings for Daisy—even though those feelings are sincere—is by showing off his possessions. Urging Daisy and Nick to explore his house, he tells them: "'It took me just three years to earn the money that bought it'" (p. 109). The very language in which Nick describes Gatsby's love for Daisy is commercial: "I think he revalued everything in his house according to the measure of response it drew from her well-loved eyes" (p. 111). Daisy responds to Gatsby's display: she cries over his beautiful shirts.

Even when the sentiments are genuine, they are formulated in monetary terms. Gatsby's love for Daisy is an intense and worked-out variety of that which lovers of all ages have felt; its expression is distinctively that of postwar America, of a society that consumes.

At this point in *The Great Gatsby* the relationship between love and money has been suggested but not enlarged, as it will be later. For one thing, we do not know about Gatsby's impoverished beginnings, and our ignorance is essential to Fitzgerald's plan. It is not simply the case, as Edith Wharton suggested in a letter to Fitzgerald, that Fitzgerald wishes to tell his story in a new fashion just to be "modern"[3]; nor can I wholly accept Fitzgerald's explanation that the reason for withholding Gatsby's past is to augment the sense of mystery surrounding him,[4] although doing so does have such an effect. Rather, withholding exactly who Gatsby is or where he comes from is a method of underscoring the rootlessness of postwar American society, its restless alienation, and its consequent reliance on money as a code for expressing emotions and identity.

Fitzgerald seems at every point to emphasize the unconnectedness of Gatsby. Gatsby has shifting identities according to which party guest one listens to, but most of the identities, even the one that turns out to be "true," have something of the unreal or fantastic about them. When they do not, they seem fantastic by being juxtaposed with others that do.

> "Who is he?" I demanded. "Do you know?"
>
> "He's just a man named Gatsby."
>
> "Where is he from, I mean? And what does he do?"
>
> "Now *you're* started on the subject," she answered with a wan smile. "Well, he told me once he was an Oxford man."
>
> A dim background started to take shape behind him, but at her next remark it faded away.
>
> "However, I don't believe it." (p. 59)

This rootlessness begins when the war ends. Before he identifies himself, the war is the subject of Gatsby's conversation with Nick, and it is the most grounded identity, until the novel's denouement, that Gatsby has.

How do the members of such a rootless, mobile, indifferent society acquire a sense of who they are? Most of them don't. The novel presents large numbers of them as comic, disembodied names of guests at dinner parties: the Chromes, the Backhyssons, and the Dennickers. Some, of course, have some measure of fame, but even Jordan Baker's reputation does not do much for her other than get her entrée to more parties. A very few, such as Gatsby, stand out by their wealth; his hospitality secures him a hold on many peoples' memories, but Fitzgerald is quick to point up the emptiness of this: Klipspringer cares more about his lost tennis shoes than Gatsby's death.

In this connection, Fitzgerald's insistence on Gatsby as a man who "sprang from his own Platonic conception of himself" is important. Conceiving one's self would seem to be a final expression of rootlessness. And it has other consequences for love, money, and aspirations as well. When one's sense of self is self-created, when one is present at one's own creation, so to speak, one is in a paradoxical position. One knows everything about oneself that can be known, and yet the significance of such knowledge is unclear, for no outside contexts exist to create meaning. The result is that a self-created man turns to the past, for he can know that. It is an inescapable context. For Gatsby and for the novel, the past is crucial.

His sense of the past as something that he not only knows but also thinks he can control sets Gatsby apart from Nick and gives him mythical, larger-than-life dimensions. When he tells Nick that "'of course'" the past can be repeated (p. 133) or that Tom's love for Daisy was "'just personal'" (p. 182), he may be compensating for his inability to recapture Daisy; but he must believe these things because the postwar world in which he, Gatsby, lives is meaningless and almost wholly loveless.

A glance at the relationships in *The Great Gatsby* proves this latter point. Daisy and Tom's marriage has gone dead; they must cover their dissatisfactions with the distractions of the idle rich. Myrtle and Tom are using one another; Myrtle hates George, who is too dull to understand her; the McKees exist in frivolous and empty triviality. Even Nick seems unsure about his feelings for the tennis girl back in the Midwest. His attraction to Jordan Baker is clearly an extension of this earlier relationship (both girls are associated with sports), but occurring as it does in the East, it partakes of the East's corruption. It too calls forth the need for money. In a draft manuscript of *The Great Gatsby*, Nick makes the link between money and desire explicit: "I thought that I loved her and I wanted money with a sudden physical pang."[5] Later Nick compares his loveless affair with Jordan to refuse the sea might sweep away, a feeling that Jordan senses and throws back at Nick with cruel irony when she accuses him of being dishonest—leading her on with no intention of marrying her—after lying to him that she is engaged to another man.

In brief, the world of *The Great Gatsby* can seem as sordid, loveless, commercial, and dead as the ash heaps presided over by the eyes of Dr. T. J. Eckleburg. Indeed, this atmosphere is so essential to *The Great Gatsby* that one of the alternative titles Fitzgerald considered for the novel was *Among the Ash-Heaps and Millionaires*.

Against this backdrop, the Gatsby–Daisy relationship seems to shine. It is at least a shared connection in which both partners respond with equal intensity. For Gatsby it has endured: He has loved Daisy for five years. And if their love is founded upon feelings from the past, these give it, notwithstanding Gatsby's insistence on being able to repeat the past, an inviolability. It exists in the world of money and corruption but is not of it.

Some implications of the inviolability Gatsby does not see. His very protesting, however, shows his sense of the impossibility of returning and makes at once more poignant and more desperate his effort to win Daisy—a poignancy further increased by the futility of his money in achieving this end.

> "I'm going to fix everything just the way it was before," he said, nodding determinedly. "She'll see."

He talked a lot about the past, and I gathered that he wanted to recover something, some idea of himself perhaps, that had gone into loving Daisy. His life had been confused and disordered since then, but if he could once return to a certain starting place and go over it all slowly, he could find out what that thing was.... (p. 133).

The last orderly period of Gatsby's life, then, was the period before he was sent to fight in the war, when he was still in the process of self-creation. The period when he loved Daisy and when Daisy loved him preceded his period of fabulous wealth. In this respect, he fits the Alger stereotype.

The period when his love becomes most intense, however, is precisely that in which he does not see Daisy. The love born in this period is therefore largely a function of his imagination. The kernel of his experience remains untouched because it is safely embedded in a previous time; the growth of the love is wild and luxuriant. It spurs him on, resulting in the glamorous world of parties and in the "huge incoherent failure" (p. 217) of his house.

The romantic and fantastic nature of Gatsby's love seems extraordinary and absurd, looked at in worldly, practical terms. Why does he wait so long to arrange a meeting and then use Jordan Baker and Nick Carraway to bring it about? A man with Gatsby's resources would surely have a hundred easier ways to do what he does in the course of this story. The answer is that the love becomes *more* important than the object of it. Gatsby has already started down this path in Louisville when he asks himself, "'What would be the use of doing great things if I could have a better time telling her what I was going to do?'" (p. 180).

If Gatsby himself is presented as curiously "unreal," the connection between Daisy and Gatsby—the unobtainable and the insubstantial—is destined to founder in a world as insistently material as the one Fitzgerald details for us. In such a world, Gatsby cannot make love to Daisy. Even earlier, during the war, when Gatsby and Daisy did make love ("took" her [p. 178]), physical contact was a limitation of his love: "He knew that when he kissed this girl, and forever wed his unutterable visions to her perishable breath, his mind would never romp again like the mind of God" (p. 134). And the moments of greatest intimacy between them are those when they neither speak nor make love: "They had never been closer in their month of love, nor communicated more profoundly one with another, than when she brushed silent lips against his coat's shoulder or when he touched the end of her fingers, gently, as though she were asleep" (p. 180). No wonder, then, that after the five-year hiatus, when Gatsby's love has had the chance to feed upon itself and nourish itself, the possibility of physical intimacy has not grown, but the love has grown beyond the merely "personal."

For these reasons Chapter 7, where Daisy, Tom, Gatsby, Nick and Jordan engage a suite at the Plaza hotel, is of greatest importance. If Daisy's love for Gatsby is to endure, it must exist in non-Platonic, physical terms. It must exist in the world of money. The scene in New York demonstrates the impossibility of this transformation and further connects Gatsby's love to his sense of fabulous, mythical riches.

If Gatsby dominates the first meeting with Daisy—the chapter ends at his house, on his territory—Tom dominates the denouement at the hotel. The change of venue allies Chapter 7 to Chapter 2, the scene of Tom's violent party with Myrtle Wilson, a connection Fitzgerald underscores by the telephone conversation about Tom Buchanan's selling his car and by the stopping for gasoline at George Wilson's station.

Daisy sees purposelessness as characterizing her whole life: "'What'll we do with ourselves this afternoon?' cried Daisy, 'and the day after that, and the next thirty years?'" (p. 141). The idleness of this remark doesn't threaten Gatsby's grandiose feelings, but Daisy inhabits the physical world of Tom, and she wants to act, not just dream, so it is she who proposes that the party move to New York—to Tom's territory. Such a move takes the day away from Gatsby. Daisy's voice ominously molds the "senselessness [of the heat] into forms" (p. 142)—i.e., abstract feelings into concrete deeds.

It is before the five characters move to New York that Gatsby makes his famous remark to Nick: "'Her voice is full of money'" (p. 144). This insight, which Fitzgerald added when the novel was in galley proof, shows Gatsby's understanding of the link between love and money. Daisy's voice has been described as the seductive, thrilling aspect of her. What Gatsby, with surprising consciousness, states is that Daisy's charm is allied to the attraction of wealth; money and love hold similar attractions.

It is true that from Wolfsheim to Nick Carraway, people are in the East to earn their livings, to pursue "the shining secrets that only Midas and Morgan and Maecenas knew" (p. 5). But Gatsby, with his boundless capacity for love, a capacity unique in the sterile world he inhabits, sees that the pursuit of money is a substitute for love. He knows himself well enough to see that his own attraction toward wealth is tied to his love for Daisy. The fact that Gatsby's money, like his love, should be self-made gives his description of her voice authority and depth.

That Daisy's voice should be full of money is a remark only Gatsby could make. It is a statement of someone alive to the possibilities of love and money and sensitive to them—perhaps too much so. Tom could never have provided the description of Daisy. His attraction to Daisy has nothing to do with her wealth. (Her family is well off, but apparently not very rich—certainly not compared to the Buchanan fortune.) And it is impossible to imagine Tom making Gatsby's remark because Tom is accustomed to having money. Money *qua* money holds no interest for him because it does not have to be chased after: His is old money simply there to be used. Tom may buy anything he wishes—from polo ponies to cufflinks—but he understands that polo ponies or cufflinks are all he is buying. His money was divested of dreams before he was even born.

Gatsby's, on the other hand, is new money, money in the process of being acquired. This newness gives the money some purpose and vitality; what Gatsby buys he buys for a purpose: to win Daisy. But there is a danger for Gatsby in this redeeming purposefulness. When he buys his fantastic house, he thinks he is buying a dream, not simply purchasing property. This direction makes Gatsby a more sympathetic man than Tom, but it is a sympathy he projects at the price of naiveté; he is completely innocent of the limits of what money can do, a man who, we feel, would believe every word of an advertisement. Daisy even makes this identification: "'You resemble the advertisement of the man'" (p. 142).

In this respect Gatsby embodies the acquisitive, consuming spirit of the rest of the characters in the novel. The characters of *The Great Gatsby* are pursuing a world of misunderstood elegance, mirrored in a thousand romantic and comic details and apotheosized, perhaps, in Nick's description of New York as made of "white heaps and sugar lumps all built with a wish out of non-olfactory money" (p. 82).

"Non-olfactory" is a curious word. It is Fitzgerald's way of using the common locution that "money smells." He is also reminding us, of course, that Gatsby's money does not "smell" right—however explicitly or tacitly condoned by the denizens of Gatsby's world, illegal and shifty means (bootlegging, stolen securities) have been used to make that wealth. Gatsby does not see that the corruption at the base of his fortune in effect compromises his vision of life with Daisy. You cannot win the ideal with the corrupt, and you cannot buy integrity or taste with dollars. When late in the story Daisy attends one of Gatsby's parties, she is repelled rather than attracted.

So stated, this has a moralistic ring, but no reader of *The Great Gatsby* could ever mistake it for a didactic work. The reader is at many points encouraged to marvel at the glitter, especially as it is the means by which Gatsby chases after Daisy. If such morality as the book conveys comes through most explicitly in the attitudes of its narrator, there are nevertheless many moments when Nick is simply overwhelmed by the astonishing freshness and strength of Gatsby's feeling. Indeed, after the remark about Daisy's voice, Nick finds himself participating in Gatsby's thinking. He finds this moment similar to an earlier one in Chapter 5 when he "was going to ask to see the rubies" (p. 113). He continues Gatsby's dream for us, recognizing the strength of Gatsby's identification of Daisy's voice and money.

That was it. I'd never understood it before. It was full of money—
that was the inexhaustible charm that rose and fell in it, the jingle
of it, the cymbals' song of it.... High in a white palace the king's
daughter, the golden girl.... (p. 144)

Here not only Nick but also we share Gatsby's dream. The man who
has asked Daisy, "'Can't you talk about crops or something?'" (p. 15) breaks
into reverie. We share in the pleasures, in the fantasies; Nick's and Gatsby's
vision becomes ours. And thus the book fosters our appreciation of Gatsby's
corrupt dream. Yet such participation can never be wholehearted and can
never be complete: Nick breaks off as Tom returns with a bottle of whiskey,
and the scene becomes Tom's again.

The novel's insistence that Tom win the struggle over Daisy is
tantamount to denying the realization of the kind of love that Gatsby is
offering Daisy and that the novel values above all others. What does remain
is the marriage of Tom and Daisy. Ironically, such love as even that
relationship may contain is embedded in the past ("'that day I carried you
down from the Punch Bowl'" [p. 159]). The future, uncertain and without
love, is a kind of death—rendering the world of *The Great Gatsby* grim
indeed. Nick sees the oncoming years as harrowing and lonely ones. What
does life hold for a decent man like Nick? He has no love, unlike Gatsby.
Nick is thirty, a number that recalls Daisy's frightening question, "'What'll
we do with ourselves ... for the next thirty years?'" (p. 144)

One answer to Nick's self-doubts might be his liaison with Jordan Baker.
That, however, has already been presented to us as a troubled one. If Jordan is
"too wise ever to carry well-forgotten dreams from age to age" (p. 163), she is
wrapped in almost impenetrable narcissism; after the disturbing events of the
day when Myrtle has been killed, Jordan is ready for a date: "'It's only half-past
nine'" (p. 171). But Nick, having watched Gatsby's love for Daisy effectively
terminated, having seen Myrtle violently run down, and wrapped in his own
loneliness, cannot accede to compulsive and indeed perverse socializing.

The novel's sense of duality, of attraction and repellence, diminishes
after the hotel scene. Instead the book proceeds with deliberate
mechanicalness to work out the consequences of Daisy's having run down
Myrtle. Wilson's dull, self-defensive grief is the embodiment of the sterility
of the valley of ashes; lacking a dream, his life itself is a kind of death. Wilson
may have been married in a church "'a long time ago'" (p. 189), but his
present God is the disembodied eyes of Dr. T. J. Eckleburg, an
advertisement. For him love has vanished, and he is left without a vision to
sustain him. The man who kills Gatsby is already dead when he commits the
murder; Nick Carraway describes him as "ashen" (p. 194), and his suicide is
simply a belated acknowledgment of his condition.

Wilson and Gatsby both die by Wilson's hand, suggesting an identification. There is one. Both have aspired to marry above their social station. Whereas Wilson borrows a suit for his wedding to conceal his low economic status, Gatsby wears his country's uniform while courting Daisy. But there the similarity ends. Yet it is worth noting that Gatsby has tried to do what probably no other developed male character in a major work of American fiction has tried to do. He has tried to marry for love into a class higher than the one he comes from. Usually women make such an attempt, namely, Sister Carrie, Lily Bart, and a host of others.

In this respect the difference between Gatsby and the hero of another book published in the same year, Theodore Dreiser's *An American Tragedy*, is instructive. Clyde Griffiths, like Gatsby, tries to rise from humble beginnings in the Midwest to a larger, more glamorous life in the East. Like Gatsby, Clyde attaches himself to a woman (Sondra Finchley) from a moneyed family. And both believe that if they only have enough money, they can buy the dream they seek.

There is a crucial difference. Clyde Griffiths is sexually attracted to Sondra Finchley, but he is not in love with her. Sondra provides the wealth and glamor that Clyde's lover Roberta, is unable to, but Clyde's feelings for Sondra are really subordinate to his sense of pleasure in her leisured environment. Of Gatsby's depth of feeling, of Gatsby's imagination, of Gatsby's genuineness of sentiment ("'I can't describe to you how surprised I was to find out I loved her, old sport'" [p. 179]), Clyde Griffiths knows nothing.

He is unaware of the fact, but Clyde is using Sondra for his own ends. Jay Gatsby is not using Daisy. He strives to move in higher circles because Daisy is there. Of course, in doing so, he violates a cultural norm. He tries to buy into a tradition instead of accepting one. Social convention and time triumph. The wearing away of freedom and the impossibility of realizing the only dreams that make life worth living are the themes of *The Great Gatsby*. The absence of great love is more painful because the sense of possibility money provides is so powerfully ambient in Gatsby's world.

Again, because the dream is unrealizable, the past becomes increasingly important to the book, for it is in memories that the dream can live. The final pages of the novel are pervaded by the consciousness of the past and the sense of history ("the dark fields of the republic" [p. 218]). For most readers these pages are the most moving and suggestive in the book, and, many would add, in the whole of F. Scott Fitzgerald's writing. The reason is that what has been felt or implied in every line earlier in the novel is expanded there in paragraphs of increasingly greater suggestiveness until the passage achieves archetypal resonances—resonances beyond even the usual national, historical ones claimed for this section of the novel.

That these final paragraphs should echo through the whole book can be illustrated bibliographically. Nick's meditation about American history and the sense of possibility originally appeared in the manuscript not as the conclusion to the whole novel, but as the end of Chapter 1, where Nick returns to West Egg from visiting Tom and Daisy and sees Gatsby attempting to "determine what share was his of our local heavens" (p. 26). All the images from the final pages—the moon rising higher, the "inessential houses" (p. 217), the "fresh, green breast of the new world" (p. 217), and so on are here, and the passage's haunting, lost feeling comes through because of them. Nick's accidental sighting of Gatsby at this point is not sufficient reason for the depth or length of the meditation, and Fitzgerald brilliantly repositioned the passage to where it now stands—but the feeling of loss was already present early in the conception. If in reading the book we find the final paragraphs a fitting conclusion, then that is so as a result of the novel's originally having hung from them, or having been composed with them already written.

From the start, therefore, Fitzgerald sensed the possibility of writing a novel whose theme embraced the notion of dreams in a general way. In letters written around the period of *The Great Gatsby*, Fitzgerald refers to the novel's being about those illusions that matter so much that you chase after them, because even though they are illusions, nothing matters as much as they do. What counts is nothing less than the profoundest experience of love. Yet what is Gatsby's love for Daisy but illusion, one fed by the dream of fulfillment America offered?

> And as the moon rose higher the inessential houses began to melt away until gradually I became aware of the old island here that flowered once for Dutch sailors' eyes—a fresh, green breast of the new world. Its vanished trees, the trees that had made way for Gatsby's house, had once pandered in whispers to the last and greatest of all human dreams; for a transitory enchanted moment man must have held his breath in the presence of this continent, compelled into an aesthetic contemplation he neither understood nor desired, face to face for the last time in history with something commensurate to his capacity for wonder. (pp. 217–18)

The love that imbues this passage, the warmth and closeness of the tone, is expressed in the imagery of birth, from the womblike feeling of holding breath, from the breast of the new world, and from the lack of understanding or desire: All these are feelings connected with being born. And because every man, including the reader, is the "last" man in history while he is alive, these sentences achieve the immediacy of myth and archetype.

The love that Gatsby has for Daisy is one whose sexual component is hidden in the inviolate past. It sees the affairs of the world as necessary but sordid. It is the love Fitzgerald felt for America, as Alfred Kazin has noted in *An American Procession*.[6] In such enclosed dreams we are children; they offer us a kind of ultimate innocence. But because such love is unconsummated and unconsummatable, it cannot express itself directly. Instead it imbues that which surrounds it with its own special quality.

This quality spills into Nick's sense of history and into the novel's feelings of what it means to be wealthy. Unsophisticated writers such as Horatio Alger made a false separation between love and money; more complex writers sublimated or subordinated the one to the other. The unique contribution of *The Great Gatsby* is the identification of them. The acquisition of money and love are both part of the same dream, the will to return to the quintessential unity that exists only at birth and at death.

The last sentence of the novel, "So we beat on, boats against the current, borne back ceaselessly into the past," points out that all of our great dreams are grounded in impossibility: We progress toward that which we want, but the natural movement of life is retrograde—we die. The water here, as in *The Waste Land*, is both life-giving amnion and a destroying force.

To say this as Fitzgerald has is to reach an insight of final proportion. For this reason, *The Great Gatsby* transcends the ideas of the 1920s, its ostensible subject. By yoking the harsher, cynical postwar judgments about love and human endeavor to the older dreams of the past, the novel makes a synthesis greater than any single period could have achieved. *The Great Gatsby* is about love and money, but its greater subject—the tragic nature of aspiration—links these two in ways that deepen in the broadest, profoundest way our sense of who we are.

NOTES

1. Mark Schorer, *Sinclair Lewis: An American Life* (New York: McGraw-Hill, 1961), p. 246.

2. Circa December 1, 1924. *The Letters of F. Scott Fitzgerald*, ed. Andrew Turnbull (New York: Scribners, 1963), p. 170.

3. "Three Letters about *The Great Gatsby*," *The Crack-Up*, ed. Edmund Wilson (New York: New Directions, 1945), p. 309.

4. To Maxwell Perkins, January 24, 1925. *Letters*, pp. 175–6.

5. F. Scott Fitzgerald, *A Facsimile of the Manuscript*, ed. Matthew J. Bruccoli (Washington, D.C.: Bruccoli Clark/Microcard, 1973), p. 123.

6. Alfred Kazin, *An American Procession* (New York: Knopf, 1984), p. 393.

RICHARD LEHAN

Inventing Gatsby

So he invented just the sort of Jay Gatsby that a seventeen-year-old boy would be likely to invent, and to this conception he was faithful to the end. (99)

At one point in his story of Gatsby, Nick tells us that "if personality is an unbroken series of successful gestures, then there was something gorgeous about him, some heightened sensitivity to the promises of life" (2). Fitzgerald's language, as always, is carefully chosen, especially the word "personality." In his early work Fitzgerald distinguished between the "egoist" and the "personage." The egoist relied on personality, which depended upon appearance, grooming, gesture—the surface aspects of self. Personage moves beyond personality to a more essential form of self—self as process, an accumulated sense of what one can become. These terms take their meaning from each other; the creation of an essential self demands the personality through which it is expressed.

Beyond the accidents of personality, we have Gatsby modeling himself on Dan Cody and, of course, having Daisy Fay for his wife. That the adolescent imagination makes something more "gorgeous" than convincing out of this notion of self is not surprising. With no real sense of the differences in class or between kinds of money, with no formal education,

From The Great Gatsby: *The Limits of Wonder.* © 1990 by G.K. Hall & Co.

with not the faintest idea of how the established rich live and act, Gatsby sets out to give personality—"gesture" as Nick calls it—to the personage he has created. The "gestures," of course, include the pink suits, the silver shirts, the gold ties, the Rolls-Royce swollen with chrome and hat boxes, the clipped speech, the "old sports," the formal intensity of manner, the gracefulness on the ballroom floor, the bending slightly forward in conversation to create the impression of an intensity of interest, the meticulous attention to detail— these and many more "gestures" complement the personage of Gatsby. Of course, the pretensions to an Oxford education seem totally out of context with this sense of self—as indeed they are. Beneath the elaborate, albeit gaudy, elegance of Gatsby looms James Gatz, the original "roughneck" that Gatsby spends so much energy trying to conceal. Nick spots the contradictions the first time he meets Gatsby:

> He smiled understandingly—much more than understandingly. It was one of those rare smiles with a quality of eternal reassurance in it, that you may come across four or five times in life. It faced—or seemed to face—the whole external world for an instant, and then concentrated on you with an irresistible prejudice in your favor. It understood you just as far as you wanted to be understood, believed in you as you would like to believe in yourself, and assured you that it had precisely the impression of you that, at your best, you hoped to convey. Precisely at that point it vanished—and I was looking at an elegant young roughneck, a year or two over thirty, whose elaborate formality of speech just missed being absurd. (48)

Gatsby does not quite bring it off, and the contradictions call attention to the seam between what he tries to be as a personage and what he is as a personality. In the ride from West Egg to Manhattan, Gatsby recites for Nick the essential self that he has created: "'I am the son of some wealthy people in the Middle West—all dead now. I was brought up in America but educated at Oxford, because all my ancestors have been educated there for many years. It is a family tradition'" (65). Like Jordan Baker, Nick does not believe him, and comes to understand why so many of Gatsby's guests feel that there is something sinister about him:

> He looked at me sideways—and I knew why Jordan Baker had believed he was lying. He hurried the phrase "educated at Oxford," or swallowed it, or choked on it, as though it had bothered him before. And with this doubt, his whole statement

fell to pieces, and I wondered if there wasn't something a little
sinister about him, after all. (65)

Gatsby begins with an element of truth (he did go to Oxford briefly after the
war on a government scholarship) and then gives way to total distortion.
Gatsby hardly comes from Midwest wealth or a tradition of genteel breeding
connected with an Oxford education. When Nick asks him where in the
Midwest he comes from, Gatsby ignorantly, but elegantly, tells him San
Francisco, geography losing to the pretensions of the romantic imagination.
The more Gatsby talks the more absurd his story becomes. Nick believes
"that he was pulling my leg" until "a glance at him convinced me otherwise."
"After that," Gatsby continues, "I lived like a young rajah in all the capitals
of Europe—Paris, Venice, Rome—collecting jewels, chiefly rubies, hunting
big game, painting a little, things for myself only, and trying to forget
something very sad that happened to me long ago" (66). By this point Nick
can hardly control his "incredulous laughter." Although well rehearsed,
Gatsby's story is so romantically exaggerated—and so historically untrue—
that Nick has the image of a "turbaned 'character' leaking sawdust at every
pore as he pursued a tiger through the Bois de Boulogne" (66). What is
happening here on the level of rhetoric will have its parallel on the level of
plot because it is Gatsby's inability to bring his romantic conception of self
in sync with historical reality that leads to his destruction.

The intensity of vision has little basis in reality, and it is exactly this
intensity that sustains Gatsby's love for Daisy Fay. As Nick tells us, "the
vitality of his illusion" went "beyond her, beyond everything. He had thrown
himself into it with a creative passion, adding to it all the time" (97). What
Fitzgerald is working with here is the romantic vision. At one point in the
novel, Daisy tells us that "it's very romantic outdoors" because there is a bird
on her lawn that "must be a nightingale come over on the Cunard or White
Star Line" (16). The allusion evokes the poetry of Keats, which Fitzgerald
knew well and which he integrated into many of his major works, especially
Tender is the Night, which takes its title from a line by Keats. Fitzgerald had
studied the romantic poets with Christian Gauss at Princeton, and when his
daughter was in college, Fitzgerald remembered that experience:

> "The Grecian Urn" is unbearably beautiful with every syllable as
> inevitable as the notes in Beethoven's Ninth Symphony…. I
> suppose I've read it a hundred times. About the tenth time I
> began to know what it was about, and caught the chime in it and
> the exquisite inner mechanics. Likewise with "The Nightingale"
> which I can never read through without tears in my eyes; likewise

the "Pot of Basil" ["Isabella"] with its great stanzas about the two brothers, "Why were they proud, etc."; and "The Eve of St. Agnes," which has the richest, most sensuous imagery in English, not excepting Shakespeare. And finally his three or four great sonnets, "Bright Star" and the others (*Letters*, 88).

It was Keats who once wrote, "there is a space of life between boyhood and maturity in which the soul is in ferment, the characters undecided, the way of life uncertain, the ambition thick-sighted."[16] This is the moment, when the romantic creates himself, that Jay Gatsby came into being. All of Fitzgerald's major characters go through this experience, as a look at his other novels quickly reveals:

[Amory Blaine, of *This Side of Paradise*] wondered how people could fail to notice that he was a boy marked for glory.

[Anthony Patch, of *The Beautiful and Damned*] thrilled to remote harmonies ... for he was young now as he would never be again, and more triumphant than death.

In the spring of 1917, when Doctor Richard Diver [of *Tender Is the Night*] first arrived in Zurich, he was twenty-six years old, a fine age for a man, indeed, the very acme of bachelorhood ... [bringing with him] the illusions of eternal strength and health, and of the essential goodness of people; illusions of a nation.

[Monroe Stahr, of *The Last Tycoon*] had flown up very high to see, on strong wings, when he was young. And while he was up there he had looked on all the kingdoms, with the kind of eyes that can stare straight into the sun.[17]

The romantic unfolding of self is inseparable from the romantic belief that the universe is alive and that fulfillment is a process of growth. The emphasis is on becoming rather than being, on expectation rather than reality. In its most radical form, as Morse Peckham has told us, "dynamic organicism results in the idea that the history of the universe is the history of God creating himself."[18] Thus the true romantic, as we have already seen in the case of Gatsby, is the son of God, repeating the godlike activity of creation. Such activity is not without its dangers. Keats's lovers—Lamia, Endymion, Hyperion—are all destroyed in this way. And when the heroes and heroines are not physically destroyed, they often experience radical disillusionment, become eternal wanderers, alienated from society, outcasts. Such is the fate of Byron's Harold, Manfred, and Cain, and of Shelley's Alastor. They wander between Carlyle's "everlasting yea" and "everlasting no" (or what Peckham calls positive and negative romanticism), seeking new commitment, often in the form of an ideal that is already exhausted. Their mortal enemy is time, ideally embodied in youth—with its romantic commitment and sense of the potential. When time is wasted it brings on romantic sadness; when it is remembered it brings on romantic nostalgia. If the idealized moment gives way to nostalgia in Fitzgerald's fiction, nostalgia in turn gives way to the horror of wasted youth, and it is within these three realms of time—time idealized, time sentimentalized, and time regretted—that Fitzgerald's fiction works.

This narrative pattern can be found repeatedly in romantic and postromantic works, and we know from reading *This Side of Paradise* that Amory Blaine (and presumably Fitzgerald himself) read such works. But one does not have to make an argument based on influence to document narrative parallels. Fitzgerald was breathing romantic air when he wrote, and works like Walter Pater's *Marius the Epicurean* and Ernest Dowson's "The Princess of Dreams" seem long stamped upon his imagination. As with Gatsby, Marius's development involves movement from romantic commitment to romantic disillusionment. Marius passes through four stages of experience: first, his boyhood and school life; then he becomes an Epicurean of the Cyrenaic school, which extols the idea of youth; next he becomes disillusioned with the Cyrenaic philosophy; and finally, he moves on to Christianity, deeply attracted to the aesthetics of the new religion but still without the faith to believe. It is in his second stage of development, his belief in Cyrenaicism, that Marius shares a state of mind with Gatsby:

> Thus the boyhood of Marius passed; on the whole more given to contemplation than to action. Less prosperous in fortune than at an earlier day there had been reason to expect ... he lived much in the realm of the imagination, and became betimes, as he was to continue all through life, something of an idealist, constructing the world for himself in great measure from within, by the exercise of meditative power.... [He had an] innate and habitual longing for a world altogether fairer than that he saw.[19]

As Gatsby created in his imagination a world that did not exist, Marius does also. And as Gatsby idealizes Daisy Fay so Marius also had "the ideal of a perfect imaginative love, centered upon a type of beauty entirely flawless and clean" (Pater, 76).

If Pater actually catches the romantic process by which a Gatsby comes into being, Ernest Dowson's "The Princess of Dreams," a prose poem, recapitulates the narrative pattern of such a story. Here the hero returns with a newly amassed treasure to a beautiful girl whom he once loved. He fails, however, to regain her love and is defeated at the hands of a cruel and "slow witted" competitor, a guardian of her tower. In a work with astonishing parallels to *The Great Gatsby* the hero disappears and the poem ends with the suggestion that the golden "princess" is fraudulently unworthy of the hero:

> For once in a dream he had seen, as they were flowers de luce, the blue lakes of her eyes, had seemed to be enveloped in a tangle of her golden hair.
>
> And he sought her through the countless windings of her forest for many moons, sought her through the morasses, sparing not his horse nor his sword.
>
> Poor legendary princess.
>
> For he did not free her and the fustian porter took his treasure and broke his stained sword in two....
>
> But there are some who say that she had no wish to be freed, and that those flowers de luce, her eyes, are a stagnant, dark pool, that her glorious golden hair was only long enough to reach her postern gate.
>
> Some say, moreover, that her tower is not of ivory and that she is not even virtuous nor a princess?[20]

When Fitzgerald was writing *The Great Gatsby* in 1923–24, he was not writing within the same cultural context as Pater and Dowson. What had radically altered the romantic vision in the intervening years was an opposing view that was itself a product of the new science with its belief in the Kingdom of Power, the Dynamics of Force. The play between a belief in romantic commitment and a belief in the limits set by force is at the very heart of modernism, expressed as a dualism between a mechanistic and organic view of the universe. The organic universe is self-contained, capable of growth, is marked by its ability to assimilate diverse material into its own substance, and relies on the spontaneous source of its own energy, as well as the interdependence of parts to parts and of the parts to the whole. The mechanistic universe presupposes a universe made up of matter in motion; such matter obeys physical laws, so that there are no miracles in nature. The organic universe is living, continually unfolding, revealing itself symbolically. The mechanistic universe is fixed, understandable through scientific laws like the law of gravity or thermodynamics, which explain matter, through which force is expressed. In literature the naturalists were trying to reduce reality to mechanistic terms, while the romantics were trying to infuse matter with spirit, energy, and life. H. G. Wells would embody the first position, while D. H. Lawrence would embody the second, and a number of other writers experimented to bridge this kind of division: Joyce, for example, with his "yes" of feminine replenishment, William James with his belief in the need for a religious state of mind that gives matter direction, Samuel Butler with his interest in creative evolution, George Bernard Shaw with his belief in the life force, and Henri Bergson with his theories of vitalism.

Henry Adams took up the argument in America. Built into Adams's vision of the universe, as in Fitzgerald's, was a sense of both systems at work. His belief in the Virgin—in the feminine principle in life, inseparable from a mythic sense of life, and from the unity of an age—revealed a deep sense of the romantic. But his awareness of the Dynamo took him into the realm of force, which, he felt, totally disrupted the possibility of romantic fulfillment. Adams had painfully discovered that history was no longer knowledge but the brute violence of irrational energies. The masculine principle (the Dynamo) had overcome the feminine principle of life (the Virgin); technology, urbanization, the rise of the corporation, and other money institutions had led to the powerhouse of change. As he put it in chapter 25 of *The Education*:

> Satisfied that the sequence of men led to nothing and the sequence of their society could lead no further, while the ... sequence of thought was chaos, he turned at last to the sequence of force; and thus it happened that, after ten years' pursuit, he found himself lying in the Gallery of Machines at the Great Exposition of 1900, his historical neck broken by the sudden irruption of forces totally new.[21]

"Chaos was the law of nature; order was the dream of man," Adams wrote. Modern technological man had gone beyond nature, had forced his mechanical will on the land, and turned that control into wealth.

What we have here is a modern, American Crusoe, who, like Defoe's prototype, had come to the new world, and then moved across a continent, eliminating the Indian and despoiling the land. Crusoe came after Nick Carraway's Dutch sailors, for whom the new world "flowered," as Daisy flowered for Gatsby (as her very name suggests). Into this world Daniel Boone entered, and out of it came William (Buffalo Bill) Cody. Gatsby embodies the beginning and end of this romantic process; his antagonist, Tom Buchanan, the kingdom of force. Nick Carraway makes the connections between these elements the night Gatsby told him the story of "Dan Cody—

told it to me because 'Jay Gatsby' had broken up like glass against Tom's hard malice" (148). The wording here is important. It is not just Jay Gatsby, but also the "idea" of "Jay Gatsby" (as Fitzgerald's quotation marks suggest) that is destroyed by Tom Buchanan. Tom incarnates the new realm of force. The first time we see him Fitzgerald emphasizes this point when Nick tells us, "Not even the effeminate swank of his riding clothes could hide the enormous power of that body—he seemed to fill those glistening boots until he strained the top lacing, and you could see a great pack of muscle shifting when his shoulder moved under his thin coat. It was a body capable of enormous leverage—a cruel body" (7). Tom puts that power to use often. He has hurt Daisy's hand (12), breaks Myrtle's nose (37), and turns Nick around with one arm, at once denying and asserting that "I'm stronger and more of a man than you are" (7).

Such physical force becomes a trope in the novel for the new America—the America in which force is embodied in corporations and in money institutions, embodied in the new urban process, and controlled by finance and the power of information. Tom defeats Gatsby with information by knowing what others do not know. By exposing the origins of Gatsby's money, he overpowers Gatsby's display of self. Although Gatsby created wild discrepancies between what he was as a "personage" and as a "personality," he held, to his credit, that sense of self together by the immense vitality of romantic will. Unfortunately for him, a greater force is at work—a mechanistic force equivalent to the working of the Dynamo, and it is against this force that Gatsby breaks "like glass" (148). In depicting the rise and fall of Gatsby, Fitzgerald not only gave us an insight into the life and death of a romantic hero, but he also gave us an insight into the cultural dynamics of the twentieth century, showing us how Henry Adams picked up where John Keats left off.

NOTES

16. John Keats, *English Poetry and Prose of the Romantic Movement*, ed. George B. Woods (New York: Scott, Foresman, 1950), 1357.

17. *This Side of Paradise* (New York: Scribner's, 1920), 17; *The Beautiful and the Damned* (New York: Scribner's, 1922), 126; *Tender is the Night* (New York: Scribner's, 1934), 115–17; *The Last Tycoon* (New York: Scribner's, 1941), 20.

18. Morse Peckham, "Toward a Theory of Romanticism," in *Romanticism: Points of View*, ed. Robert Gleckner and Gerald Enscoe (Englewood Cliffs, NJ: Prentice-Hall, 1962), 217.

19. Walter Parer, *Marius the Epicurean* (New York: Modern Library, 1921), 19, 36; hereafter cited in the text as Parer.

20. Ernest Dowson, *The Poems of Ernest Dowson*, ed. Mark Longaker (Philadelphia: University of Pennsylvania Press, 1962), 146–47.

21. Henry Adams, *The Education of Henry Adams* (Boston: Houghton Mifflin, 1946), 382.

GILES MITCHELL

The Great Narcissist:
A Study of Fitzgerald's Jay Gatsby

Many critics of *The Great Gatsby* believe, as John Chambers (1989) does, that Jay Gatsby "has a vitality and potential for intense happiness" (p. 115). A few critics, of whom Bettina (1963) is typical, believe that the best than can be said of Gatsby is that he is "a self-made phony" (p. 141). Obviously, those who admire Gatsby find Nick Carraway to be a reliable narrator, and those who deplore Gatsby's character believe Nick to be so morally obtuse that his ideas about Gatsby cannot be trusted. Critics who admire Gatsby, as well as those who do not, adduce a great deal of evidence to support their views. There is probably not a single image, act, or statement in this short novel that has not been subjected to extensive analysis in support of both the admiring and the denigrating view of Gatsby. There is at least one item lacking, however, in criticism of the novel, and that is a clinical profile of Gatsby's personality. My thesis is that the novel contains insuperable evidence that Gatsby is a pathological narcissist who by the end of the novel has lost the will to live. I do not delude myself with the belief that Fitzgerald critics the world over will welcome a psychoanalytic study of Gatsby. Nevertheless, the analysis that I propose to do provides an original context for examining Gatsby's death by comparing it with the death of the classical Narcissus. I will not deal with arguments that exonerate and praise Gatsby except, as noted above, to acknowledge their existence.

From *The American Journal of Psychoanalysis* 51, no. 4 (1991): 387–396. © 1991 by the Association for the Advancement of Psychoanalysis.

91

I realize that Gatsby is not merely a sick character who can be dismissed after diagnosis. The complexity and richness of *The Great Gatsby* resists any one approach. The analysis presented here is intended to analyze Gatsby in clinical terms only. It does not attempt to describe his entire personhood.

Although *The Great Gatsby* has been so widely read that its plot is virtually common knowledge, I will supply the following brief summary. With Nick's help, Gatsby arranges a reunion with Daisy Buchanan, whom Gatsby has loved obsessively for five years. He has bought his mansion solely because "Daisy would be just across the bay" (Fitzgerald, 1925, p. 79). At the reunion, Gatsby is disappointed with Daisy. He vows "to fix everything just the way it was" five years earlier (111). They continue to meet. Near the end of the summer, Daisy invites Gatsby and Nick to a dinner, at which she makes it plain to all present that she is in love with Gatsby. After dinner, they all go to the city and rent a hotel suite, where Gatsby informs Daisy's husband, Tom, that she is leaving him. Gatsby urges Daisy to tell Tom that she "newer loved him" so that the past will be "all wiped out forever" (p. 132), but, as later events show clearly, Daisy absolutely rejects Gatsby in saying to him, "Oh, you want too much!" (p. 133). The group then leaves to return to Long Island, and at Tom's insistence, Daisy rides with Gatsby; she is driving his car when it hits and instantly kills Myrtle Wilson, Tom's mistress. The next day, while lying in his swimming pool, Gatsby is killed by Myrtle Wilson's husband.

GATSBY'S NARCISSISTIC EGO-IDEAL:
PERFECTION AND OMNIPOTENCE

In a person with normal narcissism, the ego-ideal provides "meaning [and] self-esteem" (Menaker, 1977, p. 249). In such a person the "ego-ideal supports the ego" (Menaker, 1977, p. 250) with a realistic sense of self and realistic hopes and aspirations. However, in the narcissist, the ego-ideal becomes inflated and destructive because it is filled with images of "perfection and omnipotence" (Jasovic-Gasic and Vesel, 1981, p. 371). Such images have a "most uncompromising influence on conduct" (Menaker, 1977, p. 50). Two major themes constitute the ego-ideal of Jay Gatsby. One is the theme of perfection, which is expressed in his capacity for idealizing himself and Daisy to an extreme degree. The idealized Gatsby's perfection is manifested in the belief that as a "son of God" (Fitzgerald, 1925, p. 99) he is entitled to be exploitive in any way and to any extent consonant with his idealizations. The other major theme in Gatsby's ego-ideal is onmipotency, which is expressed in his belief that as a son of God he can control time.

Upon meeting and falling in love with Daisy, Gatsby "committed himself to the following of a grail" (Fitzgerald, 1925, p. 149), the "green light" (p. 94) that symbolizes the idealized Daisy. However, on the afternoon that Gatsby and Daisy are reunited, Gatsby begins to have trouble with his symbolism. He says to Daisy, "You always have a green light that burns all night at he end of your dock" (p. 94). Daisy is standing beside him, "her arm through his" (p. 94), as they gaze out a window of his mansion toward her house. But Gatsby seemed absorbed In what he had just said. Possibly it had occurred to him that the colossal significance of that light had now vanished forever" (94). In other words, to Gatsby the light has symbolized an ideal of perfection that has never before been tested—and threatened—because immediately after he and Daisy fell in love, the army sent him overseas, and he has not seen her for five years. Therefore, Gatsby "seemed absorbed in what he had just said" (p. 99) because believing in the dream light of the grail is much easier than believing in Daisy herself: "There must have been moments even that afternoon when Daisy tumbled short of his dreams" (p. 97). "His face shows an expression of bewilderment" (p. 97) because his "dreams ... had gone far beyond her, beyond everything" (p. 97), that is, beyond mutability and linear time. He dimly realizes, but does not yet admit, that the real Daisy is unsuitably imperfect. By the end of the novel the dream/Daisy will have diminished to the point that "perhaps he no longer cared" (p. 162) whether her call would come or not.

Daisy fails to give Gatsby the call he hopes to receive not only because she is probably deficient in "courage" (p. 135) but also because she knows she cannot live up to the needs of Gatsby's vast and rapacious idealism. He has wanted "too much!" (p. 135). He has wanted the humanly impossible. It is important to note that she has rejected Gatsby before Tom's revelations regarding Gatsby's criminality and before the accident that kills Myrtle Wilson. She rejects Gatsby because she has suddenly become acutely aware of his uncompromising demand that she obliterate an irremedial imperfection: the last four years of her life. When her "frightened eyes" (p. 135) tell Gatsby that she will not marry him, that is, that she is imperfect, he is left with nothing but a "dead dream" (p. 135).

Early in the summer, Nick observes Gatsby standing on his lawn looking across the bay at the green, grail light that symbolizes his spiritualized Daisy. He lifts his hands "in idolatrous supplication to the green light" (Dahl, 1984, p. 195). In worshipping the grail as if it were a light emanating from the idealized Daisy, Gatsby is really worshipping himself in the mirror of Daisy's symbolism. Gatsby's self-worship reveals what Sugerman (1964) aptly calls the "egotheism" of the typical narcissist (p. 82). At the end of the summer, when Daisy repudiates him and disappears behind the barricade of Buchanan wealth, the grail light also disappears, for it is Daisy's symbol. Nick says that on the night before his death, Gatsby was "clutching at some last hope" (Fitzgerald, 1925, p. 148) for Daisy's call. By the afternoon of the next day, Gatsby probably "didn't believe it would come, and perhaps he no longer cared" (p. 162). Although Nick says, on the last page of the novel, that Gatsby "believed in the green light" (p. 182), if in the last hours of his life he no longer believes that Daisy will call or cares about whether or not she will, then it follows that he no longer believes in the grail.

There is no evidence in the novel that Gatsby feels any moral conflict about urging Daisy to marry him—to marry into a life supported by criminal activities. In Rothstein's words, "People with narcissistic personality disorders feel entitled to have what they want just because they want it" (1985, p, 67). It is of crucial importance to note that Gatsby evinces no conscious sense of guilt for deceiving Daisy. Furthermore, there is no hint in the novel that he feels guilt unconsciously, because the feeling of narcissistic entitlement typically "serves as a substitute for normal repression" (Murray, 1964, p. 492).

Gatsby is a poseur in the most serious sense of the word. Therefore, he can have no genuine emotional contact with Daisy, and he compensates for this deficiency as, according to Stern, the narcissist typically does: by "making exploitive demands" (1977, p. 191) upon Daisy and upon the world in general. Exploitiveness with regard to women appears early, in his life—in his mid-teens:

> He knew women early, and ... he became contemptuous of them, of young virgins because they were ignorant, of the others because they were hysterical about things which in his overwhelming self-absorption he took for granted (Fitzgerald, 1925, p. 99)

When he first met Daisy, "He took what he could get, ravenously and unscrupulously.... He had deliberately given Daisy a sense of security; he let her believe that he was a person from much the same stratum as herself" (p. 149). Gatsby's exploitiveness derives in part from what Kernberg refers to as the narcissist's "extreme self-centeredness" (1975, p. 228), or in Fitzgerald's phrase, "overwhelming self-absorption" (1925, p. 99).

Gatsby's sense of entitlement is a major force in his character. To narcissists, entitlement means simply that they "feel entitled to have what they want just because they want it" (Rothstein, 1985, p. 67). Gatsby's entitlement justifies his grandiosity as well as his exploitiveness. The most extreme expression of his grandiosity has to do with his parentage, which "his imagination had never really accepted" (Fitzgerald, 1925, p. 99). Instead, "he sprang from his Platonic conception of himself. He was a son of God—a phrase which, if it means anything, means just that" (p. 99). The blasphemous, deific quality in Gatsby has a specific grandiose focus: "his Father's business, the service of a vast, vulgar, and meretricious beauty" (p. 99). This narcissistically inflated religious theme is elaborated in the statement that "to this conception he was faithful to the end" (p. 99). Although I have said that I would not refer to adversarial views, because I find it wonderfully extravagant and because there is all too little in literary criticism that appeals to the risible, I will quote Mellard's statement that "Gatsby bears important resemblances to the traditional Christ" and is "the archetypal scapegoat" (1966, p. 858). Of course, Gatsby is an innocent, but only in the sense that in his entire life there has been no person no event, no experience that might have made him question and revise moral values. Nevertheless, Gatsby is exploitive and dishonest, and his sense of entitlement permits him to be so. In this he is the typical narcissist.

When Gatsby tells Nick it is "God's truth" that he had been "educated at Oxford" (Fitzgerald, 1925, p. 65), like all his ancestors, he is not telling an ordinary lie, for the grandiose, deific theme is implicit in his use of the word "God's." Whether or not Gatsby is telling the truth about his ancestry and his heroic war record does not matter. The point is that when he tells Nick about it, he is planning to use Nick as an intermediary in order to see Daisy again; and he doesn't want Nick to think he is "just some nobody" (p. 67). He wants Daisy to see his house, which, he tells her, he keeps full of "celebrated people" (p. 91), special objects in his "universe of ineffable gaudiness" (p. 99). Given his poor sense of reality and his pitiable grandiosity, it is neatly appropriate that Gatsby's mansion be an "imitation," and a "colossal" (p. 5) one at that. The note inviting Nick to a party there is signed by Gatsby "in a majestic hand" (p. 41). Grandiosity is a major motive force in his idealizations of Daisy. He projects onto her a kind of royal status. To him, she is "high in a white palace the king's daughter, the golden girl (p. 120).

Gatsby is extremely adept at embuing his exploitiveness with a tawdry romanticism that Nick finds attractive. Like the typical narcissist studied by Kernberg (1975), Gatsby presents "a surface which very often is charming and engaging," and a subsurface of "coldness and ruthlessness" (p. 228). Nick says that when he first met him, Gatsby produced a smile "with a quality of eternal reassurance in it"; it concentrated on *you* with an irresistible prejudice in your favor" (Fitzgerald, 1925, p. 48). But beneath his engaging surface, Gatsby is profoundly dishonest and manipulative with Daisy both when he first meets hers and later when they are reunited. He tells her lies of a most serious nature in defending himself against Tom's revelations about how

Gatsby has made his money. In short, in asking Daisy to leave Tom, he is being morally devious. Gatsby lies to Daisy without the slightest compunction because she is the idealized object of his projections and therefore not real. Therefore, he unthinkingly assumes that he need not tell Daisy the factual truth of who he actually was when they met five years earlier and who he is now: a criminal.

If he loved her, he would want intimacy with her; but intimacy means knowing and being known, and Gatsby does not want Daisy to know him, for he is a criminal with a poor education and a background of impoverished, "shiftless and unsuccessful farm people" (p. 99). Furthermore, he does not want to know Daisy—the real Daisy—who is five years older than she was when he first met her and who had a husband whom she once loved and by whom she has had a child. The real Daisy runs far away from the scene of her crime and does not even bother to call Gatsby to say goodbye. Although she can weep over Gatsby's magniloquent display of shirts, the real Daisy has "impersonal eyes in the absence of all desire" (p. 12). It is likely that Gatsby is unknowingly attracted by Daisy's incapacity for intimacy and by the impersonality in her eyes: He discredits her love for Tom by describing it as being "just personal" (p. 152).

OMNIPOTENCE AND TIME

When Nick says to Gatsby, "You can't repeat the past" (Fitzgerald, 1925, p. 111), Gatsby is astounded at what he apparently regards as Nick's naiveté: "'Can't repeat the past?' he cried incredulously. 'Why of course you can!'" Narcissists typically believe that they can control time, for time presents "threats to omnipotence" (Stern, 1977, p. 194). Therefore, it is often the case that narcissists illogically attempt to "repeat the same experience" (p. 194) What Gatsby wants in this regard is for himself and Daisy to be in Louisville again, in love, and then to "be married from her house—just as if it were five years ago" (Fitzgerald, 1925, p. 111). Controlling time by repeating an experience would be an attempt on Gatsby's part to stop and reverse time. Therefore, Gatsby "talked a lot about the past.... [He wanted to] return to a certain starting place and go over it all slowly" (Fitzgerald, 1925, pp. 111–112). Gatsby's belief that he can delete the present and restore the idealized past reveals the perfection motif of his ego-ideal. And as Rothstein (1985) notes, "the pursuit of perfection is in itself self-destructive" (p. 99) because it radically diminishes one's humanness. But Gatsby rejects his mere humanness, and idealizes the wish to the present— in which he must live if he *does* live. At the end of the novel, therefore, Gatsby may be choosing not to live, for he is the typical narcissist in his "idealization of the omnipotent, destructive parts of the self" (Kernberg, 1984, p. 180).

Narcissists may idealize and attempt to substitute certain periods in the past for the present, and they may also attempt to erase other parts of the past. Typically, erasing takes the form of "*devaluation* of the past" (Kernberg, 1990, p. 38; emphasis added). Gatsby uses this method in regard to his parents—"his imagination had never really accepted them as his parents at all" (Fitzgerald, 1925, p. 99). He uses the same method in wanting "nothing less of Daisy than that she should go to Tom and say: 'I never loved you'" (p. 111). Gatsby believes that in uttering these words, Daisy will have "obliterated four years" (p. 111), the four years of her marriage. In the hotel room where the confrontation between Gatsby and Tom takes place, Gatsby is implacably insistent that Daisy perform this act of obliteration. Standing, as if protectively, beside her, he says, "Just tell him the truth—that you never loved him—*and it's all wiped out forever*" (p. 132; emphasis added). At this point Daisy obviously realizes that she cannot live up to Gatsby's expectations: "'Oh, you want too much!' she cried to Gatsby: 'I love you now—isn't that enough? I can't help what's past'" (p. 133). A person with normal self-esteem (normal narcissism) would theoretically find Daisy's "I love you now" sufficiently reassuring.

Another tactic that the narcissist invariably uses for controlling time is to see "all objects [including people] as images" (Lowen 1983, p. 176). The implied logic is that the reified image is beyond the laws of nature, for example, of time. Godden (1982) notes that "Reification is always a form of forgetting," for it sanctions the illusion of "buying our memory back ... time is reversible" (p. 356). Therefore, when Daisy says "I did love him once—but I loved you too" (Fitzgerald, 1925, 133), Gatsby is not reassured because she is describing the past as it really was, unmanipulated, uncontrolled by his remorselessly insistent ego-ideal. Ted Billy (1983) says that Gatsby's "attempt to alter (or obliterate) the passage of time" is a kind of "madness and despair" (p. 106). Very simply, Professor Billy's statement is a description of the uncompromising unreality that drives Gatsby's narcissism.

GATSBY AND NARCISSUS

Nick is probably right in surmising that, on the last day of his life, Gatsby "no longer cared" (p. 162) whether Daisy would call or not. (If so, Gatsby has ceased to care only a few hours after last seeing her.) The tone of the text suggests that Gatsby is grieving during the last hours of his life, but he is probably not grieving over Daisy: "When the object is lost, the narcissist mourns not the loss of the object in itself but rather the loss of the mirror" (Jasovic-Gasic and Vesel, 1981, p. 371). In other words, the narcissist does not experience loss of the person but of the person-as-mirror. The narcissist desperately needs objects that will mirror and thus validate, the ego-ideal's images of perfection and omnipotence. People with normal narcissism also need mirrors, "peers [who] play the role for us of a mirror" (Chasseguet-Smirgel 151) for purposes of self-evaluation. However, the narcissist uses people as mirrors not for gaining self-knowledge but for "self-enhancing reflection" (Kohut, 1985, p. 222), a spurious form of validation. That is to say, the narcissist sees "the object" not as itself but "as if the object were a mirror-image" of the ego-ideal (Jasovic-Gasic and Vesel, 1981, p. 370). The ultimate narcissistic crisis is the sense of loss caused by the discovery that the object is in fact *only* a mirror. For example, Narcissus does not, for a long time, realize that what he sees is only a mirror image. He idealizes the image and in so doing deceives himself with the belief that the image is actually a person, perfect, beautiful, whom he loves (wants to possess). When he realizes that the image is not what he thought it was, he loses his person-as-mirror and is left with only a mirror, that is, with nothing. In losing his person-as-mirror, he suffers unbearable mirror loss.

Perhaps the most revealing thing about Gatsby's behavior during the last hours of his life is that he tells Nick the truth about his past, about his identity. Why does he do so? He has been lying steadily to Nick all summer. Do his revelations amount to a confession and a wish to atone, at least to himself, for a life of lies? I think not. Nothing he says suggests remorse. His revelations are, on the most simple and important level, an acknowledgment that he has "paid too high a price for living with a single dream" (p. 102). The nature of the "price" is revealed in a parallel between Gatsby and the classical Narcissus.

The ultimate meaning of Gatsby's inability to care has to do with Gatsby as Narcissus. Chambers (1989, pp. 121–122) finds some subtle allusions to classical mythology in *The Great Gatsby*, but he does not mention this one. In the Narcissus myth (Ovid's version), Tiresias says that Narcissus will have a normal life span unless he comes to know himself—in the sense that he recognizes that what he sees in the pool is only a reflection. Narcissus grasps this fact when a tear drops from his eye and disturbs the water, revealing that what he has been looking at is only a mirror. He then commits suicide because he has lost the mirror that heretofore has validated his ego-ideal's sense of its perfection. I suggest that Gatsby's death also may be an indirect passive form of suicide, of which his physical death is ironically emblematic in the sense that his person-as-mirror, by acting in her real character, is a cause of his death. That is, Daisy withholds information that she was driving Gatsby's car when it struck Wilson's wife.

In telling the hopelessly unromantic truth about his identity, Gatsby is looking at the "universe of ineffable gaudiness" (p. 99) created for Daisy, and he is realizing that *it has been nothing but a mirror*. The parties for Daisy are over and Gatsby has lost all interest in time, past or present. He has wanted too much for too long, and now he apparently is unable to want anything, including Daisy. She is, after all, irremediably imperfect. The price he pays for his narcissistic dream is a form of emotional suicide: He is now unable to care, at all, about his life. The disturbance of the pool caused by Narcissus' tear is perhaps obliquely evoked by the first detail given to us concerning Gatsby's pool of death: "There was a faint, barely perceptible movement of the water" (p. 162). Fitzgerald calls special attention to the fact that Gatsby dies in his pool by having him mention that he has not "used that pool all summer" (p. 154), during which time he has struggled to maintain and consummate his idealization of Daisy.

Nick is correct—in a way that he is unaware of—in believing that on the last day of his life Gatsby remains "faithful" (Fitzgerald, 1925, p. 99). But if he no longer cares about Daisy, then he is faithful only to the anomic image of himself that he "invented" at the age of seventeen. And this is the self that lives for images of perfection, which he sees reflected in Nick's words, "You're worth the whole damn bunch put together" (p. 154). At this moment, Gatsby's "face broke into that radiant and understanding smile, as if we'd been in ecstatic cahoots on that fact all the time" (p. 154). But Nick is only a minor, satellite mirror. Gatsby apparently regards Nick as being important enough to be told his true story, but he completely disregards Nick's advice that he go into hiding for a while. Gatsby enjoys Nick's praise, for losing Daisy as his mirror of perfection does not mean than he renounces his ego-ideal's images of perfection: On the contrary, to them he is so faithful that he may very well be the typical narcissistic suicide, of whom Menaker (1977) observes, "One dies for one's ego-ideal rather than let it die" (p. 259). For Gatsby to deliberately choose to shore up his ruins and live in the natural, real world—of unmanipulated time—would be to break faith with his ego-ideal.

References

Bettina, Sister M. (1963). The artifact in imagery: Fitzgerald's The Great Gatsby. *Twentieth Century Literature: A Scholarly and Critical Journal* 9: 140–142.

Billy, Ted (1983). Agents of madness or despair: A note on The Secret Agent and *The Great Gatsby*. *Studies in American Fiction* 11: 101–106.

Chambers, John B. (1989). *The Novels of F. Scott Fitzgerald*. New York: St. Martin's Press.

Dahl, Curtis (1984). Fitzgerald's use of architectural styles in *The Great Gatsby*. *American Studies* 25: 91–102.

Fitzgerald, F. Scott (1925). *The Great Gatsby*. New York: Charles Scribner's Sons.

Godden, Richard (1982). *The Great Gatsby:* Glamor on the turn. *Journal of American Studies* 16: 343–371.

Jasovic-Gasic, Miroslava, and Vesel, Josif (1981). Fear of death and narcissism. *Psychology Today* 4: 369–372 (published in Prague).

Kernberg, Otto F. (1975). *Borderline Conditions and Pathological Narcissism*. New York: Jason Aronson, Inc.

Kernberg, Otto F. (1984). *Severe Personality Disorders: Psychotherapeutic Strategies*. New Haven: Yale University Press.

Kernberg, Otto F. *Internal World and External Reality: Object Relations Theory Applied*. New York: Jason Aronson.

Kohut, Heinz (1985). *How Does Analysis Cure?* A. Goldberg and P. Stepansky (eds.). Chicago: University of Chicago Press.

Lowen, Alexander (1983). *Narcissism: Denial of the True Self*. New York: Macmillan.

Mellard, James (1966). Counterpoint as technique in *The Great Gatsby*. *The English Journal* 55: 53–859.

Menaker, Ruth (1977). The ego-ideal: An aspect of narcissism. In *The Narcissistic Condition: A Fact of Our Lives and Times*, M. L. Nelson (ed.). New York: Human Sciences Press.

Murray, John (1984). Narcissism and the ego-ideal. *Journal of the American Psychoanalytic Association* 12: 477–511.

Rothstein, Arnold (1985). *The Narcissistic Pursuit of Perfection*. New York: International Universities Press.

Sugerman, Shirley (1964). *Sin and Madness: Studies in Narcissism*. Philadelphia: Westminster Press.

Stern, Mark E. Narcissism and the defiance of time. In *The Narcissistic Condition: A Fact of Our Lives and Times*, M. L. Nelson (ed.). New York: Human Sciences Press.

EDWARD WASIOLEK

The Sexual Drama of Nick and Gatsby

Nick is our narrator in F. Scott Fitzgerald's *The Great Gatsby*, and we see
pretty much what he sees. Nick sees, and we with him, that Gatsby is naive,
posturing, and a little ridiculous, but also someone charged with colossal
vitality and in the end morally superior to those about him because of his
fidelity to his dream. Nick's summation is explicit: "No—Gatsby turned out
all right in the end; it is what preyed on Gatsby, what foul dust floated in the
wake of his dreams that temporarily closed out my interest in the abortive
sorrows and short-winded elations of men."[1] Part of that foul dust is
certainly the Buchanans and especially Tom. The contrast for Nick between
Toni and Gatsby is stark, blunt, and uncompromising. Gatsby has
"something gorgeous about him, some heightened sensitivity to the promises
of life" (2), and "an extraordinary gift for hope, a romantic readiness such as
I have never found in any other person" (2), but Tom has a hard mouth and
supercilious manner, two shining arrogant eyes, and a cruel body. One is
sensitive and the other coarse, one idealistic and romantic and the other
literal, cruel, and arrogant. One has an idealistic love, the other a dirty love;
one reaches for the stars, and the other for the ash heap. Gatsby's love for
Daisy may be misplaced, foolish, and unrealistic; but for Nick, and the
critics, the fidelity and vitality of Gatsby's dream are not foolish. The dream
for Nick is incorruptible, even if the object of the dream, Daisy, is

From *The International Fiction Review* 19, no. 1 (1992): 14–22. © 1992 by International Fiction
Association.

corruptible. I know of no defense of Toni, whatever the reservations about Gatsby.[2] Yet there is something wrong with the contrast. By the end of the novel Nick's attachment to Gatsby, and ours, has reached almost heroic proportions. Gatsby sacrifices himself for his love and awaits his autumnal death with calm and dignity, while Tom, selfish and mean to the end, slinks away, almost a murderer, to continue his self indulgent life. The contrast is too sharp and extreme, and Nick has too much at stake in making it. It is also at variance with the facts. It takes some effort to separate oneself from what Nick sees and how he sees it. He is after all our narrative voice and he seems to be sane, judicious, and fair. In the tradition of commentary on Nick, he is our "moral norm." But he seems less than fair in the contrast he makes between Tom and Gatsby.

Gatsby is, after all, a bootlegger, a criminal, perhaps even a murderer or someone who threatens murder, if Tom's report of Walter Chase's fear is accurate. Tom makes love to another man's wife, but so does Gatsby; Tom buys Myrtle for a few trinkets and Daisy for a $350,000 dollar necklace; Gatsby tries to buy her with his magnificent mansion. Tom orchestrates a rather messy party in which people get sloppy, drunk, and violent, but so does Gatsby. Only the scale is greater. Tom may be insensitive to people, but Gatsby hardly seems to be aware that anyone other than Daisy exists. There are reasons surely to disapprove of Tom, but something more than objective approval and reliability are at work in the intense and unqualified way in which Nick approves of Gatsby and disapproves of Tom. There is ample justification for Nick to speak of others as a "rotten crowd" (154) but no justification to exonerate Gatsby. There is the possibility that Nick's defense of Gatsby and his eagerness to think the best of him and the worst of Tom, hide reasons other than those general, impersonal, and honorific reasons that Nick gives.

It can be argued—and a legion of critics following Nick have argued—that Gatsby is to be exonerated because of his "incorruptible dream," that in an age of cynicism, boredom, and unbelief, he is unique because he believes in something. No matter that the object of the dream, Daisy, is tawdry and that the means to pursue the dream sordid, the colossal freshness of his faith justifies everything. Even when a critic sees him in a harsh light, as in the following passage, he finds him "uplifted" by "the magnitude of his ambition and the glamor of his illusion." Thus, "Gatsby is a boor, a roughneck, a fraud, a criminal. His taste is vulgar, his behavior ostentatious, his love adolescent, his business dealings ruthless, and dishonest. He is interested in people—most notably Carraway himself—only when he wants to use them. His nice gestures stem from the fact that, as one character comments, 'he doesn't want any trouble with anybody.' Like other paranoiacs, he lives in a childish tissue of lies and is unaware of the existence of an independent reality in which other people have separate existences. What lifts him above ordinary viciousness is the magnitude of his ambition and the glamor of his illusion."[3] Nick and the critics have faulted Gatsby for many things, but not for his "incorruptible dream."

But it is not easy to specify what that dream is. Lockridge calls it "a dream of human order amid chaos";[4] Marius Bewley, "the withering of the American dream";[5] Ornstein, Gatsby's "fictional past";[6] and for Trilling, Gatsby and the dream "comes inevitably to stand for America itself."[7] The novel may be all these things, but it is first and foremost about Gatsby's love for Daisy, a point that must be insisted on, because it has been regularly and summarily dismissed. Not only does the novel say this in the most direct and literal manner, but Fitzgerald himself knew it and regretted that he had not somehow elaborated the idea and explained the idea more fully. What is more it is a real love, that is, a love with a sexual basis. Lionel Trilling's remark that it was remarkable how little sex Fitzgerald puts into his stories may be asserted about *The Great Gatsby* only if one ignores much of the novel (237). Tom sleeps with a chambermaid shortly after his marriage; the Buchanans leave Chicago because of one of his flings; he fornicates with Myrtle while Nick goes out to buy a pack of cigarettes; Nick has an affair with a girl from Jersey City; and the parties Gatsby gives are whatever else, sexual orgies. When the novel is over in an image sexually explicit, Myrtle kneels in her own blood with her naked breast partly severed and flapping. These examples are only the rim of the caldron. The caldron is Gatsby's love of Daisy and those relationships that Fitzgerald regretted not having explained more fully. It is Gatsby's love for Daisy that explains why Nick loves Gatsby and hates Tom.

There is of course, in the vast literature on Gatsby some noting of sexual motifs. But they have been, with few exceptions, scattered and casual. The exceptions have been pieces by Murray Levith, Patricia Pacey Thornton, and Keath Fraser. Murray Levith notes, among other things, that Fitzgerald's Long Island is phallic in description, the two eggs suggests male genitals, and Gatsby's car is "a rich cream color." He repeats Trilling's characterization of Jordan Baker as "vaguely homosexual," and takes note of McKee as "a pale feminine man." Most suggestively he calls Gatsby's romantic dream for Daisy "radically prepubescent—indeed infantile." His conclusion is that "Fitzgerald leaves us with a sterile and clearly masturbatory image: 'So we beat on, boats against the current, borne back ceaselessly into the past.'"[8] But the details remain details and throw no light on the larger issues of the novel.

Patricia Pacey Thornton pays the most detailed attention to sexual motifs. She notes correctly that Fitzgerald's guest list is filled with sexual hybrids: "The women are 'defeminized'—Mrs. Ulysses Swett, Francis Bull, Faustina O'Brien—and men are emasculated—Newton Orchid, Earnes Lilly, and Russell Betty." She calls Nick and Jordan "androgynous twins."[9] They "cannot properly be called opposite sex since they seem to have equally divided between them masculine and feminine genes. They are, in fact, androgynous twins, and their attraction–repulsion results from their shared and divided natures" (PT 464). Also "Nick's is a divided nature, torn between traditional and experimental, masculine and feminine, moral and immoral" (PT 466). Thornton sees Nick's masculine qualities in his ambition, desire to acquire money and power and his feminine virtues in his ability to listen to others, his providing food and nourishment to Daisy and Gatsby, and his human warmth. She has high praise for Nick, and in that sense continues the tradition of uncritical acceptance of Nick as the moral center of the novel: "Apart from Gatsby and his imagination, both sexes are intellectually barren and mindless. Nick is the only one to qualify as a thinker, as a moral philosopher" (PT 467).

She is most original in the similarities she notes between Myrtle and Gatsby. The two never meet and have nothing to do with each other until the fateful accident. She notes that the speech of both just misses being absurd, that both wear the clothes of the wealthy, and that both are ambitious. She might have summarized all this by saying what is implied, that is, that both want to leave the valley of ashes behind. What she does not say and does not suspect is a deeper relationship: in his psyche Myrtle is the sexual woman that Gatsby has left behind and is terrified of meeting again. If Daisy is the tip of the caldron for Gatsby, Myrtle is the caldron, which is to say that Daisy and Myrtle are deeply and inextricably related in Gatsby's psyche.

Gatsby loves Daisy with an ideal love: unswerving, undeviating, and overwhelming. Gatsby must make her what she is not and must give her every perfection; his love for Daisy has to be lifted above time and reality. Gatsby is determined that the real Daisy—bored, spoiled cynical, and uncaring—must not appear, and when she does, he has to deny her. She must always be for him the Daisy of white innocence and first love. If this obsession has been called innocence and faith, it is also a compulsive and determined flight before reality and into a dream purged of change and blemish. It is a colossal faith and a colossal flight. What is he running from? The answer is everywhere in the novel. Wolfsheim tells us that he would never so much as look at another man's wife and Jordan Baker is only a name for him. Gatsby flees from Myrtle, from the women at his parties, and from the real Daisy. He flees from women and sex. Why? The perfect woman, elevated by abstraction to sainthood, the quest for whom is associated with the quest for the holy Grail, may be beautiful, but she also represents a split in his psyche and a sign of a severe psychic disorder, a nascent form of emotional suicide.

The cool unconcern of Gatsby hides rage and terror underneath. This is why everything must be reinforced; he can have no traffic with ordinary women; Daisy cannot be just wonderful but must be perfect; the car and his clothes spotless; the parties the biggest; and the house bigger and better than everyone else's. The split in his inner life is reflected in his outer life. The novel is built on a pattern of surface and underground, bright and dull, cleanliness and dirtiness, white and dark. Gatsby wears white or pink suits; his shirts are beautiful; and only the telephone calls connect him to his sleazy underground. He lives on the fringes of the Buchanan's glamorous world and moves between the glamor of East and West Egg and New York. The economic underground between them is the valley of ashes, where there is dirt, junk cars, pale faces, listless people and sex. Tom has no problem in stopping off at the valley of the ashes and embracing the "dirty" woman, Myrtle, and Nick, the voyeur, has no trouble accompanying him. But Gatsby's car spreads wings when it passes the valley of the ashes and Myrtle's smouldering sensuality. He wants nothing to do with the valley of ashes or the sexual woman who lives there. Gatsby wants to climb to the secret place above the trees and "suck on the pap of life, gulp down the incomparable milk of wonder" (112) where Daisy and the saintly woman lives. The image is clearly sexual, though mixed with stardust and idealism, evoking the serene and ideal moment of the child at peace on his mother's breast. Levith is right in calling the image prepubescent and infantile, but it is precisely because it is these things that it has immense significance.

One will want to object that Daisy is no mother, but the fact of the matter is that Daisy is a mother, the only mother in the novel. In Gatsby's psychic projection she is the ideal woman, fixed in timelessness and perfection and raised above the sordidness of sex. Many have remarked on the retreat of Daisy before the "raw emotion" and into phantasy and purity. Daisy is presented to us always in white, and more than once floating above the earth. Richard A. Koenigsberg was the first to discern the split in Gatsby's psyche of the degraded and idealized representation of the mother, and he is right when he says: "If Myrtle Wilson stands as the degraded half of this split image of the mother, then Daisy Buchanan—especially from the narrator's point of view—represents her counterpart: the unreachable, idealized mother."[10] He goes on: "For Daisy is really a first love; to which he remains so intensely faithful that we wonder if it is not some earlier woman—that *first* 'first love' of all little boys—to whom he is so fanatically devoted" (323). But Koenigsberg does not show how this split fuels his love for Daisy, and how that sexual complex explains Nick's devotion to him. Gatsby will have nothing to do with "dirty" women and everything to do with the "clean" woman, who is then raised to a saintly and perfect image.

Gatsby suffers from a "madonna complex," that use of the idealized perfect woman to keep at bay, in the psyche, the pain and terror of the "sordid" or sexual woman. Such a flight from the "dirty" woman to the clean woman is a form of homosexuality. Homosexuality? Freudian reasoning may lead us there, but does the text. There is more than a hint of it in Gatsby's distaste for women. We are told that on Dan Cody's yacht women spoiled Gatsby early and he contracted a contempt for them; and at Gatsby's parties, where sex swirls about him, "no French bob touched his shoulder" (50). There is more than a hint, too, in that series of surrogate fathers Gatsby has sought out to compensate for the weak and ineffectual actual father, the first of which, Dan Cody, dresses him and employs him in a vague and unspecified capacity. Later he will do the same with Klipspringer, who is everywhere present in Gatsby's house, and who seems to be employed in a vague and unspecified capacity and has the air of a kept guest. The most telling evidence of Gatsby's repressed homosexuality comes from Nick himself, as do the reasons why Gatsby is so important to Nick, important enough to give up his "girl" and to stand with Gatsby against the world in the crisis days of Gatsby's life. At the end of the novel, it is Gatsby and Nick against the world. I am suggesting that the reason Nick feels sympathy for Gatsby and distaste for Tom has less to do with what Gatsby and Tom are in themselves and everything to do with Nick's psychological needs. Nick favors Gatsby because he favors what Gatsby is, feels so intensely for Gatsby because he feels what Gatsby feels. Put bluntly we are confronted with the sympathy of one homosexual for another. Is there anything in or text to support this. Yes, rather blatantly so.

Nick shows something of his homosexual leanings in the distaste that he registers for the aggressive masculinity of Tom and the repugnance he feels for Tom's dirty love. But these proclivities become overt at the party in Tom and Myrtle's apartment and in his relationship to Mr. McKee. According to Nick, Mrs. McKee is shrill, languid, and horrible; Catherine is rather grotesque with her sticky bob of red hair, her rakish eyebrows, and blurred expression on her face. Mr. McKee, on the other hand, is respectful to everyone, and Nick notices the intimate detail of lather on McKee's cheekbone. Nick is tender and attentive to his effeminate gentleman, who is in the artistic game. So attentive that when McKee leaves, he leaves with him, and as subsequent events show, for a purpose. It is McKee who suggests to Nick to come and have lunch with him "anywhere," and it is the elevator boy who—and in this context the image must be sexual—orders McKee to take his hands off the lever. And it is we who read after three dots about Nick standing beside McKee's bed and McKee apparently sitting up between the sheets clad in his underwear. The last paragraph of Chapter II has Nick half asleep in the cold lower level of Penn station waiting for the four o'clock train.

How strange that in the vast critical literature of commentary on *The Great Gatsby*, there is hardly a mention of this scene![11] Keath Fraser in "Another Reading of *The Great Gatsby*" is almost alone in pointing to the sexual implications of the scene that ends Chapter II, but concludes that one doesn't quite know how to read the scene. Nick is less straightforward than he puts himself forth for Fraser, and he plays with the sexual ambiguities of Nick's character and behavior.[12] He is especially acute in his analysis of Nick and Jordan Baker's relationship. But he never brings his excellent perceptions to bear on the central issues of the novel: he has nothing to say about Nick and Gatsby's relationship and Gatsby and Daisy's love. He is too timid, also, in my view in making firm and definite Nick's homosexual proclivities. I do not know how one can read the scene in McKee's bedroom in any other way, especially when so many other facts about his behavior support such a conclusion. The ties he feels to Gatsby explain not only his overt defense of Gatsby, but his behavior in the novel with other people. Like Gatsby he acts out something of the same kind of pattern of flight and defense. We have to remind ourselves that he has come East not only to sell bonds, but also to flee from a romantic entanglement, and later he flees the entanglement of the brief Jersey City affair. Most clearly, however he imitates Gatsby's love for Daisy by his love affair with Jordan. Jordan has something of the same brand of sophistication as Daisy. We are introduced to both in images of sensuous purity; both are dressed in white and so free of earthly dross that they seem to float in the air. They passed their youth together; they have the same friends, move in the same circles, have something of the same brittle beauty and insouciance, and if Nick is a little in love with his cousin, he is a little more in love with Jordan Baker. Gatsby, to be sure, "idealizes" Daisy and one cannot stretch Nick's interest in Jordan to idealization. He is intrigued by her: by her dishonesty and carelessness, and also by the world of beautiful, wealthy, and glamorous people she moves in. Yet this difference aside, Nick chooses Jordan for some of the same reasons Gatsby chose Daisy. Daisy is Gatsby's defense against women, and Jordan is Nick's against women. It cannot escape our attention that Jordan has the body of a boy and that she has qualities of character that are conventionally considered to be masculine. She is aggressive, cynical, and engaged in sports at a time when few women were. She wears all her clothes as if they were sport clothes, and walks as if she had learned to walk on a golf course. When she perspires the suggestion of a moustache appears on her upper lip. Nick doesn't have to feel the emotions one usually feels for a woman: tenderness, affection, love. Jordan protects him from these by her cynicism and proud and haughty face. He can participate with impunity in that dishonesty, cynicism, and carelessness which he energetically excludes from his characterization of himself. It is as if the insensitivity and homosexuality hidden in Gatsby's love of Daisy is partially revealed in Nick's "love" for Jordan. It is not without significance that when Gatsby is abandoned by his love, Daisy, Nick abandons his love, Jordan. It is easier for Nick to give up Jordan than for Gatsby to give up Daisy. The screen is thinner, the flight more obvious, and the repression less deep. Nick acts out his homosexuality and Gatsby does not. Gatsby's is shielded by the intensity and energy of his idealistic love and his incorruptible dream. At the end it is Nick and Gatsby alone against a cold and uncaring world. The fidelity that Gatsby had shown to Daisy, Nick shows to Gatsby, rationalized, of course, by Nick as basic human decency.

If Nick's feelings for Gatsby are intense, they are equally intense for Tom. And they are intense for the same reason. Tom pursues the coarse sexuality, which Gatsby has excluded from his consciousness by idealization and repression. Tom, too, in his compulsive and promiscuous sexuality enacts a flight from real love as much as does Gatsby. Gatsby will have nothing to do with real women and Tom will have nothing to do with them. Gatsby divides women into pure and dirty, and Tom divides women into pure and dirty. But Tom acts out what is deeply hidden in Gatsby's psyche. Tom embraces the dirty women and Gatsby keeps her at bay with idealization. Is it any wonder that they both love the same woman, Daisy. She is sufficiently removed from reality to meet the needs of both. Despite his aversion to Tom's aggressive masculinity and primeval thinking, Nick accompanies Tom on his rounds, participating vicariously in his sexual exploits, even to the point of providing Tom and Myrtle with the time and space to complete their fornications. Indeed, in what appears to be almost a primal scene, he is just outside the door where Tom and Myrtle effect their sexual union. And he is just outside the door when Daisy and Gatsby celebrate their "idealistic" union. Nick is the enabler and observer in both unions. For Nick, Gatsby and Tom seem to function somewhat like good and bad fathers. Tom is called paternal more than once by Nick, and he seems to have a kind of power and authority over Nick. Nick does pretty much what he is told, Tom has all the attributes that one associates with the hated father: he is authoritative, opinionated, domineering, and very much the no-sayer. In fact it is he who says no to both Gatsby's bid to claim Daisy and Myrtle's bid to replace Daisy. If Gatsby deep in his psyche has identified Daisy with the first love, where he had sucked "on the pap of life" (112) and gulped "down the incomparable milk of wonder" (112), Tom is the hated father, who denies him that love.

Myrtle is Tom's dirty woman and as the image of underground and dirty sex, she embodies what Gatsby has repressed in his consciousness and symbolizes what Gatsby has attempted to kill in himself. It is no accident, then, that Myrtle mistakes Gatsby for Tom on the fateful night of her death. Gatsby has the "pure" woman, Daisy, by his side, and the "dirty" woman appears out of the dark in the light of the vehicle guided by Daisy. The "pure" woman brings her out of the dark and kills her, and as at the parties, Gatsby sits passively by her side. Myrtle kneeling in her own blood, her dress ripped and her breast flapping helplessly is an image of sex punished and punished by the pure woman, with the instruments of Gatsby's power. Gatsby protects the ideal woman and flees from the sexual woman. This climactic scene reenacts the drama of Gatsby's psychic structure. Deep in his psyche he had killed the dirty woman in himself by giving all his power to the pure woman, and by doing so he had killed himself. Gatsby is mistaken by Wilson to be the murderer of Myrtle, but in a psychoanalytic sense it is not a mistake. The keeper of the "dirty" woman, Wilson (Gatsby), kills the keeper of the clean woman Gatsby. The psychic suicide is corroborated by the actual murder-suicide. When it is all over and only Nick remains, the dirt that has been kept at bay returns: an obscene word is found scrawled on the sidewalk before the house, and Nick finds dust (from the valley of ashes?) settling over the furniture in Gatsby's house.

Nick, of course, loves Gatsby and hates Tom, but this is so because Gatsby throws a veil of glamor and fateful romance over his displaced homosexuality, while Tom reveals it in a vulgar irredeemable form. The same split of dirty and clean woman exists in Tom, too, and his exaggerated masculinity is as much a sign of his homosexuality as is Gatsby's idealism. But Tom exposes the dirty woman by seeking her out and embracing her, and it is the exposure that Nick finds intolerable, especially in such a vulgar and naked form. Tom acts out what Gatsby is terrified of. Gatsby's dirty woman is deeply repressed and surfaces in his consciousness in the sexual violence he orchestrates but does not participate in at his parties. These parties have a dreamlike quality to them, and Gatsby's part in the parties are analogous to the distancing of responsibility in repression. Nick is in the psychic drama what he has been in the economic drama: the voyeur timidly playing all bases and striving to have it both ways, while elevating this strategy to honesty and good sense. Perhaps it is good sense, but it is not honest. His bourgeois background where the family fortune has been put together by small economics and few risks has served him well. In the end Nick is cowed by the hated father and the seigneur of the castle, and shakes hands with him, all rationalized, of course, as largeness of spirit.

It may be objected that a psychoanalytic reading of the novel diminishes the significance of the hero, and that it gives him a less lofty part than he has as an embodiment of the American dream. It certainly makes Nick something other than that impartial observer and objective reporter that he puts himself forth as, and that a tradition of criticism has taken at face value. It does not and should not exclude from our readings and understandings other Gatsbys. There is no doubt that Gatsby enacts a social and economic drama of mythic proportions. He is the self-made man who rattles the doors of the rich and almost makes it to the castle's center. He is Nick's economic and social phantasy, as well as his psychological phantasy. Fitzgerald knew that in his attempts to seize and hold what America and his age meant to him, he had to struggle with destructive urges that overwhelmed his mind and spirit. Fitzgerald's descent from *This Side of Paradise* to *Tender is the Night* can be looked at as a progressive sweeping of the romanticizations of love and a franker and deeper examination of sex. The incest motive that lies beneath Gatsby's idealization of Daisy is addressed in *Tender is the Night*, where Nicole sleeps with her father and Dick sleeps with his surrogate daughter, Rosemary.

If Daisy is Gatsby's dream, and Gatsby is Nick's dream, both of them are Fitzgerald's dream. If Freud is right that we are all the actors in our dreams, then Fitzgerald is all the actors in *The Great Gatsby*. As he had to be. We know enough about his love life to know how destructive and futile it was, how desperately and emptily he slept with whatever came his way; and if there was no overt homosexuality—and there probably was—there was enough in covert fantasy to fuel his destructive loves. Sex was frightening to Fitzgerald and he tempted and confronted his fears by laying them bare in the novels; and because he was human, very human, he kept his fears at bay by hatred and repugnance. And for a while it worked. The controlled fantasy of art helped him keep his life under control. But when the art was gone, so was the life.

NOTES

1. F. Scott Fitzgerald, *The Great Gatsby* (New York: Scribners, 1953); all references are to this edition.

2. The following quotation is representative: "Tom Buchanan is gross sensuality, a beast lacking in imagination, incapable of clear sight, much less vision." Kenneth Eble, *F. Scott Fitzgerald* (Boston: Twayne, 1963) 94.

3. Gary J. Scrimgeour, "Against *The Great Gatsby*," *Criticism*, 8 (Winter, 1966): 79.

4. Ernest Lockridge, "Introduction," *Twentieth Century Interpretations of The Great Gatsby* (Englewood Cliffs, NJ: Prentice Hall, 1968) 11.

5. Marius Bewley, "Scott Fitzgerald's criticism of America," *Sewanee Review* 62 (Spring 1954): 713.

6. Robert Ornstein, "Scott Fitzgerald's Fable of East and West," *College English* 17 (1956–57): 142.

7. Lionel Trilling, *The Liberal Imagination* (Garden City, NY: Doubleday, 1953) 242.

8. Murray J. Levith, "Fitzgerald's *The Great Gatsby*," *Explicator*, 37 (April 1979), item 7.

9. Patricia Pacey Thornton, "Sexual Roles in *The Great Gatsby*," *English Studies in Canada* 5.4 (Winter 1979): 457. Subsequent references are to this edition and will appear in the text after 'PT'.

10. Richard A. Koenigsberg, "F. Scott Fitzgerald: Literature and the Work of Mourning," *American Imago* 24 (1967): 323.

11. Henry Idema III in *Freud, Religion, and The Roaring Twenties* (Savage, MD: Rowan and Littlefield, 1990) notes the scene in the railway station and considers briefly the possibility that Nick is a homosexual, but does not go into the effect of this upon his relationship with Gatsby. He is careful to note also that he has taken the idea of homosexuality from a class he took from me at the University of Chicago.

12. Keath Fraser, "Another Reading of *The Great Gatsby*," *English Studies in Canada* 5.3 (Autumn 1979): 330–43.

THOMAS H. PAULY

Gatsby as Gangster

In an article entitled "The Passing of the Gangster," published in the March 1925 issue of *American Mercury*, Herbert Asbury confidently offered the remarkable assertion: "there are now no more gangs in New York and no gangsters in the sense that the newspapers use the word." The surprising disparity between this contemporary evaluation of the crime scene and our perception of the 1920s as the heyday of gangsters hinges upon Asbury's belief that the gangsters of his age owed their notoriety to ambitious journalists, novelists, playwrights, and scriptwriters fiercely competing for audiences and paychecks. Asbury viewed these accounts as distortions of truth in support of a threadbare stereotype. "The moving picture and the stage," he pointed out, "have always portrayed the gangster as a low-browed person with an evilly glinting eye, a plaid cap drawn down over beetling brows and a swagger that in itself is enough to inform the world that here is a man bent on devilment." With obvious contempt, he counters: "in the main, the really dangerous gangster, the killer, was apt to be something of a dandy."[1] Asbury invoked his stylish gangster to return enthusiasts for these fictions to the hard fact that truly successful gangsters didn't make brazen displays of their intent.

Even though his article shrewdly appealed to the same interest in gangsters he was criticizing, Asbury little suspected that his revisionist

From *Studies in American Fiction* 21, no. 2 (Autumn 1993): 225–236. © 1993 by Northeastern University.

proposal would be quickly embraced. Unwittingly his "dandy" anticipated the innovative gangster which F. Scott Fitzgerald introduced a few weeks later with the publication of *The Great Gatsby*. Jay Gatsby effectively overturned the dated assumption that gangsters were lowlifes from the Bowery and replaced it with an upscale figure who was enviably wealthy and fashionably stylish. Significantly, this portrayal was an outgrowth of actual changes in existing criminal conditions. Fitzgerald understood better than Asbury that since the advent of Prohibition, gangsters were, in fact, on the rise; not only were they gaining more wealth and power, but they were presuming to status and respectability as well. If Fitzgerald's Gatsby was solidly grounded in these historical developments, he too came perilously close to being an implausible gangster and a distortion of fact. Though readers still find Gatsby too romantic, too idealistic, and too naive to be a criminal success, Fitzgerald counteracted this impression by cloaking his gangster in mystery, then frustrating Nick's efforts to penetrate it, and finally suggesting that Gatsby, like Asbury's dandy, may be more dangerous than Nick realizes. If this elusive figure involved a significant modification of the actual gangsters on which Fitzgerald was drawing, he was not the specious fabrication that Asbury was decrying.

To characterize Gatsby as a "dandy" might seem inappropriate since clothing is rather incidental to his depiction. This quality is communicated to Nick more by his other possessions than by his white suit, silver shirt, and gold tie—his palatial house, his grand parties, his fancy automobile, his hydroplane, and his library of real books. His flourish of expensive shirts late in the novel merely embellishes this image. This Gatsby is an ideal consumer in his expenditure of so much on the nonessential. He is a dandy who buys expensive merchandise to take on its desirability and to convince Daisy of his worthiness. These traits confirm the potency of a consumer culture and illuminate the social instability generated by the age's myriad products and aggressive advertising. The new credit economy of the 1920s accelerated social mobility and empowered a new ethos whereby merchandise rivaled background, profession, and merit as a determinant of status.[2]

All around him Fitzgerald beheld people who had risen from commonplace backgrounds to affluence and prominence.[3] His own success as a writer validated this new upward mobility. Still, the advances of gangsters were truly extraordinary. In 1920 George Remus was a small-time criminal lawyer who purchased a distillery for medicinal spirits in order to circumvent the recently passed Volstead Act. Though today's readers are often confused by the connection between Gatsby's bootlegging and his drugstores, Fitzgerald was merely registering the widespread exploitation of pharmacies' exemption from Prohibition law due to the large quantities of alcohol used in their prescriptions. Remus' success was to make drug stores as well-known for alcohol as speakeasies. Within four years, he controlled fourteen distilleries, a sprawling network of pharmacies and some 3000 employees. He had cornered one-seventh of the national market for medicinal alcohol and realized a gross income of some twenty-five million dollars. His accumulated holdings were estimated at forty million.[4] With this fortune Remus built a huge mansion and filled it with lavish furnishings that included expensive paintings, a solid gold piano, an arboretum of exotic plants, and a marble indoor pool costing over $125,000.[5] Among the two hundred guests in attendance at one of his numerous parties, he distributed $25,000 worth of jewelry to the men and then presented each woman with a new automobile. Unfortunately this extravagant life style drew the attention of the Department of Justice, and after a 1924 trial extensively covered by newspapers, he was sent to prison for three years.[6]

Arnold Rothstein afforded another example of gangster wealth with a stronger, more direct influence upon Fitzgerald's novel. In a letter written in 1937, in which he reflected on *The Great Gatsby*, Fitzgerald wrote: "I selected the stuff to fit a given mood or 'hauntedness' or whatever you might call it, rejecting in advance in *Gatsby*, for instance, all of the ordinary material for Long Island, bit crooks, adultery theme and always starting from the small focal point that impressed me—my own meeting with Arnold Rothstein for instance."[7] Just prior to World War I, Rothstein was a small time gambler whose livelihood was jeopardized by the reckless actions of his hot-headed friend Herman Rosenthal. This crucial turning point in Rothstein's career is referred to in the initial conversation between Nick and Meyer Wolfsheim:

"What place is that?" I asked.

"The old Metropole."

"The old Metropole," brooded Mr. Wolfsheim gloomily. "Filled with faces dead and gone. Filled with friends gone now forever. I can't forget so long as I live the night they shot Rosy Rosenthal there. It was six of us at the table, and Rosy had eat and drunk a lot all evening. When it was almost morning the waiter came up to him with a funny look and says somebody wants to speak to him outside. 'All right,' says Rosy … He turned around in the door and says: 'Don't let that waiter take away my coffee!' Then he went out on the sidewalk, and they shot him three times in his full belly and drove away."

"Four of them were electrocuted," I said, remembering.

"Five, with Becker." His nostrils turned to me in an interested way (pp. 84–85).[8]

The wave of reform set off by these events propelled Rothstein to close his modest gambling parlor and initiate a system of floating games like those memorialized in *Guys and Dolls*. When Rothstein returned to a permanent facility several years later, he relocated outside the city, first with an elegant casino created from a Long Island estate and then with the "Brook" in Saratoga which, at the time of its opening in 1919, was the most luxurious gaming house in the country.[9] Meanwhile Rothstein's diversification into sports betting climaxed with his reputed fixing of the 1919 World Series.[10] For Fitzgerald and most Americans at the time, this was a breathtaking exemplification of Rothstein's power. As Nick explains:

> The idea staggered me. I remembered, of course, that the World's Series had been fixed in 1919, but if I had thought of it at all I would have thought of it as a thing that merely happened, the end of some inevitable chain. It never occurred to me that one man could start to play with the faith of fifty million people— with the single-mindedness of a burglar blowing a safe" (p. 88).

Though Rothstein was to reap handsome profits from Prohibition, his emergence during the 1920s as the most important underworld figure in New York City owed more to an involvement with stolen bonds like the ones Gatsby is peddling at the time of his death. During the same year as the World Series fix, Jules "Nicky" Arnstein, a long-time gambling friend of Rothstein's, stole some five million dollars worth of Liberty bonds from vulnerable errand boys relaying them between brokerage houses and banks. Since these losses were covered by surety companies and Rothstein's experience with bail bonding provided him with an insider's knowledge of these companies, Rothstein may have provided Arnstein with confidential knowledge about these transfers. Whether or not he actually alerted Arnstein to this prospect, he quickly sprang to Arnstein's defense when a minor criminal fingered him as the one responsible for these thefts. Significantly, these bonds were never recovered; meanwhile Liberty bonds played a role in several important Rothstein deals.[11] Rothstein's take from these bonds vastly exceeded his return from the fixed Series and was perhaps his single most lucrative venture.[12] Indeed, Tom Buchanan's sources appear most reliable in his characterization of Gatsby's drug store chain as "just small change" (p. 161) compared to his stolen bonds.

In their exemplification of the staggering wealth and elevated status attained by gangsters of the 20s, Remus and Rothstein furnished Fitzgerald with valuable raw material for his novel. However, Fitzgerald's encounter with a minor bootlegger was equally important and much more revealing about his attitude toward this material. This figure, whom Matthew Bruccoli has identified as Max Gerlach,[13] is described in Edmund Wilson's play *The Crime in the Whistler Room*.

> He's a gentleman bootlegger: his name is Max Fleischman. He lives like a millionaire. Gosh, I haven't seen so much to drink since Prohibition. I've never seen so much to drink! ... Well, Fleischman was making a damn ass of himself bragging about how much his tapestries were worth and how much his bathroom was worth and how he never wore a shirt twice—and he had a revolver studded with diamonds that he insisted on showing everybody. And he finally got on my nerves—I was a little bit stewed—and I told him I wasn't impressed by his ermine-lined revolver: I told him he was nothing but a bootlegger, no matter how much money he made. Of course that made him sore as hell, and he ordered me out of the house. I told him I never would have come into his damn house if it hadn't been to be polite and that it was torture to stay in a place where everything was in such terrible taste.[14]

Authenticated by Fitzgerald's marginal notation "I had told Bunny my plan for Gatsby" in his copy of the play,[15] this description evidences telling anticipations of his novel. First, Fleischman's party bears a striking resemblance to Gatsby's in providing guests with an endless flow of liquor in open defiance of Prohibition law. This Nick-like narrator doesn't say that the party was open to all comers, but he seems an outsider—probably uninvited and certainly a stranger to the host. He also doesn't mention the size of Fleischman's house, but his comments on its tapestries and bathroom suggest that it was on the scale of Gatsby's. Finally, Gatsby's display of his shirts for Daisy is a variation upon Fleischman's proclaimed refusal to wear a shirt twice.

Still, these anticipations of Gatsby are offset by the indignation of this observer at Fleischman's vulgarity and "terrible taste," unlike Nick's reactions to Gatsby. Contrary to his intentions, Fleischman's expensive purchases simply confirm his origins to be well down the social ladder. The speaker's characterization of Fleischman as "a gentleman bootlegger" shades into irony as it becomes clear that he doesn't consider his loud host a gentleman at all. His obsession with his tapestries, diamond-studded revolver, and once-worn shirts become damning evidence of his poor taste and shallow values. "He got on my nerves," the speaker summarizes. In a telling self-definition, he then adds that he came to the party only "to be polite." Despite his acknowledged drunkenness, he clearly feels socially superior to this self-promoting possessor of staggering wealth.

With its evocation of the tipsy, party-going Fitzgerald and Nick's eye for social pretense, this speech reads as though Wilson wrote up Fitzgerald's report pretty much as he heard it. True or not, this passage's connection to Fitzgerald's plans merits reflection, for in shaping his diverse examples of gangster wealth into the hero of his novel, Fitzgerald took great pains to endow his Gatsby with an attitude that sharply differentiated him from gangsters like the flamboyant Remus and the crass Fleischman. Significantly, Gatsby scrupulously avoids Remus' efforts to make himself the center of attention and Fleischman's offensive insistence upon the cost of everything he owns. He becomes almost unbelievable in his low, self-effacing profile at his parties and his extreme reluctance to comment on his possessions, especially since they have been purchased for the sole purpose of communicating his improved status. The reader learns that his mansion was selected for its location directly across the bay from Daisy's residence in hopes that it might catch her eye and signal his change in status. When this doesn't happen, Gatsby seeks out Nick and Jordan and recruits them into a complicated scenario so that Daisy can be brought to Nick's house and see his mansion. The whole purpose of this elaborate maneuvering is to inform Daisy of his success without personally doing so.

This tight-lipped discretion and intricate planning lends much-needed credibility to his pretense of being a true gentleman and sets Gatsby apart from the Remuses, Fleischmans, and his own gangster associates. Readers are led to believe that Gatsby's wealth derives from serving as a front of respectability for Meyer Wolfsheim, a "man bent on devilment" who badly needs someone to mask his blatant criminality. The narrator's aversion so manifest in Wilson's account of Fleischman and so withheld from Nick's portrayal of Gatsby comes spilling out in Nick's reaction to Meyer Wolfsheim. Unlike the Waspish Gatsby, whose smile of greeting warmly acknowledges Nick, this "small flat-nosed Jew ... with two fine growths of hair which luxuriated in either nostril" (p. 83) ignores him and continues with his account of a recent payoff. He only responds to Nick when he shows knowledge of the Rosenthal affair. Wolfsheim's one effort to engage Nick consists of calling attention to himself and pointing out how his cuff links are made of human molars. His ensuing characterization of Gatsby as "a perfect gentleman," a "man of fine breeding" who went to "Oggsford College" (p. 86), suggests the propriety Wolfsheim seeks from Gatsby while simultaneously establishing his distance from it. Nick's account implies that Wolfsheim owes his success more to a brazen disregard for the law than any perceptive reading of character or subtle scheming.

The implication of Wolfsheim's example—that most gangsters are obtuse, intractable lowlifes—is further reinforced by the phone call that Nick intercepts following Gatsby's death. Without ever confirming that he is speaking to Gatsby, the caller blurts out how his disposal of the stolen bonds has miscarried. His characterization of Chicago as a "hick town" (p. 200) by way of justification only confirms his ignorance and incompetence.

Alongside these figures, Gatsby almost succeeds at being the possessor of manners and refinement he strives to appear, so much so that he comes across as a rather implausible gangster. Those same qualities which differentiate Gatsby from his criminal associates threaten his believability as the effective gangster he is supposed to be—unless, of course, there is more to Gatsby than his ungangsterish appearance and manner. Critics usually assume that Fitzgerald channeled the model of Arnold Rothstein into his characterization of Meyer Wolfsheim. While it is true that Wolfsheim is identified as the man who fixed the 1919 World Series, it is also true that Gatsby was associated with the stolen bonds that were more crucial to Rothstein's successful career. The presumed linkage of Wolfsheim and Rothstein also disregards the significant fact that the crude Wolfsheim was nothing like the actual Rothstein, who was something of a Gatsby to those who knew him. Ironically, Rothstein's skills at engineering social mobility so far surpassed those of Gatsby that he would have had no need for him.

When he served as Fitzgerald's inspiration, Rothstein was a man of enormous experience and sophistication. His early success at high-stakes gambling came from considerable intelligence and chameleon-like adjustment to the conditions of his profession. Well before he opened his own gambling parlor, he acquired the dress and demeanor of a man about town and successfully won the confidence of the well-to-do who made his games profitable. If the decidedly conservative cast of Rothstein's dress, deportment, and choice of residences belied his aggressive pursuit of money and useful connections, it was cultivated not just to suggest well-heeled respectability but even more to avoid the kind of attention that Fleischman and Remus so hungrily sought.[16] Typically Rothstein eschewed notoriety and public adulation, believing quite correctly that they led to convictions. One reason historians have had such difficulty determining what crimes Rothstein actually committed is that he made such a concerted effort to mask his involvement and to obscure what he was doing. Rothstein maintained a fully staffed business office amidst all the busy commercial activity of West 57th St. All his important records were kept in secret code.[17] He countered the adverse publicity of his involvement in the World Series fix with an announcement of plans to retire. Echoing a point that he himself made to the press on countless occasions, the *New York Times* reported in 1920 that "he has faced many charges, some of which were born in malice, but he has stuck to his guns and not once has any charge, legally made against him, been sustained."[18]

Although Rothstein differed from Gatsby in his metropolitan background, his more refined tastes, his vast network of criminal associates, and his calloused selfishness, he was that paradoxical blend of gentleman "dandy" and criminal success at the heart of Gatsby's characterization. This aspect of Rothstein draws attention to a frequently overlooked aspect of Fitzgerald's presentation, Gatsby's evasiveness. Given all the confusion created by Gatsby's "old sport" affectation, his indirect mode of communication, alongside all that is not known about him, Gatsby probably practices the same deception which made Rothstein so successful. At issue here is the central question of Gatsby's function as a front. Many readers, like Nick, tend to assume that Gatsby's wealth derives from facilitating a necessary liaison between the crude Wolfsheim and the proprieties of respectable society. Presumably Gatsby handles all public relations for the alcohol and stolen bonds that Wolfsheim supplies. This unexamined assumption never considers that behind his shaky facade of Waspish gentility Gatsby would have needed to be a more cunning criminal than Nick allows to have amassed so much wealth. Obviously a good front doesn't just *look* impressive—he capitalizes on his impressiveness to gain the confidence of his victims and to mask his crafty maneuvering.[19]

Artist that he was, Fitzgerald was sufficiently concerned about Gatsby's implausibility as a gangster and his own limited knowledge of underworld operations that he made a concerted effort to obscure the course of events that transformed his innocent product of midwestern morality into a big time metropolitan gangster. Throughout the first half of the book, much of what the reader learns about Gatsby's background is a crazy-quilt collection of rumors whose sum result is confusion and unbelievability. Gatsby is said to have been a German spy, to have gone to Oxford, and to have killed a man. His house and parties establish that he is very rich and cause him to be known by people from every level of society. However, few have actually met him and fewer have any reliable knowledge about the sources of his vast wealth. None of the many guests at his party can identify him. Significantly, the dust cover of the original edition of the novel accentuated this obscurity: "it is the story of Jay Gatsby who came so mysteriously to West Egg."[20] Reviewers of the novel noticed as well; *The Saturday Review*, for example, noted "all the cleverness of his [Gatsby's] hinted nefarious proceedings" and suggested that "the mystery of Gatsby is a mystery saliently characteristic of this age in America."[21]

Much of the success of these jumbled suggestions derive from

Fitzgerald's use of Nick Carraway as a narrator who struggles to make sense of his confusing neighbor. Fitzgerald adds to the mystery surrounding Gatsby by first making Nick an outsider who learns about Gatsby as he is generally known (or not known). As he registers these baffling shreds of information, he naturally struggles to make sense of them. Meanwhile Fitzgerald teases his curiosity, along with that of the reader, by allowing him limited contact with Gatsby. The result of these suspect bits of information and brief glimpses is at best an impression.

Fitzgerald characterizes Nick as a person more intent upon learning than deciding. As he says in the novel's introductory paragraphs, accentuating his mediation in our understanding of Gatsby, "I'm inclined to reserve all judgements."[22] In contrast to Wilson's speaker describing Fleishman, he is far more tentative in his evaluation of the gangster he meets because he stands so far outside his experience and values. In sharp contrast to Gatsby, Nick comes from a very proper background that has carried him from Yale to the respectable but unprofitable career of a bond salesman. His inside knowledge of Eastern society and its mores enables him to see Gatsby for the "roughneck" he is. At the same time, his growing reservations about this society set off a reaction that invests Gatsby with greater significance and greater worth. "I wanted the world to be in uniform and at a sort of moral attention forever" (p. 2), he admits in a frequently cited comment. Not unsurprisingly, this longing for a world that is pure and decent makes him acutely aware of the ways in which it isn't. Troubled by his age's award of respectability to the Buchanans and wealth to gangsters, Nick can't help admiring Gatsby's resolute commitment to success, love, and dreams. This Gatsby evidences traits which Nick deeply respects but finds sorely lacking in everyone else around him. Measured by this bias, Gatsby's excesses and unbelievability validate his reassuring uniqueness.

Ultimately Nick does pass judgement without ever reckoning with these biases. In spite of Gatsby's extensive involvement with crime, Nick arrives at the startling conclusion that he is essentially an innocent victim of other people's heartlessness, a true believer destroyed by the cynicism of his age. "You're worth the whole damn bunch put together," Nick tells Gatsby at his last meeting, in a comment that vents his mounting disillusionment with his own social circle. Later he stamps out the obscene desecration scrawled on the steps of Gatsby's empty house and offers his final association of Gatsby with the original beholder of the new world he imagines. Even though Gatsby's loss of Daisy and ensuing death confirm Nick's worst fears, he concludes that Gatsby "turned out all right at the end" (p. 3) because his death saved him from the demoralizing disillusionment that haunts Nick's consciousness.

Because Nick's estimate of Gatsby stems from such limited understanding of Gatsby and absorbs so many concerns peculiar to himself, one cannot help wondering if the man at the center of the mystery is really the one he finds. The novel offers at least one telling suggestion that Nick may have overlooked qualities that would make Gatsby more sinister than he has allowed. Nick shows surprisingly little reaction to Tom's revelation of Gatsby's involvement with stolen bonds and to the phone call following Gatsby's death that reveals how his plans for disposing of them have miscarried. To the extent that he makes anything of these revelations, they reinforce his belief that Gatsby's death saved him from having to face his across-the-board defeat.

True as this may be, Nick never suspects that Gatsby's elaborate plans may have involved using him as an agent for his bonds. After all, Nick is a bond salesman. Moreover, he is too trusting and uncritical to question Gatsby's persistent offers of help. "I'm going to make a big request of you today," Gatsby explains before he takes Nick to meet Wolfsheim, "so I thought you ought to know something about me. I didn't want you to think I was just some nobody" (p. 81). Nick decides that Gatsby's objective will be fulfilled when he later learns about the undisclosed "matter" from Jordan. Consequently, he is confused by Wolfsheim's assumption that he is seeking "a business connection." It never occurs to him that Gatsby, like the reader, might have perceived Nick's uneasiness with Wolfsheim and thus squelched part of his plan with his hurried dismissal of Wolfsheim's comment as a "mistake." That Gatsby may have been cultivating Nick as a possible outlet for his bonds is made even more likely in his later remarks on the eve of his meeting with Daisy.

> "Why, I thought—why, look here, old sport, you don't make much money, do you?"
>
> "Not very much."
>
> This seemed to reassure him and he continued more confidently.
>
> "I thought you didn't if you'll pardon my—you see, I carry on a little business on the side, a sort of side line, you understand. And I thought that if you don't make very much—you're selling bonds, aren't you, old sport?"
>
> "Trying to."
>
> "Well, this would interest you. It wouldn't take up much of your time and you might pick up a nice bit of money. it happens to be a rather confidential sort of thing." (p. 100)

For the reader bothered by Nick's retreat from his ingrained skepticism in the case of Gatsby, this man of mystery seems more scheming and duplicitous than Nick acknowledges, if only because Gatsby's extravagant possessions attest so eloquently to his success with crime. Nick simply cannot conceive that Gatsby would exploit others to achieve his objectives—nor that Nick's own innocence and propriety might have carried Gatsby elsewhere to dispose of his bonds. *The Great Gatsby* poses a central question: is Gatsby, as Nick assumes, one of the last romantics wholly dedicated to the love of his life, or is he perhaps, as Nick never really considers, a devious criminal who pursues his business with the same evasion and intrigue shown in his plotted reunion with Daisy? Of course, it is quite possible that he could be both. To see Gatsby as both lover and gangster would demand that this figure be recognized as having more in common with both the criminal Meyer Wolfsheim and the conniving Arnold Rothstein than Nick ever allows. Fitzgerald encourages his reader to consider this possibility. Although this Gatsby is as obsessed with the girl of his dreams as Nick believes, he also appears to be someone who is more intent upon his own objectives and more manipulative than Nick comprehends. This Gatsby is at once more sinister and more believably unbelievable, a true product of Prohibition's criminal conditions.

NOTES

1. Herbert Asbury, "The Passing of the Gangster," *American Mercury*, 4 (1925), 358, 362.

2. William E. Leuchtenburg, *The Perils of Prosperity* (Chicago: Univ. of Chicago Press, 1958), pp. 178–203, and Roland Marchand, *Advertising the American Dream: Making Way for Modernity 1920–40* (Berkeley: Univ. of California Press, 1985).

3. Henry Dan Piper, *F. Scott Fitzgerald: A Critical Portrait* (New York: Holt, Rinehart, Winston, 1965), pp. 114–15.

4. John Kobler, *Ardent Spirits: The Rise and Fall of Prohibition* (New York: Putnam, 1973), pp. 315–16.

5. *This Fabulous Century: 1920–1930*, Vol. 3 (New York: Time-Life, 1969), pp. 172–73 (includes photographs of Remus' mansion).

6. Kobler, p. 318. See also *New York Times*, May 17, 1924, p. 1.

7. *The Letters of F. Scott Fitzgerald*, ed. Andrew Turnbull (New York: Scribners, 1963), p. 551.

8. *The Great Gatsby* (New York: Scribners, 1925), pp. 84–85. Ensuing references are noted parenthetically in the text. Despite some minor factual errors, this account confirms Fitzgerald's extensive knowledge about Rothstein. For a thorough discussion of this episode see Leo Katcher, *The Big Bankroll: The Life and Times of Arnold Rothstein* (New York: Harper, 1959), pp. 72–97.

9. Katcher, pp. 109–12.

10. Rothstein was approached during the planning, but refused to participate and

therefore was not involved in the actual fix. However, he used his knowledge to profit handsomely in the betting. See Katcher, pp. 138–48.

11. Scholars have never tracked Fitzgerald's idea for the stolen bonds beyond his interest in the Fuller–McGee case. However, the main issue of this case was the fact that Fuller & Co. was a "bucket shop," a brokerage house that pocketed customer money without actually buying the intended securities. Bonds figured into this case only peripherally but sensationally, when it was revealed that Arnold Rothstein owed Fuller $187,000 and that liberty bonds worth $58,925 that he had posted as collateral were missing. See *New York Times*, January 26, 1923, p. 1.

12. Katcher, pp. 98–99, 170–79.

13. Matthew Bruccoli, "How Are You and the Family Old Sport—Gerlach and Gatsby," *Fitzgerald/Hemingway Annual*, 1975, pp. 33–36.

14. Edmund Wilson, "The Crime in the Whistler Room" in *This Room and This Gin and These Sandwiches* (New York: New Republic, 1937), pp. 75–76.

15. Quoted in Arthur Mizener, *The Far Side of Paradise: A Bibliography of F. Scott Fitzgerald* (Boston: Houghton Mifflin, 1951), p. 171.

16. Craig Thompson and Allen Raymond, *Gang Rule in New York* (New York: Dial, 1940), pp. 53–55, 59. See also Katcher, pp. 41, 53, 106, 115, 166.

17. Katcher, pp. 166 and 301.

18. *New York Times*, October 20, 1920, p. 14.

19. As one of the few fronts whom Rothstein did employ, Dapper Dan Collins (Robert Tourbillon) offers some compelling reasons to suspect Nick's perception of Gatsby. Collins was a tall man whose striking good looks owed much to his well barbered, peroxide blonde hair. As a life-long con artist and legendary womanizer, Collins invested enormous care in his grooming and attire in order to deceive and exploit his victims. He actively preyed on women, robbing some of their money and turning others into prostitutes. In sharp contrast to Gatsby and his unselfish devotion to Daisy, Collins sought what he wanted from his prey. He was a particularly good front because he was so adept at exploiting those taken in by his attractiveness; Katcher, pp. 241–42.

20. Matthew J. Bruccoli, *F. Scott Fitzgerald: A Descriptive Bibliography* (Pittsburgh: Univ. of Pittsburgh Press, 1987), p. 66.

21. *Saturday Review* (May 9, 1925), 740. See also *New York Times*, April 19, 1925, p. 9; *Dial* 79 (August 25, 1920), 163; and *International Book Review* (May 25, 1925), 426.

22. Nick's mediation in the reader's understanding of Gatsby has been the subject of numerous articles; see especially Scott Donaldson, "The Trouble with Nick," in *Critical Essays on F. Scott Fitzgerald's The Great Gatsby*, ed. Scott Donaldson (Boston: G.K. Hall, 1984), pp. 131–39; Kent Cartwright, "Nick Carraway as an Unreliable Narrator," *PLL*, 20 (1984), 218–232; Barry Gross, "Our Gatsby, Our Nick," *CentR*, 14 (1970), 331–40; and T. A. Hanzo, "The Theme and the Narrator of 'The Great Gatsby,'" *MFS*, 2 (1956–57), 183–90.

RONALD BERMAN

The Great Gatsby
and the Good American Life

F. Scott Fitzgerald wanted to make *The Great Gatsby* the great American novel of his century. He succeeded for certain reasons, among them was his understanding that a new novel required a new mode to be provided by modernism. And he deployed a set of enormously important ideas at a moment when they were being debated by the nation.

The Great Gatsby is often said to be an evolutionary form of Fitzgerald's work, but I think that it is a mutation. He agreed with his friend and critic Edmund Wilson who had encouraged him to forget his earlier writing and move on to new plots, characters, and ideas. In fact, he instructed his editor Max Perkins to have the jacket for his 1926 volume of stories, *All the Sad Young Men*, "show transition from his early exuberant stories of youth which created a new type of American girl and the later and more serious mood which produced *The Great Gatsby* and marked him as one of the half dozen masters of English prose now writing in America"[1]—a nice assessment on both points. There is much in *The Great Gatsby* that does not have a literary history. It is as accurate and self-justifying as a photograph—something often encountered in its pages.

Fitzgerald's choice of place and subject was itself a statement of purpose. H. L. Mencken had in 1924 identified the life of post-war New York City as the natural new subject of the American novel. That life was

From *Fitzgerald, Hemingway, and The Twenties*. © 2001 by The University of Alabama Press.

monied, vulgar, noisy, chaotic, and immoral; hence it was more interesting than anything that could be served up by the literature of gentility. He was fascinated by the same New York crowds that provide the background for Fitzgerald. He too understood their figurative meaning. The frenzied life of Manhattan, its open pursuit of sex, money, and booze was, Mencken wrote, a "spectacle, lush and barbaric in its every detail, [which] offers the material for a great imaginative literature." A new kind of American novel might not only capture the moment but comprehend a new experience in American history, the replacement of Victorian public conscience by modern subjectivity. Mencken told aspiring writers that the New York scene—democracy in its current incarnation—"ought to be far more attractive to novelists than it is."[2]

An enormous amount of the telling of Fitzgerald's story is about New York as well as about Gatsby. The modern moment had after all found its correlative: the great literary and artistic movement of the century's beginnings saw the social world from the urban, dislocated point of view of *The Waste Land*. Modernism provided Fitzgerald, Hemingway, and other writers with not only tactics but also a new sensibility. For example, as Susan Sontag writes of cityscape in photography, "bleak factory buildings and billboard-cluttered avenues look as beautiful, through the camera's eye, as churches and pastoral landscapes. More beautiful, by modern taste."[3] Ezra Pound had written about the aesthetic power of city lights; Hemingway began his description of Paris in *The Sun Also Rises* with its "electric signs"; Blaise Cendrars theorized that billboard-cluttered avenues had for the first time made urban landscape visually interesting. Ordinary things were accepted—welcomed—by modernist writers. They challenged the high seriousness of art and artiness. In *The Great Gatsby* Fitzgerald writes with authority about ads, photos, automobiles, magazines, and Broadway musicals as if these things too fuel the energies of art: "the cars from New York are parked five deep in the drive, and already the halls and salons and verandas are gaudy with primary colors and hair shorn in strange new ways and shawls beyond the dreams of Castile" (34).[4] Production, entertainment, style, and consumption are native subjects of modernism, often displacing what is merely natural. In the case of a certain billboard featuring Doctor T. J. Eckleburg—both symbol and sign of the times—they become part of the weave of a great American novel.

Like any other intellectual movement, modernism had its sacred texts. From its use of Baudelaire to that of T. S. Eliot it was self-referential. *The Great Gatsby* calls attention to its intellectual allegiances, and as Robert Emmet Long has observed, Fitzgerald brings the plot and idealistic idea of *Almayer's Folly* up to date: A young adventurer falls in love, at first succeeds, then loses everything.[5] New ideas of form are displayed, and throughout Fitzgerald's deeply symbolic novel, we become aware of how far we have gone from the values of realism. As for subject, Mencken may have wanted a Great American Novel on social life in New York, but when it came out, he did not recognize it. I think he expected something that might have been called *Prohibition on Broadway*. He did not expect a romance or a myth as powerful as that of *The Waste Land*—what Nick Carraway calls a quest for the grail. As for style, Fitzgerald's novel of New York is nowhere more modernist than in its impressionism. Expecting hard-edged delineation of the manners and mores of the Jazz Age, we find instead evocations of yellow cocktail music and trembling opal and a moon produced out of a caterer's basket. The Jazz Age is there, but the story is its own telling.

Fitzgerald's characters are more than the sum of their own experiences: they constitute America itself as it moves into the Jazz Age. A larger story swirls around them, however, and its meaning is suggested by an early, unused title for the novel: *Under the Red, White, and Blue.*

The Great Gatsby reflects national issues. Just before Fitzgerald came of age, Walter Lippmann had stated that "those who are young today are born into a world in which the foundations of the older order survive only as habits or by default." And soon after the publication of *The Great Gatsby*, John Dewey was to write that "the loyalties which once held individuals, which gave them support, direction, and unity of outlook on life, have well-nigh disappeared."[6] *The Great Gatsby* shows a version of the new social world criticized by the Public Philosophy that Lippmann and Dewey represented. It is a world of broken relationships and false relationships, a world of money and success rather than of social responsibility, a world in which individuals are all too free to determine their moral destinies. Daisy warns Nick and the reader about this world when she says, in the first chapter, "I think everything's terrible anyhow" (17). Because she believes that, she is free to act any way she wants.

One issue of the novel is loyalty to love, another is loyalty to friendship. Nick himself exemplifies loyalty to people and ideas, whereas Daisy and Tom have freed themselves from troublesome conscience and from even more troublesome self-awareness. They will be loyal neither to idea nor person. They have no significant sense of self to which they can be true. Important referents are involved, because Americans had for some time been advised of the perilous subjectivity of their lives and the absence of will. The Public Philosophy often called the nation to account for the way it made and spent money, about its class relationships, about the state of our national character. Here is how Josiah Royce described American uncertainties a year or two before Fitzgerald went to Princeton: "Since the war, our transformed and restless people has been seeking not only for religious, but for moral guidance. What are the principles that can show us the course to follow in the often pathless wilderness of the new democracy? It frequently seems as if, in every crisis of our greater social affairs, we needed somebody to tell us both our dream and the interpretation thereof. We are eager to have life.... But what life?"[7] Readers who now come to Fitzgerald's novel and to the twenties are inclined to think that the oft-mentioned subject of the American Dream is a matter of personal freedom and financial success; however, writers like Royce and Lippmann described the dream in different terms. They related it to the building of the nation in the eighteenth century and to the qualities of character that nation building implied. They also suggested that it was disappearing into history.

Perhaps it was already gone. Were there even models left for us to understand? Milton R. Stern agrees in *The Golden Moment* that the possibility of even *understanding* the dream had disappeared. Here is how he describes a central problem in Fitzgerald's novel: "The poor, naive, believing son of a bitch. He dreamed of a country in the mind and he got East and West Egg. He dreamed of a future magic self and he got the history of Dan Cody. He dreamed of a life of unlimited possibility and he got Hopalong Cassidy, Horatio Alger, and Ben Franklin's 'The Way to Wealth.' What else could he imitate?"[8] Gatsby is a hero in a world without heroism, unable to connect "with the past and the eternities."[9]

For Fitzgerald himself the dream was quite literally about the vanishing quality of greatness. It meant displaying in private life those daring unselfish qualities that had made America possible. This was a subject on Fitzgerald's mind in the twenties. We are fortunate that he defined it in the conclusion of his short story "The Swimmers" (1929)[10]: "France was a land, England was a people, but America, having about it still that quality of the idea, was harder to utter—it was the graves at Shiloh and the tired, drawn, nervous faces of its great men, and the country boys dying in the Argonne for a phrase that was empty before their bodies withered. It was a willingness of the heart" (512). It would be difficult to understand *The Great Gatsby* without that last line. Nevertheless, as good as that line is, it is not entirely original. It comes from a good deal of reading about the nation. Harold E. Stearns, one of the most thoughtful critics of Americanism in the early twenties, identified "willingness" as "the old and traditional American" style of spiritual generosity in a material world. If affirmed character and will, resisting what seemed to be unalterable "economic and social forces." "Willingness" was, according to Stearns, part (and the best part) of our national character.[11] It was clearly a form of greatness, part of the reason why Gatsby is the Great Gatsby.

First, however, we must examine the opposite of this idea of greatness: Against Royce's panoramic vision of national development, responsibility, and obligation, a character like that of Tom Buchanan is a compendium of American failures. He is rich with no conscience, moralistic without being moral, exclusionary, racist, and, above all, untrue to any self-conception. He is Royce's nightmare and the nightmare of the Public Philosophy, a figure of resentment and of absolute, solipsistic subjectivity.

How is Gatsby himself to be measured? The values that Fitzgerald recalled from the years before the Jazz Age did not consist wholly of moral prohibitions, although clearly they derive from a traditional morality "based upon spirit over matter."[12] William James did indeed preach fully conscious responsibility for our moral decisions; George Santayana did lecture the American public about its responsibility to create a meaningful social order; and John Dewey did repeatedly outline the conditions for an informed public adapting to necessary social change. But more was implied than these things. James, in a letter to H. G. Wells that has become part of our intellectual history, remarked on the new, and alarming "worship of the bitch-goddess SUCCESS" in America.[13] He saw that prosperity and power might in themselves become trivial and boring. Life demanded intense powers of imagination, even romantic love and devotion. He argued for dedication to people and ideas and against the state of mind that lost itself in meaningless subjectivity, which would prove to be a form of unconsciousness not simply metaphorical. Life demanded goals, sacrifice, and a certain amount of risk. In fact, James once wondered idly if the last heroes in America might not be outside the law, choosing not to be prudentially middle-class. So far as James could see, there was nothing wrong (excess and ignorance apart) in emotional dedication to a cause. The characters of *The Great Gatsby* enact many a drama scripted by American philosophy, and its language mirrors the language of debate about a country becoming ever more monied and less heroic, less true—except for Jay Gatsby—to the grand passions of its past.

Gatsby has the capacity for the pursuit of happiness. He believes in his dream and in Daisy as its object. He has a passion for belief, and although he may be wrong about the kind of happiness that is possible and about the woman who represents that happiness, he has committed himself to the dream. Gatsby's pursuit of Daisy against impossible odds is perhaps the final form of the American will to wring a new life from destiny.

Of course, Gatsby is imperfect. In spite of his idealism, his idea of the good life seems merely to be the acquisition of money, things, property. Possibly the most famous literary possession of our century is his car in "a rich cream color, bright with nickel, swollen here and there in its monstrous length with triumphant hatboxes and supper-boxes and tool-boxes, and terraced with a labyrinth of wind-shields that mirrored a dozen suns" (51). In this book we tend to see the sun as it is reflected by produced things. Gatsby's house (like Myrtle's apartment) is a showcase of consumption. Nevertheless, an enormously shrewd essay by Santayana in 1920 (its title, fittingly, is "Materialism and Idealism in American Life") had pointed out that one of these quantities did not necessarily cancel out the other. Gatsby is materialistic because Americans do not have many other alternatives. Material life offers one of the few recognized ways in which the American can express his idealism. This is how Santayana describes the issue:

> For the American the urgency of his novel attack upon matter, his zeal in gathering its fruits, precludes meanderings in primrose paths; devices must be short cuts.... There is an enthusiasm in his sympathetic handling of material forces which goes far to cancel the illiberal character which it might otherwise assume.... his ideals fall into the form of premonitions and prophecies; and his studious prophecies often come true. So do the happy workmanlike ideals of the American. When a poor boy, perhaps, he dreams of an education, and presently he gets an education, or at least a degree; he dreams of growing rich, and he grows rich.... He dreams of helping to carry on and, to accelerate the movement of a vast, seething progressive society, and he actually does so. Ideals clinging so close to nature are almost sure of fulfillment; the American beams with a certain self-confidence and sense of mastery; he feels that God and nature are working with him.[14]

Money, after all, has been only a means to express otherwise inchoate ideas. Santayana, famously, was convinced that this was a kind of secular theology, which suggests one way to approach Jay Gatsby's own ideas. One of the central themes of Fitzgerald's novel is the application of religious feeling to secular experience; one of the central themes of Santayana is the representativeness of this American conception.

What are the obstacles to Gatsby's dream, apart from intractable human nature, time, and chance? Gatsby does not want only to be a success, he wants to be a gentleman. Meyer Wolfshiem reminds us several times that he has fulfilled *both* of his desires, but Wolfshiem turns out to be less than a reliable judge. One of the most important things for readers at our end of the century to remember is that democratic life was different in 1922. Throughout Fitzgerald's novels and stories we see aspiration meeting rejection. The text refers to a democracy that current readers may not recognize. Nick, Wolfshiem, Tom, and even Myrtle Wilson have an ideal social type in mind. So does Gatsby. We might be disposed to think that, especially in America, a self-made man would be proud of his achievement. But Gatsby hides his past—although it has been interesting enough to have provided the material for a dozen novels. He begins life on a worked-out farm, learns how to read and think with not much help, goes on his *wahnderjahre*, becomes irresistible to women, rescues a yacht from disaster, tops it all off by becoming (Basil Duke Lee dreams of this) a gentleman criminal. If this reminds us of famous lives and books, it is intended to. Every literary-biographical theme we can imagine has been part of his forgotten life: there are echoes of David Copperfield, Julien Sorel, Compton Mackenzie, Horatio Alger, Joseph Conrad, and even Raffles, the suave society crook admired by Fitzgerald and also by George Orwell when they were schoolboys. But this adventurous story remains profoundly uninteresting to Gatsby, although it fascinates Nick.

Gatsby does not want to be praised for what he is, but for what he is not. In this, he represents the tensions of the early twenties. Wolfshiem, who respects social standards (admittedly from a distance), thinks about Gatsby being "a perfect gentleman" and "a man of fine breeding" (57). Myrtle Wilson has married her husband George "because I thought he was a gentleman." She pumps gas, but says the same thing as Wolfshiem about the ideal social type: "I thought he knew something about breeding" (30). Her friend Lucille McKee, who is by no means Mrs. Astor, has dropped a suitor, she says, because "he was way below" (29) her. Even Tom Buchanan, with his delusions of science and art and all that, wants badly to assert patrician responsibility and to assert the values of his social class.

When Gatsby says, "Here's another thing I always carry" (53), it is final proof that his early life has disappeared, a photo of "Oxford days" showing that he has always belonged, so to speak, among his peers. Gatsby is not only the leading man of the Jazz Age but the last great figure of the gentleman hero. He understands and accepts that inequality is characteristic of his democratic moment. Such inequality is unfair, but there is a benefit: his character is thickened, made more intense, by obsolete qualities of courtesy, thoughtfulness, and honor. Whether dealing with Nick Carraway or Daisy or, a girl who has torn her gown at his party, he has that nobility unknown to West Egg, forgotten by East Egg and by our national memory. The irony of the novel is that he has become far more of a gentleman than his social adversaries—"the whole damn bunch" (120) of them.

Before *The Great Gatsby*, Fitzgerald dealt with the educated and literate world. He told us possibly more than we want to know about the privileged life of Princeton and its college-boy weekends in Manhattan. The creation of Jimmy Gatz, Myrtle Wilson, and George Wilson shows how far his understanding developed. In his correspondence with Max Perkins, his editor at Scribner's, Fitzgerald went so far as to state that Myrtle Wilson was a more achieved character than Daisy Fay Buchanan. There are reasons for that: Daisy and Gatsby do not have the same hard delineation as their surrounding cast. They are partly mythical and even allegorical. Myrtle belongs to the everyday world. Fitzgerald's tactic in establishing her is to describe in detail her relationship to that world and to allow her to reveal her taste and style. Daisy, rarely described directly, is part idea; Myrtle, often described directly, is understood through her countless acquisitions. Her apartment has as much to say about her conception of herself as Gatsby's palace has to say about his:

> The apartment was on the top floor—a small living room, a small dining room, a small bedroom and a bath. The living room was crowded to the doors with a set of tapestried furniture entirely too large for it so that to move about was to stumble continually over scenes of ladies swinging in the gardens of Versailles.... Several old copies of "Town Tattle" lay on the table together with a copy of "Simon called Peter" and some of the small scandal magazines of Broadway. Mrs. Wilson was first concerned with the dog. A reluctant elevator boy went for a box full of straw and some milk to which he added on his own initiative a tin of large hard dog biscuits—one of which decomposed apathetically in the saucer of milk all afternoon. (25)

When we see Myrtle's arrangements we see the inside of her mind. There are many things that are admirable about her, but, like Gatsby, she has never understood essential models of style. He wants to be a gentleman; she wants to be a lady: what are the odds? Myrtle, who is blue-collar, has surrounded herself with the artifacts of the middle class. She does not understand even these things very well, which argues that her understanding of Tom (who exists many levels above the middle class) is itself deficient. Everything about the apartment suggests that Myrtle, like Gatsby, has gotten her ideas about style and class from the mass market. Not only are the magazines and books in plain sight, the furnishings are a demonstration of what she has learned from newsstand culture.

There are more objects and things described in this apartment than the mind can easily register. Myrtle has tried to *accumulate* her social character. She has bought the tapestries because they provide her self image, more grandiose than we might guess at first sight, when all she seems to have is carnal intelligence. She has bought books, magazines, furniture, pictures, and "police dog" because of the urgings of advertisements that promise status through acquisition. Her catalogue of all the things she's "got to get" (31)—a massage, a wave, a collar for the dog, a wreath, an ash tray—is a blueprint for becoming what that she knows she is not. But as Stern suggests, even the possibilities of imitation have diminished. That phrase "small," repeated four times in a paragraph, says something about great expectations compressed into limited psychological space.

Beneath the skin of the novel is a powerful opposition between the language of navigation and will, of drift and unconsciousness. That opposition comes, I think, from discourse of the Public Philosophy.[15] Vital energy, for example, implies strength of character. That energy in Jay Gatsby, in Myrtle Wilson and, from time to time, in Nick Carraway suggests the ability to lead a life of feeling. It states the intensity and emotional commitment that are so rare among others in this story. So, when we see Gatsby at rest—as near to rest as he gets—we see his *American* readiness for experience: "He was balancing himself on the dashboard of his car with that resourcefulness of movement that is so peculiarly American—that comes, I suppose, with the absence of lifting work or rigid sitting in youth and, even more, with the formless grace of our nervous, sporadic games. This quality was continually breaking through his punctilious manner in the shape of restlessness. He was never quite still; there was always a tapping foot somewhere or the impatient opening and closing of a hand" (51). "Vitality," "energy," and the "restlessness" that Gatsby displays are common phrases of the early twentieth century. Such phrases are shorthand (as in the speeches and writings of Teddy Roosevelt), for American creative possibility. Always in motion, Gatsby is intended to remind us of qualities praised not only by novelists but also by those who believed that in order to have a moral life one had first to have great energy, concentrated will, and high resolution. Against the language of this passage we need to poise the language describing others in the text. They are (except for Jordan's ungoverned will) sensed through terms of indolence, inertia, withdrawal, and even paralysis. Daisy Fay Buchanan's languor—"What do people plan?" (13)—shows the life of the Lotos-eaters. Even Jordan becomes not only situationally "bored" but existentially; and she is, of course, too wise or, like Daisy, perhaps too "sophisticated" to dream at all. Background figures are sick, silent, "lethargic," or paralytically drunk.

Tom and Daisy lead quintessentially unexamined lives. As Nick puts it, they act and seem to live "for no particular reason" (9)—anathema to the philosophy of vital energy. That phrase "drift," used repeatedly in the opening of *The Great Gatsby*, reminds Fitzgerald's readers of American debates very much unfinished: I have mentioned Lippmann, who had recently written of America as a "nation of uncritical drifters," mindless and self-absorbed.[16] There were political implications, for he concluded that a democracy so diminished might not survive or deserve to survive. On the personal scale, a fatal lack of moral tension is necessarily implied: Fitzgerald's allusive descriptions tell us, a long time before Tom and Daisy and Jordan ever make decisions, how those decisions are likely to be made.

The people at both of Gatsby's parties (and at Myrtle's dissolvent party also) represent "New York," a place but also an idea. "New York" is itself problematic, it being widely understood in the twenties that the city was no longer white, native, or Christian. In fact, according to Charles Merz, "the most fundamental charge being brought by its critics against New York is the charge that here is an 'alien' city, literally un-American and anti-American in its make-up.... the city has gone foreign."[17] That is one of the reasons why the language of the novel applied to the life of New York is "tumultuous" and chaotic and why the air is alive with dissonant sounds unheard in the provinces. New York names are among these dissonant sounds, rejecting both familiarity and iambic pentameter. In addition, Meyer Wolfshiem, Gulick, Eckhaust, and Beluga the tobacco importer are objects of suspicion both to Tom Buchanan and to the framers of the Immigration Bill of 1924, the year of the novel's composition. The splendidly mixed and unbalanced procession of names that begins Fitzgerald's fourth chapter implies the uneasy presence in America of those who have come (all too recently) from the wrong parts of Europe. In Manhattan, Nick and Jordan hear that "foreign clamor on the sidewalk" (106), which has made everyone uneasy. It is in the course of things that "Gatz" from *Mitteleuropa* should become the mellifluous, anglophone "Gatsby." Lily Shiel (Fitzgerald's Jewish-Cockney lover, with a name difficult to scan) becomes Sheilah Graham, metrically socially a happier choice.

Breakdown is characteristic of the story and also of its language. We begin with harmonic, rhythmic statement, with long, assured and sweeping sentences, with language that easily imitates music: "And so with the sunshine and the great bursts of leaves growing on the trees" (7). But both story and language move inexorably from harmony to chaos. Starting with the sober, careful, and practiced enunciations of Jay Gatsby we go to another mode that dominates the later telling and experiencing of the story. The language moves from rhythmic precision of statement to cacophony as the narrative moves from day to night and from the description of dreams to that of nightmares.

Fitzgerald opposes harmony and dissonance in both literal and figurative forms, just as he does drift and its mastery. By the end of Gatsby's first party, "most of the remaining women were now having fights with men said to be their husbands" (42). One particular song ends in "gasping broken sobs" (42), and we exit to a "bizarre and tumultuous scene" of collision amid the "harsh discordant din" of auto horns (44). Those "caterwauling horns" are in themselves allusions. Amanda Vaill has recently written that this particular kind of dissonance was in the modernist domain by mid-twenties: Fitzgerald's friend Gerald Murphy collaborated with Fernand Leger in a film of *Ballet mécanique* that featured the sound of machinery, including the "automobile horn."[18] (The original score by George Antheil, played in Paris in 1924, featured among other sounds that of an electric fan disguised as an airplane propeller and also a "battery of cacophones." Aaron Copeland witnessed the performance and thought that it "outsacked the *Sacre*," which had until then set the international standard for modernist polemic dissonance).[19] The discordant sounds of the film's uncaring mechanical "moving objects" were intended to imply not only human experience in cities but also the meaning of lives in them. There was a great deal of musical dissonance in the first quarter of the new century. The opposition of harmony and disorder was especially useful to modernism, with atonality being understood as "a critique of society" as well as a description of it.[20] Stravinsky invoked the sewing-machine, Honegger the locomotive, and Antheil the machine-gun. The object was, Stravinsky said, that of "producing noise" that characterized the way we live now, and what our lives meant.[21] On this, Eliot was definitive: "the scream of the motor-horn, the rattle of machinery, the grind of wheels" are both facts and symbols "of modern life."[22] Closer to home, Jelly Roll Morton's *Sidewalk Blues* (recorded for Victor in 1926) starts off with a blaring automobile horn, which is a way of letting us know existentially as well as musically where we are. Nick Carraway realizes that the "many-keyed commotion" (81) at Gatsby's second party has explicit social meaning: Daisy hears it and intuitively understands the danger it poses to the soft rhythms of her unconsidered life. In terms of music, what follows is a parable out of Mahler and Schoenberg. Dissonance becomes a trope of social disorder, a warning about fate—and always a reminder of the allusive tactics of modernism.

NOTES

1. *F. Scott Fitzgerald: A Life in Letters*, ed. Matthew J. Bruccoli (New York: Touchstone, 1995), 122.

2. H. L. Mencken, "Totentanz," in *second Mencken Chrestomathy*, ed. Terry Teachoot (New York: Alfred A. Knopf, 1995), 181; Mencken, "Metropolis," 189.

3. Susan Sontag, *On Photography* (New York: Dell, 1973), 78.

4. All Citations fro *the Great Gatsby* in this chapter are in the edition edited by Matthew J. Bruccoli (Cambridge: Cambridge University Press, 1991).

5. Robert Emmet Long, *The Achieving of "The Grat Gatsby"* (Lewisburg: Bucknell University Press, 1979), 118.

6. Lippman, *Drift and Mastery*, xvii–xviii; from John Dewey. *The Public and its Problems* (1927), cited by Christopher Lasch in *The Revolt of the Elites* (New York: W.W. Norton, 1995), 84.

7. Royce, "William James and the Philosophy of Life," 1:215. this essay refers to the Spanish-American War of 1898.

8. Milton R. Stern, *The Golden Moment: The Novels of F. Scott Fitzgerald* (Urbana: University of Illinois Press, 1971), 247.

9. Robert Sklar, *F. Scott Fitzgerald: The Last Tycoon* (New York: Oxford University Press, 1967), 169. See also the survey of theme and idea in Richard Lehan, *"The Great Gatsby": The Limits of Wonder* (Boston: Twayne, 1990), 58–66.

10. All citations fro "The Swimmers" are from *the Short Stories of F. Scott Fitzgerald*, ed. Matthew J. Bruccoli (New York: Charles Scribner's Sons, 1989).

11. Harold E. Sterns, *The Street I Know* (New York: Lee Furman, Inc., 1935), 101. See also Stearns on the enormous influence of James, Lippman, and Santayana, 69, 98.

12. Kenneth E. Eble, *F. Scott Fitzgerald* (Boston: Twayne, 1977), 95.

13. Quoted in George Cotkin, *William James, Public Philosopher* (Baltimore: Johns Hopkins University Press, 1990), 91. See my discussion of "Success" in *"The Great Gatsby" and Modern Times* (Urbana: University of Illinois Press, 1994), 166–67.

14. Santayana, *Character and Opinion in the United States*, 108–9.

15. see my discussion of the relationship of will to act in *"The Great Gatsby" and Fitzgerald's World of Ideas*, 192–200.

16. Lippman, *Drift and Mastery*, xvii.

17. Charles Merz, *The Great American Band Wagon* (Garden City: Garden City Publishing, 1928), 235–36.

18. See Amanada Vaill, *Everybody Was So Young: Gerald and Sara Murphy, A Lost Generation Love Story* (Boston: Houghton Mifflin. 1998), 189. There were several versions of this film.

19. See Peter Conrad, *Modern Times, Modern Places* (New York: Alfred A. Knopf, 1999), 386–87.

20. See the discussion of harmony and dissonance in early modernism by Allan Janik and Stephen Toulmin, *Wittgenstein's Vienna* (Chicago: Ivan R. Dee, 1996), 102–12. The idea of harmony as metaphor is Platonic: see section 411 of most editions of the *Republic*. I have used *The Republic*, trans. G.M.A. Grube (Indianapolis: Hackett, 1983). This section shows the correspondence between music, the individual mind, and the polity.

21. Conrad, *Modern Times, Modern Places*, 412.

22. Eliot's remarks on Stravinsky from the *Dial* (July–December 1921) and *Criterion* (October 1924) are cited in Lyndall Gordon, *T.S. Eliot: An Imperfect Life* (New York: W.W. Norton, 1998). 176.

Character Profile

Jay Gatsby is a self-invented millionaire, a middle-class Midwesterner turned wealthy Easterner. He lives in a "colossal" mansion in West Egg, New York, and is famous for his extravagant parties. In his early thirties, Gatsby is tanned with short hair, and Nick Carraway, the narrator, can find "nothing sinister about him." When Nick meets him for the first time, Gatsby's smile "was one of those rare smiles with a quality of eternal reassurance in it, that you may come across four or five times in life. It faced—or seemed to face— the whole external world for an instant, and then concentrated on *you* with an irresistible prejudice in your favor."

Gatsby's identity is built upon "romantic speculations" and "bizarre accusations," as the exact nature of his past is shrouded in mystery. While known for his famous parties, "always full of interesting people," Gatsby stands alone from the crowd "looking from one group to another with approving eyes."

Gatsby's "incorrigible dream," is to be reunited with Daisy Buchanan, the love he had lost five years earlier. He admires that "her voice was full of money." When Gatsby first met Daisy, he was too poor for her tastes, and while he was an officer overseas, she married Tom Buchanan, a wealthy but careless man. Gatsby has shaped his identity over the years, erasing his past as if he "sprang from his Platonic conception of himself," in hopes to impress Daisy and to possess the elusive American dream. He changed his name from Gatz to Gatsby, accumulated wealth, and joined the ranks of the rich. Yet beneath the elaborate elegance of Gatsby, the silk shirts and the clipped speech, the "roughneck" still looms, the part of him which he tries so desperately, yet unsuccessfully, to conceal.

Gatsby is a complex character, filled with contradictions. Nick portrays him as both naïve and exploitative. His unshakable sense of entitlement leads Gatsby to believe he can possess Daisy's love and approval. Even when he first met her, "He took what he could get, ravenously and unscrupulously." When he sees Daisy for the first time since their youth, he shows her his silk shirts and she cries at their sheer beauty. Gatsby "revealed everything in his house according to the measure of response it drew from her well-loved eyes." Gatsby blindly ignores the possibility that Daisy will not leave her husband and child for a newly moneyed man, possibly one involved in criminal activities. When Nick tells him that he cannot change the past, Gatsby is adamant: "Why of course you can!"

Nick's reactions to Gatsby waver between skepticism and faith. He suspects Gatsby lies about his "education at Oxford," even though he swears it is the "God's truth." Yet Nick also feels that Gatsby possesses an innocence; that Gatsby, a bootlegger (nobody knows for sure the extent of his possible other crimes) maintains a "capacity for wonder." He postures, exaggerates, and lies about himself, but Nick recognizes that Gatsby has "something gorgeous about him, some heightened sensitivity to the promises of life" and describes him as "a son of God." Although Gatsby's love for Daisy may be misplaced and foolish, Nick notes that Gatsby has "an extraordinary gift for hope, a romantic readiness that I have never found in any other person." A flawed hero, Gatsby's idealism, "overwhelming self-absorption," and fidelity to this impossible dream eventually destroy him. Nick explains, "Gatsby believed in the green light, the orgiastic future that year by year recedes before us. It eluded us then, but that's no matter—tomorrow we will run faster, stretch out our arms farther."

On the night before his death, Gatsby continues "clutching at some last hope." However, his wealthy lifestyle, and his faith in an idealistic, invented life, has led to his own end. Jay Gatsby has chased after the illusory American dream, a quest that leads him from poverty to wealth, briefly into the arms of his beloved, and eventually to death.

Contributors

HAROLD BLOOM is Sterling Professor of the Humanities at Yale University and Henry W. and Albert A. Berg Professor of English at the New York University Graduate School. He is the author of over 20 books, including *Shelley's Mythmaking* (1959), *The Visionary Company* (1961), *Blake's Apocalypse* (1963), *Yeats* (1970), *A Map of Misreading* (1975), *Kabbalah and Criticism* (1975), *Agon: Toward a Theory of Revisionism* (1982), *The American Religion* (1992), *The Western Canon* (1994), and *Omens of Millennium: The Gnosis of Angels, Dreams, and Resurrection* (1996). *The Anxiety of Influence* (1973) sets forth Professor Bloom's provocative theory of the literary relationships between the great writers and their predecessors. His most recent books include *Shakespeare: The Invention of the Human* (1998), a 1998 National Book Award finalist, *How to Read and Why* (2000), *Genius: A Mosaic of One Hundred Exemplary Creative Minds* (2002), and *Hamlet: Poem Unlimited* (2003). In 1999, Professor Bloom received the prestigious American Academy of Arts and Letters Gold Medal for Criticism, and in 2002 he received the Catalonia International Prize.

EDWIN S. FUSSELL taught American Literature at University of California, San Diego. His publications include *Frontier: American Literature and the American West* (1965), *Lucifer in Harness: American Meter, Metaphor, and Diction* (1973), *The French Side of Henry James* (1990), and *The Catholic Side of Henry James* (1993).

HENRY DAN PIPER taught English at Southern Illinois University where he also served as dean of liberal arts and sciences. Prior to his career as an

English teacher, he was an accomplished chemist for DuPont and worked on the Manhattan Project.

NEILA SESHACHARI taught in the English Department at Weber State University. She published short stories and critical essays, and won critical acclaim for her book on conversations with William Kennedy. She was also a nationally reputed F. Scott Fitzgerald Scholar. Dr. Seshachari died in March 2002.

BRIAN WAY is a former Senior Lecturer in English at University College in Swansea, England. He is the author of *Audience Participation*, *Development through Drama*, and *F. Scott Fitzgerald and the Art of Social Fiction*.

BRUCE BAWER is the author of *Diminishing Fictions* and *Prophets and Professors*. He also authored *A Place at the Table: The Gay Individual in American Society* and *Stealing Jesus: How Fundamentalism Betrays Christianity*.

ROGER LATHBURY is a member of the English Department at George Mason University. He has published a critical study on *The Great Gatsby*.

RICHARD LEHAN is Professor Emeritus of English at the University of California, Los Angeles. He is the author of *Theodore Dreiser: His World and His Novels*, and has published works on Fitzgerald and Hemingway.

GILES MITCHELL teaches at the University of North Texas. In addition to publishing scholarly articles, he is a poet whose collections include *Love Among the Mad* and *Some Green Laurel*.

EDWARD WASIOLEK is Professor Emeritus of Slavic Languages & Literatures at the University of Chicago. He has edited books on Dostoyevsky.

THOMAS H. PAULY is the Associate Chair of the English Department at the University of Delaware. He is the author of *An American Odyssey: Elia Kazan and American Culture*. He has published over thirty articles and is currently writing a biography of Zane Grey.

RONALD BERMAN is Professor of English Literature at the University of California, San Diego. He is the author of *Public Policy and the Aesthetic Interest* (1992), *The Great Gatsby and Modern Times* (1994), and *The Great Gatsby and Fitzgerald's World of Ideas* (1996).

Bibliography

Allen, Joan. *Candles and Carnival Lights*. New York: New York University Press, 1978.

Bawer, Bruce. "'I Could Still Hear The Music': Jay Gatsby and the Musical Metaphor." *Notes on Modern American Literature* 5, no. 4 (Fall 1981)

Bell, Ian F. A. "Newnesses of Beginning: The Violent Phantasies of Willa Cather and F. Scott Fitzgerald." From *The Insular Dream: Obsession and Resistance*. Ed: Kristiaan Versluys. Amsterdam: VU University, 1995: 242–260.

Berman, Ronald. *The Great Gatsby and Modern Times*. Urbana: University of Illinois Press, 1994.

———. *Fitzgerald, Hemingway, and the Twenties*. Tuscaloosa: University of Alabama Press, 2001.

———. *The Great Gatsby and Fitzgerald's World of Ideas*. Tuscaloosa, AL: University of Alabama Press, 1997.

Bloom, Harold, ed. *Modern Critical Interpretations: The Great Gatsby*. New York: Chelsea House, 1988.

———. *Bloom's Notes: F. Scott Fitzgerald's The Great Gatsby*. New York: Chelsea House, 1996.

Breitwieser, Mitchell. "*The Great Gatsby*: Grief, Jazz and the Eye-Witness." *Arizona Quarterly* 47, no. 3 (Autumn 1991): 17–70.

Bruccoli, Matthew, ed. *New Essays on The Great Gatsby*. New York: Cambridge University Press, 1985.

————. *Some Sort of Epic Grandeur: The Life of F. Scott Fitzgerald*. New York: Carroll & Graf, 1994.

Bryer, Jackson R., Alan Margolies, and Ruth Prigozy, eds. *F. Scott Fitzgerald: New Perspectives*. Athens: University of Georgia Press, 2000.

Chambers, John B. *The Novels of F. Scott Fitzgerald*. New York: St. Martin's Press, 1989.

Claridge, Henry, ed. *F. Scott Fitzgerald: Critical Assessments*. Mountfield, UK: Helm Information, 1991. 4 vols.

Clymer, Jeffory A. "'Mr. Nobody from Nowhere': Rudolph Valentino, Jay Gatsby, and the End of the American Race." *Genre: Forms of Discourse and Culture* 29, no 1–2 (Spring-Summer 1996): 161–92.

Coleman, Dan. "'A World Complete in Itself': Gatsby's Elegiac Narration." *Journal of Narrative Technique* 27, no. 2 (Spring 1997): 207–33.

de Koster, Katie, ed. *Readings on F. Scott Fitzgerald*. San Diego: Greenhaven, 1998.

Dillon, Andrew. "The Great Gatsby: The Vitality of Illusion." *Arizona Quarterly* 44 (1988): 49–61.

Dixon, Wheeler Winston. *The Cinematic Vision of F. Scott Fitzgerald*. Ann Arbor, MI: UMI Research P, 1986.

Donaldson, Scott. *Critical Essays on F. Scott Fitzgerald's* The Great Gatsby. Boston: G.K. Hall & Co, 1984.

————. "Possessions in *The Great Gatsby*." *Southern Review* 37, no 2 (Spring 2001): 187–210.

Fussell, Edwin S. "Fitzgerald's Brave New World." *ELH* 19, no. 4 (December, 1952): 291–306.

Gervais, Ronald J. "Gatsby's Extra Gardener: Pastoral Order in the Jazz Age." *Illinois Quarterly* 43, no. 3 (Spring 1981): 38–47.

Hoffman, Frederick J., ed. *The Great Gatsby: A Study*. New York: Scribners, 1962.

Holquist, Michael. "Stereotyping in Autobiography and Historiography: Colonialism in *The Great Gatsby*." *Poetics Today* 9, no. 2 (1988): 453–72.

Hook, Andrew. *F. Scott Fitzgerald*. Modern Fiction series. London: Edward Arnold, 1992.

Kerr, Frances. "'Feeling Half Feminine': Modernism and the Politics of Emotion in *The Great Gatsby*." *American Literature* 68, no. 2 (June 1996): 405–31.

Lee, Robert A. *Scott Fitzgerald: The Promises of Life*. London: Vision Press, 1989.

Lehan, Richard. The Great Gatsby: *The Limits of Wonder*. Boston: Twayne Publishers, 1990.

Long, Robert Emmet. *The Achieving of The Great Gatsby*. Lewisburg, PA: Bucknell University Press, 1979.

Marren, Susan Marie. *Passing for American: Establishing American Identity in the Work of James Weldon Johnson, F. Scott Fitzgerald, Nella Larsen, and Gertrude Stein*. Dissertation: The University of Michigan, 1995.

Matterson, Stephen. *The Great Gatsby*. London: Macmillan, 1990.

Meyers, Jeffery. *Scott Fitzgerald: A Biography*. New York: Harpercollins, 1994.

Mitchell, Giles. "The Great Narcissist: A Study of Fitzgerald's Jay Gatsby." *The American Journal of Psychoanalysis* 51, no. 4 (1991): 387–96.

Moore, Benita A. *Escape into a Labyrinth: F. Scott Fitzgerald, Catholic Sensibility, and the American Way*. New York: Garland, 1988.

Pauly, Thomas H. "Gatsby as Gangster." *Studies in American Fiction* 21, no. 2 (Autumn 1993): 225–36.

Pendelton, Thomas. *I'm Sorry About the Clock: Chronology, Composition, and Narrative Technique in the Great Gatsby*. London: Associated University Press, 1993.

Phillips, Gene D. *Fiction, Film, and F.S. Fitzgerald*. Chicago: Loyala University Press, 1986.

Piper, Henry Dan. *F. Scott Fitzgerald: A Critical Portrait*. New York: Holt, Reinhart and Winston, 1965.

Roulston, Robert and Helen H. Roulston. *The Winding Road to West Egg: The Artistic Development of F. Scott Fitzgerald*. London: Associated University Presses, 1995.

Samuels, Charles T. "The Greatness of Gatsby." *Massachusetts Review* 7 (Autumn 1966): 783–794.

Seiters, Dan. *Image Patterns in the Novels of F. Scott Fitzgerald*. Ann Arbor, MI: UMI Research P, 1986.

Seshachari, Neila. "*The Great Gatsby*: Apogee of Fitzgerald's Mythopoeia." Matthew J. Bruccoli, ed. *Fitzgerald/Hemingway Annual 1976*.

Tredell, Nicolas, ed. *F. Scott Fitzgerald: "The Great Gatsby."* New York: Columbia: UP, 1997.

Wasiolek, Edward. "The Sexual Drama of Nick and Gatsby." *The International Fiction Review* 19, no. 1 (1992): 14–22.

Way, Brian. *F. Scott Fitzgerald and the Art of Social Fiction*. London: Edward Arnold Ltd., 1980.

White, Patti. *Gatsby's Party*. West Lafayette, IN: Purdue University Press, 1992.

Whitley, John S. *F. Scott Fitzgerald: "The Great Gatsby."* London: Edward Arnold, 1976.

Acknowledgements

"Fitzgerald's Brave New World," by Edwin S. Fussell. From *ELH* 19, no. 4 (December, 1952): 291–306. © by The Johns Hopkins University Press. Reprinted with permission of the Johns Hopkins University Press.

"*The Great Gatsby*: Finding a Hero," by Henry Dan Piper. *F. Scott Fitzgerald: A Critical Portrait*. © 1965 by Henry Dan Piper. Reprinted by permission.

"*The Great Gatsby*: Apogee of Fitzgerald's Mythopoeia," by Neila Seshachari. From *Fitzgerald/Hemingway Annual 1976*, ed. Matthew J. Bruccoli. © 1978 by Indian Head Inc. Reprinted by permission.

"The Great Gatsby," by Brian Way. From *F. Scott Fitzgerald and the Art of Social Fiction* © 1980 by Brian Way. Reprinted by permission.

"'I Could Still Hear The Music': Jay Gatsby and the Musical Metaphor," by Bruce Bawer. From *NMAL* 5, no. 4 (Fall, 1981): 25–26. © 1981 by Bruce Bawer. Reprinted by permission.

"Money, Love, and Aspiration in *The Great Gatsby*," by Roger Lathbury. *New Essays on The Great Gatsby*, ed. Matthew J. Bruccoli. © 1985 by Cambridge University Press. Reprinted with permission of Cambridge University Press.

145

"Inventing Gatsby" by Richard Lehan. From *The Great Gatsby: The Limits of Wonder*. © 1990 by G.K. Hall & Co. Reprinted by permission of the Gale Group.

"The Great Narcissist: A Study of Fitzgerald's Jay Gatsby," by Giles Mitchell. From *The American Journal of Psychoanalysis* 51, no. 4 (1991): 387–396. © 1991 by Kluwer Acadamic Publishers. Reprinted by permission.

"The Sexual Drama of Nick and Gatsby," by Edward Wasiolek. From *The International Fiction Review* 19, no. 1 (1992): 14–22. © 1992 by International Fiction Association. Reprinted by permission.

"Gatsby as Gangster," by Thomas H. Pauly. From *Studies in American Fiction* 21, no. 2 (Autumn 1993): 225–236. © 1993 by Northeastern University. Reprinted by permission.

"*The Great Gatsby* and the Good American Life," by Ronald Berman. *Fitzgerald, Hemingway, and The Twenties*. © 2001 by The University of Alabama Press. Reprinted by permission.

Index

Aarne, Antti A., 35
Aarne-Thompson märchens, 35
"Absolution," 15, 24
The Achieving of "The Great Gatsby"
(Long), 126–127, 136
Adams, Henry, 56, 89, 90
"Against *The Great Gatsby*"
(Scrimgeour), 103, 110
"Agents of madness or despair: A note
on *The Secret Agent* and *The
Great Gatsby* (Billy), 97, 99
"Akimcanna: Self-Naughting"
(Coomaraswamy), 34, 37
Alger, Horatio, 24, 41, 69, 71, 76, 82,
128
All the Sad Young Men, 125
Almayer's Folly (Conrad), 126–127
The Ambassadors (James), 69
America/Americanism
credit economy, 114
criticism of, 2–3, 27
Emersonian influence, 1–2
loss of innocence and illusion, 52
resourcefulness of movement, 133
as "willingness of the heart," 128,
129
the American Dream
expansion of male self, glory, 28–29
of freedom, 4–5, 80
of fulfillment, 81
Gatsby's personal quest vs., 28, 36
historical meaning of, 28
as modern secular myth, 23, 27,
128

quest for mythic ideal vs., 29–31
rags to riches story, 9, 23–24
as terrifying, 10
tragedy of belief in, 24–25, 36
values of, 8, 36, 96
wealth and, 11, 16, 41–45
World War I, effect of, 70
The American (James), 69
Amory Blaine *(This Side of Paradise)*,
23, 32, 86
An American Procession (Kazin), 82
An American Tragedy (Dreiser), 80
Anderson, Sherwood, 23
"Another Reading of *The Great
Gatsby*" (Fraser), 107, 111
Antheil, George, 135
Anthony Patch *(The Beautiful and the
Damned)*, 86
apotheosis, 33, 35–36
*Apparatus for F. Scott Fitzgerald's 'The
Great Gatsby'* (Bruccoli), 58, 62
aquaplane, 32
*Ardent Spirits: The Rise and Fall of
Prohibition* (Kobler), 115, 123
aristocracy, 45
Arnstein, Jules "Nicky," 116
"The artifact in imagery: Fitzgerald's
The Great Gatsby" (Bettina), 91, 99
The Art of the Novel (James), 39–40,
41, 61
Asbury, Herbert, 113–114, 123
ashes, valley of, 46, 75, 105
A Study of History (Toynbee), 25
The Autobiography of Benjamin

Franklin, 9
The Awkward Age (James), 39–40, 41

Baker, Jordan *(The Great Gatsby)*. *see* Jordan Baker
Ballet mécanique (film), 135
Barrie, Sir James, 23
Bawer, Bruce
  biographical info, 140
  "'I Could Still Hear the Music': Jay Gatsby and the Musical Metaphor," 63–67
Beaudelaire, Charles, 126
The Beautiful and the Damned, 86
La Belle Dame Sans Merci (Celtic fairy tale), 8, 35
The Beloved Vagabond, 23
Bergson, Henri, 89
Berman, Ronald
  biographical info, 140
  "Success," 129, 136
  "The Great Gatsby" and Fitzgerald's World of Ideas, 133, 136
  "*The Great Gatsby* and the Good American Life," 125–135
Bettina, Sister M., 91, 99
Bewley, Marius, 2–3, 27, 37, 103, 110
The Big Bankroll: The Life and Times of Arnold Rothstein (Katcher), 116–117, 119, 123–124
Billy, Ted, 97, 99
Bishop, John Peale, 21–22
Bits of Paradise (Bruccoli, ed.), 46–47, 61
Blakean emanation, 2
blasphemy, 8, 95
Blatchford Sarnemington ("Absolution"), 15
Bloom, Harold
  biographical info, 139
  "Introduction," 1–5
Bob, Charles Victor, 15
Boone, Daniel, 89
Borderline Conditions and Pathological Narcissism (Kernberg), 94, 95, 100
Bound to Rise (Alger), 24
Brawne, Fanny, 3
"Bright Star" (Keats), 86

Bruccoli, Matthew J.
  Apparatus for F. Scott Fitzgerald's 'The Great Gatsby,' 58, 62
  Bits of Paradise, 46–47, 61
  F. Scott Fitzgerald: A Descriptive Bibliography, 120, 124
  F. Scott Fitzgerald: A Life in Letters, 125, 135
  The Great Gatsby, A Facsimile of the Manuscript, 75, 82
  "How Are You and the Family Old Sport—Gerlach and Gatsby," 117, 124
  New Essays on The Great Gatsby, 69
  Short Stories of F. Scott Fitzgerald, 128, 136
Bruestle, B.B., 22, 25
Buchanan *(The Great Gatsby)*. *see* Daisy Buchanan; Tom Buchanan
Burke, Nellie, 18–19
Butler, Samuel, 89
Byron, Lord, 87

C.A. Stoneham and Co. (New York), 18
Campbell, Joseph, 29, 31, 33–34, 36, 37
Carlyle, Arthur, 87
Carraway, Nick. *see* Nick Carraway *(The Great Gatsby)*
Cartwright, Kent, 121, 124
Cendrars, Blaise, 126
Cervantes, Miguel de, 2
Character and Opinion in the United States (Santayana), 130, 136
Chasseguet-Smirgel, Janine, 98
Christianity, 23, 33, 35, 65, 95
"Christian Myth and Naturalistic Deity: *The Great Gatsby*" (Guerin), 33, 37
Christopher Newman *(The American)*, 69
Citizen Kane (Welles), 57
Clyde Griffiths *(An American Tragedy)*, 80
Cody, William "Buffalo Bill," 89
Coffin, Tristram P., 35, 37

Collins, Dapper Dan, 124
comedy
    Falstaff parallel, 55–56
    Gatsby's meeting with Daisy, 53
    Myrtle buys a dog, 53–54
    Nick's disappointment as, 45
    party settings as, 57–59
    rottenness of Buchanans, 43
Commercial and Financial Chronicle
    Annual Index, 1922–24, 17, 25
commercialization of love, youth and
    beauty, 11, 73, 75, 114
Conrad, Joseph, 2, 48, 126–127
Conrad, Peter, 135, 136
contrasts
    Gatz and Gatsby, 84, 134
    harmony and dissonance, 134–135
    Tom and Gatsby, 101–102
    wild jazz and church bells, 65
Coomaraswamy, Ananda K., 34, 37
Copeland, Aaron, 135
Cotkin, George, 129, 136
"Counterpoint as technique in *The
    Great Gatsby*" (Mellard), 95, 100
The Crack-Up (Wilson, ed.), 32, 37,
    54, 62, 73, 82
Crevecoeur, J. Hector St. John De, 9
"The Crime in the Whistler Room"
    (Wilson), 117–118, 124
Critical Essays on F. Scott Fitzgerald
    (Donaldson, ed.), 121, 124
Cyrenaicism, 87

Dahl, Curtis, 99
Daisy Buchanan *(The Great Gatsby)*.
    see also Gatsby: Daisy
    Daisy Miller compared to, 2
    double view of, 72–73
    as fusion of sex and money, 42, 72
    motherhood of, 105–106
    Myrtle and, 52, 108–109
    negativity of, 127
    Nick and, 3–4, 40, 42, 50–51,
        71–72, 76, 79
    tawdriness of, 102
    Tom and, 28, 52, 75, 77
    unexamined life of, 52, 133–134,
        135

vagueness of, 132
voice "full of money," 8, 35, 42, 77,
    79
Wedding March and, 66
Daisy Miller (James), 2
Dan Cody *(The Great Gatsby)*, 20, 31,
    34, 41–42, 83, 128
Dapper Dan Collins, 124
Defoe, Daniel, 89
Dewey, John, 127, 129
Dexter Green ("Winter Dreams"), 71
Dickens, Charles, 54, 55–56
Dickens, Money, Society (Smith), 54, 55,
    62
Dick Humbird *(This Side of Paradise)*,
    45
Dictionary of National Biography, 24, 26
dissonance, 134–135
Donaldson, Scott, 124
Don Quixote (Cervantes), 2
Dowson, Ernest, 87, 88, 90
dramatic scenes, 40–41, 55–58, 84, 95.
    see also Parties
dreams. *see also the* American Dream
    buying fulfillment of, 11, 78, 80,
        102
    Gatsby's, 11, 24, 36, 42, 45–46, 80,
        93, 101, 102, 128, 129, 137
    grounded in impossibility, 82
    Keatsian, of love, 1, 3
    as theme of *The Great Gatsby*, 81
Dreiser, Theodore, 14, 42, 80
Drift and Mastery (Lippmann), 127,
    133–134, 136
duality of characters, 71–73, 79
Dulcinea *(Don Quixote)*, 2
dynamic organicism, 86
Dynamo, force of, 89, 90

East Egg, 32, 46, 105, 128
*Editor to Author: The Letters of Maxwell
    E. Perkins* (Whelk, ed.), 13, 14–16,
    25
The Education of Henry Adams
    (Adams), 89, 90
ego-ideal, 92, 96, 97–98, 99
"The ego-ideal: An aspect of
    narcissism" (Menaker), 92, 99, 100

egoist vs. personage, 83, 90
egotheism, 93
"Elavoe," 23
Elbe, Kenneth, 102, 110, 129, 136
Eliot, T.S., 4, 46, 82, 126, 127, 135,
    136
E.M. Fuller and Co. (New York), 16,
    18
Emerson, Ralph Waldo, 9
Emersonianism, 1–2
Emma *(Madame Bovary)*, 48–49
*English Poetry and Prose of the Romantic
    Movement* (Woods, ed.), 86, 90
Enscoe, Gerald, 86, 90
Ernest Lilly *(The Great Gatsby)*, 104
Eschenbach, Wolfram von, 23
"The Eve of St. Agnes" (Keats), 86
*Everybody Was So Young: Gerald and
    Sara Murphy, A Last Generation
    Love Story* (Vaill), 135, 136
eyes of Dr. T.J. Eckleburg, 75, 79, 126

F. Scott Fitzgerald: A Critical Portrait
    (Piper), 114, 123
*F. Scott Fitzgerald: A Descriptive
    Bibliography* (Bruccoli), 120, 124
F. Scott Fitzgerald: A Life in Letters
    (Bruccoli, ed.), 125, 135
"F. Scott Fitzgerald: Literature and
    the Work of Mourning"
    (Koenigsberg), 105, 111
F. Scott Fitzgerald: The Last Tycoon
    (Sklar), 128, 136
*F. Scott Fitzgerald: The Man and His
    Work* (Kazin, ed.), 31, 37
*F. Scott Fitzgerald and the Craft of
    Fiction* (Lehan), 27, 37
F. Scott Fitzgerald (Elbe), 102, 110,
    129, 136
The Fall of Hyperion (Keats), 3–4
Fallon, William J., 17
Falstaff *(Henry IV)*, 55–56, 59, 62
*The Far Side of Paradise: A Bibliography
    of F. Scott Fitzgerald* (Mizener), 48,
    61, 117, 124
Faustina O'Brien *(The Great Gatsby)*,
    104
"Fear of death and narcissism"

(Jasovic-Gasic and Vesel), 92,
    97–98, 99
femininity and masculinity, 28–29, 89,
    90, 103–104, 107–108
first kiss, 35, 42, 50–51, 76
Fitzgerald, F. Scott
    on Anderson's *Many Marriages*, 23
    Bishop and, 21–22
    Eliot's influence on, 4
    favorite scene of, 73
    Flaubert compared to, 5
    Gatsby as projection of self, 21–22,
        23, 25
    Gerlach and, 116–117
    interest in society scandals, 15–16,
        20
    James compared to, 39–40, 41
    Lardner and, 16
    love for America, 82, 110
    obsession with youth, 9, 11, 28, 87
    Perkins and, 13–14, 15–16, 132
    personal symbols of, 31–32
    Rothstein and, 115
    sexuality of, 110
    on triumph and romance, 31–32
Fitzgerald, F. Scott, style of. *see also*
    Comedy; Irony; Symbolism;
    Themes
    contrasts, 65, 84, 101–102,
        134–135
    dramatic scenes, 55–58, 84, 95 *(see
        also* Parties)
    duality of characters, 71–73, 79
    egoist vs. personage, 83, 90
    evolution of, 131–132
    Gatsby's as pervasive social pattern,
        9
    language, carefully chosen, 41,
        46–50, 51, 83, 133, 134
    modernism, 88–89, 125, 126–127,
        135
    sexual motifs, 103–110
    tasteless and self-indulgent, 47
    three realms of time, 87
    vicious forms artistically written,
        46–48, 51, 52, 61, 102–103
Fitzgerald, F. Scott, works of, See also
    The Great Gatsby; This Side of

Paradise
"Absolution," 15, 24
All the Sad Young Men, 125
The Beautiful and the Damned, 86
"Elavoe," 23
"Forging Ahead," 24–25
The Last Tycoon, 86
"Love in the Night," 46–47, 61
"May Day," 10
"My Lost City," 11, 32
"The Offshore Pirate," 24
"The Popular Girl," 24–25
"The Swimmers," 128, 136
Tender is the Night, 86
Trimalchio, 58–59
The Vegetable, 24–25
"Winter Dreams," 71
"Fitzgerald's Brave New World"
    (Fussell), 7–11, 27, 37
"Fitzgerald's *The Great Gatsby*"
    (Levith), 103, 111
"Fitzgerald's Use of Architectural
    Styles in *The Great Gatsby*" (Dahl),
    99
Flaubert, Gustave, 5, 49, 61
Foley, Thomas F., 18
*"The Fool of Nature" in the English
    Drama of Our Day* (Bruestle), 22,
    25
"Forging Ahead," 24–25
Fowler, Gene, 18, 25
Francis Bull *(The Great Gatsby)*, 104
Frank and Fearless (Alger), 24
Franklin, Benjamin, 9, 11, 24, 41, 128
Franz, Marie-Louis Van, 36, 37
Fraser, Keath, 107, 111
freedom, 4, 80
*Freud, Religion, and The Roaring
    Twenties* (Idema), 107, 111
Freud, Sigmund, 4, 107, 110
From Canal Boy to President (Alger), 24
From Ritual to Romance (Weston), 22,
    25
Fuller, Edward M., 16–20, 20–21
Fuller-McGee case, 16–20, 124
Fussell, Edwin S.
    biographical info, 139
    "Fitzgerald's Brave New World,"
        7–11, 27, 28, 37

Gang Rule in New York (Thompson
    and Raymond), 119, 124
gangsters, 113–123
"Gatsby as Gangster" (Pauly),
    113–123
"Gatsby's Fairy Lover" (Coffin), 35.37
Gatsby *(The Great Gatsby)*
    Americanism of, 1–2
    as archetypal Great or Noble Fool,
        22–23
    as archetypal hero, 1, 22, 28,
        34–36, 52, 131
    as archetypal scapegoat, 95
    autobiography of, 47–48, 84–85,
        120
    "aware of own doubleness," 71
    blasphemy of, 8, 95
    born James Gatz, 31, 34, 42, 134
    Clyde Griffiths compared to, 80
    comic nature of, 52–59, 53, 55–59
    critics' view of, 91, 102
    Daisy and, 30, 34–35, 56, 77, 92
    Daisy, attitude toward, 2, 3, 8–9,
        25, 29–31, 42, 73, 76–77, 94,
        95, 104–105, 138
    Daisy, attitude toward post affair,
        50, 51–52, 93, 98–99
    Daisy, first kiss of, 35, 42, 50–51,
        76
    Daisy, original romance with,
        34–35, 42, 50–51, 95
    Dan Cody and, 20, 31, 34, 41–42,
        83, 128
    as a "dandy," 114
    death of, 33, 35–36, 98–99
    disillusion of, 10, 51–52, 97–98
    Don Quixote compared to, 2
    dream, buying his, 11, 78, 80, 102
    dream of, 11, 24, 36, 42, 45–46, 80,
        93, 101, 102, 128, 129, 137
    ego-ideal of, 92, 96, 97–98, 99
    egotheism of, 93
    Falstaff compared to, 55–56, 59
    as Fitzgerald's projection of self,
        21–22, 23, 25
    flight and defense patterns, 107
    Fuller as model for, 20–21
    funeral of, 32–33, 67

as gangster, 20, 114–123, 131
George and, 79–80
God and, 34, 65, 67, 86, 92, 93, 95
Hamlet compared to, 2
hero in "The Princess of Dreams"
   compared to, 88
homosexuality of, 108, 109
imaginative inner life of, 42, 45–52,
   65, 76, 94–95
individual tragedy equated to
   society's, 9
Madonna complex, 106
mansion of, 95
Marius compared to, 87
microcosmic and macrocosmic
   levels of, 36
money and, 78, 90, 94, 95–96,
   129–130
Myrtle and, 104
mythic projection of self (goodness,
   optimism, hope), 2, 7, 71,
   84–85, 97–99, 101, 110
mythic quest of, 4, 23, 28–31
Nick and, 4, 40, 48, 60, 67, 70–71,
   78, 98, 99, 108, 122–123, 138
   (see also Nick Carraway: on
   Gatsby)
nobility of, 131
parties of, 40–41, 56–58, 64–65, 74,
   109, 117, 118, 134–135
Perkins critique of, 13–14
psychoanalysis of, 91–99, 103,
   105–106
romanticism of, 7, 65, 85, 95
romantic process and, 89
rootlessness of, 74
Rothstein as model for, 119–120
self-improvement rules, 24
theatrical gestures of, 55–58, 84, 95
Tom and, 35, 51, 101–102, 108,
   116
unrealistic nature of, 2, 22, 65–66,
   97, 102–103
vagueness of, 13–14, 21–22, 114,
   120, 132, 137
values of, 36, 96
Wolfshiem and, 118, 120, 130
wonder, capacity for, 10, 45, 49–50,

52, 91
Gatz. see Jimmy Gatz; Mr. Gatz
Gauss, Christian, 85–86
geography
   East and West Egg, 32, 46, 105,
      128
   New York, 11, 15, 78, 125–127,
      134
   San Francisco in the Midwest, 85
   valley of ashes, 46, 75, 105
George Wilson (The Great Gatsby), 46,
   79–80
Gerlach, Max, 116–117
Gerontion (Eliot), 46
Gleckner, Robert, 86, 90
Godden, Richard, 97, 99
The Golden Moment: The Novels of F.
   Scott Fitzgerald (Stern), 128, 136
Goodrich, Norma Lorre, 31, 37
Goody, Louise, 17
Gordon, Lyndall, 135, 136
The Grail Legend (Jung and Franz), 36,
   37
grandiosity, 55–58, 84, 95. see also
   Parties
The Great American Band Wagon
   (Merz), 134, 136
Great Fool as archetypal, 22–23
"The Great Gatsby: Finding a Hero"
   (Piper), 13–25
The Great Gatsby, A Facsimile of the
   Manuscript (Bruccoli), 75, 82
"The Great Gatsby: Apogee of
   Fitzgerald's Mythopoeia"
   (Seshachari), 27–36
The Great Gatsby: A Study (Hoffman),
   27, 37
The Great Gatsby: Glamour on the
   turn" (Godden), 97, 99
"The Great Gatsby: The Limits of
   Wonder" (Lehan), 136
The Great Gatsby
   The Awkward Age compared to,
      39–40
   Citizen Kane compared to, 57
   drama and organization of, 39–41,
      81
   exploration of American

civilization, 49
Gatsby and Daisy's first kiss, 35,
    42, 50–51, 76
language of, 41, 46
Lord Jim compared to, 2
Madame Bovary compared to, 5,
    48–49, 61
mediation of Gatsby, 2
mirror and forecaster of 1920s,
    20–21
music as imaginistic device, 63–67
as mutation of Fitzgerald's work,
    125
mythology from Fitzgerald's life,
    25
pattern of surface and
    underground, 105
place in literature of, 61
Plaza Hotel scene, 66, 77, 92, 97
relationships in, 75
sexual motifs in, 42, 72, 103–110
as social comedy, 45, 53–54
sordid backdrop, 75
synopsis, 92
theatrical gestures in, 55–58, 84, 95
Tom's violence as trope of new
    America, 90
Trimalchio compared to, 58–59
water, significance of, 32–33
The Great Gatsby, characters of. *see also*
    Daisy Buchanan; Gatsby; Jordan
    Baker; Meyer Wolfshiem; Myrtle
    Wilson; Nick Carraway; Tom
    Buchanan
Dan Cody, 20, 31, 34, 41–42, 83,
    128
Ernest Lilly, 104
Faustina O'Brien, 104
Francis Bull, 104
George Wilson, 46, 79–80
James Gatz, 31, 34, 42, 84, 134
James J. Hill, 15
Klipspringer, 74
McKees, 75, 106–107, 131
Mr. Gatz, 15, 41
Mrs. Ulysses Swett, 104
Newton Orchid, 104
Owl Eyes, 32, 58

Russell Betty, 104
Walter Chase, 20, 102
*"The Great Gatsby" and Fitzgerald's
    World of Ideas* (Berman), 133, 136
"The Great Gatsby" and Modern Times
    (Berman), 129, 136
"The Great Gatsby and the Good
    American Life" (Berman), 125–135
"The Great Gatsby" (Way), 39–61
*The Great Masterpiece: A Life Story of
    William J. Fallon* (Fowler), 18, 25
"The Great Narcissist: A Study of
    Fitzgerald's Jay Gatsby" (Mitchell),
    91–99
Great Neck, NY, 15–18
green light
    as focus of Gatsby's dream, 45
    as Gatsby's devotion to history, 9
    Gatsby telling Daisy about, 50
    symbol of idealized Daisy, 93, 94
    triviality of, 52
Gross, Barry, 121, 124
Guerin, Wilfred Louis, 33, 37
guests and gossip columns, 46
Guys and Dolls, 116

Hamlet (Shakespeare), 2
Hanzo, T. A., 121, 124
Hemingway, Ernest, 126
Henry IV (Shakespeare), 55–56, 62
*The Hero: A Study in Tradition, Myth
    and Drama* (Raglan), 22, 25
The Hero: Myth/Image/Symbol
    (Norman), 33, 37
heroes in mythology. *see also* Myths
    apotheosis of, 33, 35–36
    archetypal hero, 1, 22, 28, 34–36,
        52, 131
    archetypal scapegoat, 95
    boat as ferry across turbulent
        waters, 31
    call to adventure, 34–35
    Campbell's description of, 33–34
    conquest of women = conquest of
        world, 35
    death as triumph, 36
    Great or Noble Fool, 22–23

women and, 28–31, 34–35
The Hero with a Thousand Faces
    (Campbell), 29, 31, 33–34, 36, 37
The History of Sir Richard Whittington
    (Wheatley, ed.), 23–24, 26
Hoffman, Daniel F., 26
Hoffman, Frederick J., 27, 37
homosexuality, 106–107, 111
Honegger, Arthur, 135
Horatio *(Hamlet)*, 2
"How Are You and the Family Old
    Sport—Gerlach and Gatsby"
    (Bruccoli), 117, 124
How Does Analysis Cure? (Kohut), 98,
    100

"'I Could Still Hear the Music': Jay
    Gatsby and the Musical Metaphor"
    (Bawer), 63–67
Idema, Henry, 107, 111
illusions, 81, 85, 103
Immigration Bill of 1924, 134
*Internal World and External Reality:
    Object Relations Theory Applied*
    (Kernberg), 100
International Book Review, 124
"Introduction" (Bloom), 1–5
"Introduction" to *The Great Gatsby: A
    Study* (Hoffman), 27, 37
"Introduction" to *Twentieth Century
    Interpretations of The Great Gatsby*
    (Lockridge), 103, 110
"Inventing Gatsby" (Lehan), 83–90
irony in *The Great Gatsby*
    American dream as terrifying, 10
    balancing illusion and reality,
        45–46
    control of, 47
    fusion of wonder and vulgarity, 10,
        48, 49–50
    Gatsby buying his dream, 11, 78,
        80, 102
    Gatsby's romantic idealism, 65–66
    Jordan accusing Nick of
        dishonesty, 75
"Isabella; or, The Pot of Basil"
    (Keats), 86
Ivanhoe (Scott), 23

James, Henry, 2, 39–40, 41, 42, 56,
    61, 69, 82
James, William, 89, 129
James Gatz *(The Great Gatsby)*, 31, 34,
    42, 84, 134. *see also* Gatsby
James J. Hill *(The Great Gatsby)*, 15
Janik, Allan, 135, 136
Jasovic-Gasic, Miroslava, 92, 97–98,
    99
Jay Gatsby *(The Great Gatsby)*. *see*
    Gatsby
jazz, 64–65
Jesus, 35, 65, 95
Jimmy Gatz *(The Great Gatsby)*, 31,
    34, 42, 84, 134. *see also* Gatsby
Jordan Baker *(The Great Gatsby)*
    Dick Humbird compared to, 45
    dishonesty and glamour of,
        107–108
    eavesdropping shamelessly, 43
    on Gatsby's romance with Daisy,
        40
    masculinity of, 107–108
    Nick and, 44–45, 61, 65, 75, 79,
        104, 107–108
    reputation of, 74
    sophistication of, 133
Joyce, James, 89
Judy Jones ("Winter Dreams"), 71
Jung, Emma, 36, 37

Katcher, Leo, 116–117, 119, 123–124
Kazin, Alfred, 82
Keats, John, 85, 86–87, 90
Keatsian dream of love, 1, 3
Kernberg, Otto F., 94, 95, 96–97, 100
the kiss of Gatsby and Daisy, 35, 42,
    50–51, 76
Klipspringer *(The Great Gatsby)*, 74
Kobler, John, 115, 123
Koenigsberg, Richard A., 105, 111
Kohut, Heinz, 98, 100

Lambert Strether *(The Ambassadors)*,
    69
language, use of, 41, 46–50, 51, 83,
    133, 134
Lardner, Ring, 13, 16

The Last Tycoon, 86
Lathbury, Roger
  biographical info, 140
  "Money, Love and Aspiration in
    The Great Gatsby", 69–82
Lawrence, D. H., 89
Leger, Fernand, 135
Lehan, Richard
  biographical info, 140
  *F. Scott Fitzgerald and the Craft of
    Fiction,* 27, 37
  "Inventing Gatsby," 83–90
  *"The Great Gatsby: The Limits of
    Wonder,"* 136
Lemming, David Adams, 34, 37
Leon, Ponce de, 11
Letters from an American Farmer
  (Crevecoeur), 9
The Letters of F. Scott Fitzgerald
  (Turnbull, ed.), 73, 82, 115, 123
Leuchtenburg, William E., 114, 123
Levith, Murray J., 103, 111
The Liberal Imagination (Trilling), 103,
  110
Lippmann, Walter, 127, 128,
  134–135, 136
The Little Minister (Barrie), 23
Locke, John William, 23
Lockridge, Ernest, 103, 110
Long, Robert Emmet, 126–127, 136
Lord Jim (Conrad), 2
love and money, 69–70, 71, 77, 82
"Love in the Night," 46–47, 47, 61
Lowen, Alexander, 97, 100
loyalty, 127–128
Lysons, Rev. Samuel, 24, 26

macrocosmic mythologies, 34, 36
Madame Bovary (Flaubert), 5, 48–49,
  61
Making His Way (Alger), 24
mansion, 95
Many Marriages (Anderson), 23
"Marie Antoinette Music Room," 66
Marius the Epicurean (Parer), 87, 90
masculinity and femininity, 28–29, 89,
  90, 103–104, 107–108
"Materialism and Idealism in

American Life" (Santayana), 130
Max Fleischman ("The Crime in the
  Whistler Room"), 117–118, 121
"May Day," 10
McGee, William F., 17–20
McKees *(The Great Gatsby),* 75,
  106–107, 131
mechanistic vs. organic, 88–89
Mellard, James, 95, 100
memories/the past, 80, 96–97
men, belief in glory of the self, 28–29
Menaker, Ruth, 92, 99, 100
Mencken, H. L., 52, 126, 127, 135
Mendelssohn, Felix, 66
Merz, Charles, 134, 136
metaphors, 8, 64
Meyer Wolfshiem *(The Great Gatsby)*
  eulogy for Rosenthal, 21, 115
  Gatsby and, 118, 120, 130
  lunch in New York, 40
  Nick and, 54, 115, 118–119
  Rothstein as model for, 20, 119
*Middle Class Culture in Elizabethan
  England* (Wright), 26
Mitchell, Giles
  biographical info, 140
  "The Great Narcissist: A Study of
    Fitzgerald's Jay Gatsby," 91–99
Mizener, Arthur, 48, 61, 117, 124
The Model Merchant (Lysons), 24, 26
modernism, 88–89, 125, 126–127, 135
Modern Times, Modern Places (Conrad),
  135, 136
money. *see also* Wealth
  Daisy's voice as, 8, 35, 42, 72, 77,
    79
  as focus of society, 77, 114, 127,
    129–130
  Gatsby's, 78, 90
  love and, 69–70, 71, 77, 82
  sense of possibility from, 80
  sentiments as, 73
  sex and, 42, 75
"Money, Love and Aspiration in *The
  Great Gatsby*" (Lathbury), 69–82
monomyths, 33–34
Monroe Stahr *(The Last Tycoon),* 86
Morris, Lloyd, 19, 25

Morton, Jelly Roll, 135
motifs, 22–23, 32–33
Mr. Gatz *(The Great Gatsby)*, 15, 41
Mrs. Ulysses Swett *(The Great Gatsby)*,
    104
Murphy, Gerald, 135
Murray, John, 100
music, 63–67, 135
"My Lost City," 11, 32
Myrtle Wilson *(The Great Gatsby)*
    buys a dog, 53–54
    Daisy and, 52, 108–109
    Gatsby and, 104
    raucous party of, 40
    relationships of, 75
    respect for social standards, 131
    solidity of, 132–133
    Tom and, 54
Mythology: The Voyage of the Hero
    (Lemming), 34.37
myths. *see also* Heroes in mythology
    blending myths of Franklin and
        Leon, 11
    creation legends, 33
    death by water-rebirth myth, 33
    Gatsby's quest for mythic ideal,
        28–31
    multilevel interpretations, 27
    Narcissus, 92–99
    Parzival, 23
    yacht as symbol, 31
Myths of the Hero (Goodrich), 31, 37

narcissism, 32, 92–99
Narcissism: Denial of the True Self
    (Lowen), 97, 100
"Narcissism and the defiance of time"
    (Stern), 94, 100
"Narcissism and the ego-ideal"
    (Murray), 100
*The Narcissistic Condition: A Fact of Our
    Lives and Times* (Nelson, ed.), 100
The Narcissistic Pursuit of Perfection
    (Rothstein), 94, 96, 100
Narcissus, 32, 98
Nelson, M.L., 100
New England Quarterly (Watkins), 24,
    26

New Essays on The Great Gatsby
    (Bruccoli, ed.), 69–82
Newton Orchid *(The Great Gatsby)*,
    104
New York scene, 11, 15, 78, 125–127,
    134
New York Times, 18, 25, 119–120, 124
*New York Times Annual Index, 1920
    1928*, 17, 25
"Nick Carraway as an Unreliable
    Narrator" (Cartwright), 121, 124
Nick Carraway *(The Great Gatsby)*
    on Daisy, 3–4, 40, 42, 50–51,
        71–72, 76, 79
    description of New York, 78
    disillusionment of, 43–45, 121–122
    flight and defense patterns, 107,
        108
    Gatsby and, 4, 40, 48, 60, 67,
        70–71, 78, 108, 122–123, 138
    on Gatsby, 76, 83, 84, 94, 95, 101,
        137
    on Gatsby as son of God, 34
    on Gatsby's death, 36
    on Gatsby's parties, 56–57, 57–58
    as homosexual, 106–107, 111
    Horatio compared to, 2
    Jordan and, 44–45, 61, 65, 75, 79,
        104, 107–108
    Marlow compared to, 2
    Midwest culture of, 60–61
    role, establish structure and tone,
        41, 55, 81, 121
    role, moral critic, 42–43, 44–45,
        59–60, 70–71, 102, 104,
        121–122
    role, narrator, 60–61, 121, 124
    self-doubts of, 79
    Tom and, 3, 43, 90, 106, 108
    on Western spirit of characters, 15
    Wolfshiem and, 54, 115, 118–119
The Night Club Era (Walker), 19, 25
Noble Fool as archetypal, 22–23
Norman, Dorothy, 33, 37
Nostromo (Conrad), 48
noveau riche, 16
The Novels of F. Scott Fitzgerald
    (Chambers), 91, 98, 99

"Ode on a Grecian Urn" (Keats), 85
"Ode to a Nightingale" (Keats), 85
"The Offshore Pirate," 24
O'Hara, John, 21
omnipotency, 65, 92
On Photography (Sontag), 126, 135
organic vs. mechanistic, 88–89
Ornstein, Robert, 103, 110
"Our Gatsby, Our Nick" (Gross), 121, 124
Owl Eyes *(The Great Gatsby)*, 32, 58

"pander," 11
Parer, Walter, 87, 90
parody of guests/gossip columns, 46
parties, 40–41, 56–58, 64–65, 74, 109, 117, 118, 134–135
Parzival (Eschenbach), 23
"The Passing of the Gangster" (Asbury), 113–114, 123
Pater, Walter, 87, 90
Paul Bunyon: Last of the Frontier Demi Gods (Hoffman), 26
Pauly, Thomas H.
    biographical info, 140
    "Gatsby as Gangster," 113–123
Peckham, Morse, 86–87, 90
The Perils of Prosperity (Leuchtenburg), 114, 123
Perkins, Max, 13–14, 15–16, 132
personage vs. egoist, 83, 90
Petronius, 58–59
Piper, Henry Dan
    biographical info, 139–140
    F. Scott Fitzgerald: A Critical Portrait, 114, 123
    "*The Great Gatsby:* Finding a Hero," 13–25
Platonism, 1–2, 34, 74, 95, 135, 136, 137
Plaza Hotel, 66, 77, 92, 97
The Poems of Ernest Dowson (Longaker, ed.), 88, 90
Poor Richard's Almanac (Franklin), 24
"The Popular Girl," 24–25
Postscript to Yesterday (Morris), 19, 25
Pound, Ezra, 126
"The Princess of Dreams" (Dowson), 87
Prohibition, 114–116, 123
psychoanalysis, 91–99, 103, 105–106

Ragged Dick (Alger), 24
Raglan, Lord, 22, 25
Raymond, Allen, 119, 124
religious allusions
    Christianity, 23, 33, 35, 65, 95
    death as crucifixion, 35–36
    Gatsby and, 34, 65, 67, 86, 92, 95
    God as eternal, 65, 92
    myth of the grail knight, 23
    three trips around the world, 31
    water as cleansing, life-giving, 32–33
    "worship" of green light, 9, 93
Remus, George, 114–115, 116–117, 118
repression, 4
The Republic (Plato), 135, 136
Richard Diver *(Tender is the Night)*, 86
Rig Veda, 33
Robinson Crusoe (Defoe), 89
Romanticism
    dangers of, 86–87
    of Flaubert and Fitzgerald, 48–49
    Gatsby and, 7, 65, 85
    Keatsian dream of love, 1
    modernism and, 88–89, 125, 126–127, 135
    moral realism vs., 2, 78
    possibilities in Gatsby's world, 56
Romanticism: Points of View (Gleckner and Enscoe, eds.), 86, 90
rootlessness of postwar society, 73–74, 127–128
"The Rosary" (song), 67
Rosenthal, Herman "Rosy," 21, 115
Rothstein, Arnold, 19, 21, 94, 96, 100, 115–117, 119–120, 123, 124
Royce, Josiah, 127–128, 129, 136
Russell Betty *(The Great Gatsby)*, 104

"Salt," 14
San Francisco in the Midwest, 85
Santayana, George, 129, 130, 136
The Saturday Evening Post, 24

Saturday Review, 120, 124
Schorer, Mark, 70, 82
Scott, Sir Walter, 23
"Scott Fitzgerald's Criticism of
    America" (Bewley), 27, 37, 103,
    110
"Scott Fitzgerald's Fable of East and
    West" (Ornstein), 103, 110
Scrimgeour, Gary J., 103, 110
Seabury, Samuel, 21
A Second Mencken Chrestomathy
    (Teachoot, ed.), 126, 135
Sentimental Tommy (Barrie), 23
separation of love and money, 69–70
Seshachari, Neila
    biographical info, 140
    "*The Great Gatsby*: Apogee of
        Fitzgerald's Mythopoeia," 27–36
*Severe Personality Disorders:
    Psychotherapeutic Strategies*
    (Kernberg), 96–97, 100
"The Sexual Drama of Nick and
    Gatsby" (Wasiolek), 101–110
sexual motifs, 103–110
"Sexual Roles in *The Great Gatsby*"
    (Thornton), 103–104, 111
Shakespeare, William, 2, 55, 62
Shaw, George Bernard, 89
Sheean, Nellie, 18
Shelley, Percy Bysshe, 87
Short Stories of F. Scott Fitzgerald
    (Bruccoli, ed.), 128, 136
Sidewalk Blues (Morton), 135
Silkworth, Walter, 16, 20
Sin and Madness: Studies in Narcissism
    (Sugerman), 93, 100
Sinclair Lewis: An American Life
    (Schorer), 70, 82
"Sir Richard Whittington" (*Dictionary
    of National Biography*), 23–24, 26
Sister Carrie (Dreiser), 14, 80
Sklar, Robert, 128, 136
"The Sleepers" (Whitman), 4
Smith, Grahame, 54, 55, 62
social standing, 45, 131
Sondra Finchley (*An American
    Tragedy*), 80
Sontag, Susan, 126, 135

Stern, Mark E., 94, 100
Stern, Milton R., 128, 133, 136
Sterns, Harold E., 128, 136
Stoneham, Charles A., 18, 20
Stravinsky, Igor, 135
The Street I Know (Sterns), 128, 136
Strive and Succeed (Alger), 24
"Success" (Berman), 129, 136
Sugerman, Shirley, 93, 100
The Sun Also Rises (Hemingway), 126
"The Swimmers," 128, 136
swimming pool, 32
symbolism, 28, 31–32, 32–33. *see also*
    Green light

Teachoot, Terry, 126, 135
Tender is the Night, 86
Thackeray, William Makepeace, 48
theatrical gestures, 55–58, 84, 95. *see
    also* Parties
"The Theme and the Narrator of *The
    Great Gatsby*" (Hanzo), 121, 124
themes. *see also* America/Americanism;
    Dreams; Geography; Money;
    Myths; Religious allusions; Wealth
    commercialization of love, youth
    and beauty, 11, 73, 75, 114
    eternal youth, 9, 11, 28
    femininity and masculinity, 28–29,
        89, 90, 103–104, 107–108
    loyalty, 127–128
    parties, 40–41, 56–58, 64–65, 74,
        109, 117, 118, 134–135
    perfection, 92, 106
    social standing, 45, 131
    symbolism, 28, 31–32, 32–33 (*see
        also* Green light)
    time, as mortal enemy, 87, 93,
        96–97
    valley of ashes, 46, 75, 105
    water as *leit motif*, 32–33
This Fabulous Century: 1920-1930
    (Time-Life), 115, 123
This Side of Paradise
    Amory's list of favorite books, 23
    attempt at styles of dominance, 45
    Fitzgerald's style in, 71
    romantic aspects of, 32, 86, 87

Thompson, Craig, 119, 124
Thompson, Stith, 35
Thoreau, Henry David, 9
Thornton, Patricia Pacey, 103–104,
    111
"Three Letters about *The Great
    Gatsby*" (Wilson, ed.), 73, 82
time, as mortal enemy, 87, 93, 96–97
Time (magazine), 15, 25
Tom Buchanan (*The Great Gatsby*)
    brutality of, 44, 90, 110
    compendium of American failures,
        129
    Daisy and, 28, 52, 75, 77
    domination of, 77, 79, 89–90
    father attributes of, 108
    Gatsby and, 35, 51, 101–102, 108,
        116
    money of, 77–78
    Myrtle and, 54
    as mythic ogre, 35
    Nick and, 3, 43, 90, 106, 108
    relationships of, 75
    restlessness, futility of, 42–43
    unexamined life of, 52, 133–134
    Walter Chase and, 20
"Totentanz" (Mencken), 126, 127, 135
Toulmin, Stephen, 135, 136
Tourbillon, Robert "Dapper Dan
    Collins," 124
"Toward a Theory of Romanticism"
    (Peckham), 86, 90
Toynbee, Arnold, 25
Trilling, Lionel, 103, 110
Trimalchio, 58–59
"The Trouble with Nick"
    (Donaldson), 121, 124
T.S. Eliot: An Imperfect Life (Gordon),
    135, 136
Turnbull, Andrew, 73, 82, 115, 123

upper class fails at aristocracy, 45

Vaill, Amanda, 135, 136
Vanity Fair (Thackeray), 48
The Vedas, 33
The Vegetable, 24–25
Vesel, Josif, 92, 97–98, 99

Volstead Act, 114–115

Walker, Jimmy, 21
Walker, Stanley, 19, 25
Walter Chase (*The Great Gatsby*), 20,
    102
Wasiolek, Edward
    biographical info, 140
    "The Sexual Drama of Nick and
        Gatsby," 101–110
The Waste Land (Eliot), 4, 82, 126, 127
water as *leit motif*, 32–33
Watkins, E.C., 24, 26
Way, Brian
    on the American rich, 41–45
    biographical info, 140
    on Gatsby's comic nature, 52–59
    on Gatsby's inner life, 42, 45–52
    on James and Fitzgerald, 39–41
    "The Great Gatsby," 39–61
"The Way to Wealth" (Franklin), 128
wealth. *see also* Money
    the American Dream and, 11, 16,
        41–45
    duality of, 71
    emptiness of, 74
    nouveau riche, 15–16
    novel's feelings of, 82
    rags to riches story, 9, 23–24
    shortcomings of the rich, 42–43,
        44–45, 51–52
    women as, 28
"Wedding March" (Mendelssohn), 66
Welles, Orson, 57
Wells, H. G., 89
West Egg, 32, 46, 105, 128
Weston, Jessie L., 22, 25
Wharton, Edith, 42, 52, 54, 73
"When Lilacs Last in the Dooryard
    Bloom'd" (Whitman), 4
Whitman, Walt, 4
William James, Public Philosopher
    (Cotkin), 129, 136
"William James and the Philosophy of
    Life" (Royce), 127–128, 136
Wilson, Edmund
    The Crack-Up, 32, 37, 54, 62, 73,
        82

"The Crime in the Whistler
   Room," 117–118, 121, 124
"Three Letters about *The Great
   Gatsby*", 73, 82
Wilson *(The Great Gatsby)*. *see* George
   Wilson; Myrtle Wilson
"Winter Dreams," 71
Wittgenstein's Vienna (Janik and
   Toulmin), 135, 136
Wolfshiem. *see* Meyer Wolfshiem *(The
   Great Gatsby)*
women

as adjunct to amassing wealth, 28
exploitation of, 94
as ultimate quest of hero, 29–31,
   34–35
Wordsworthian solitary, 2
World Series fix, 116
World War I, 70, 73–74
Wright, Louis B., 26
Wynn, Ed, 16

yacht, 31

DATE DUE

GAYLORD			PRINTED IN U.S.A.